Deborah Kay has three adult children and three grandchildren, and has made it a lifelong goal to be vigilant over their safety. Although she grew up in a quiet, rural setting in Central Queensland, she has travelled widely through Australia and overseas, including living in Malaysia for three years, which has broadened her appreciation of different cultures. Currently Deborah works with small children as a teacher aide in Ipswich. Having now told her story in print, Deborah is keen to talk publicly on child sex abuse and do what she can to impact positively, and highlight the issue. As she puts it: 'I am no longer silent... I now have the freedom to speak out for the sanctity of childhood'.

Barry Levy is a prize-winning journalist, including the Australian Human Rights Award for Journalism – for a multiple series of stories on child sex abuse, domestic violence and homelessness; the Anning Barton Memorial Award for Outstanding Journalism (Central Queensland) – for a series on child sex abuse (incest-rape); and a Walkley Awards Queensland State finalist – for a series on homelessness. Levy's works of fiction include: The Terrorist, *the story of what happens when you drop an Arab Muslim student into a Western Jewish home;* Shades of Exodus, *a portrait of migrants, particularly South Africans, who have come to Australia;* As If! *a realistic depiction of life on the streets for Australian kids; and* Burning Bright, *a story of young love, hate and child abuse.*

Glass House Books
Brisbane

Sawdust

...when the dust has settled

Deborah Kay

with Barry Levy

Glass House Books
Brisbane

Glass House Books
an imprint of IP (Interactive Publications Pty Ltd)
Treetop Studio • 9 Kuhler Court
Carindale, Queensland, Australia 4152
sales@ipoz.biz
ipoz.biz/IP/IP.htm

First published by IP in 2013
© Deborah Kay, Barry Levy, 2013

Printed in 12 pt Cochin on 14 pt Myriad Pro.

National Library of Australia Cataloguing-in-Publication entry

Author:	Kay, Deborah, author.
Title:	Sawdust : ...when the dust has settled / Deborah Kay, Barry Levy.
ISBN:	9781922120373 (pbk.)
Notes:	Includes bibliographical references.
Subjects:	Child sexual abuse.
Other Authors/Contributors:	
	Levy, Barry, author.
Dewey Number:	362.76

Also by Barry Levy from IP
As If!
Shades of Exodus
The Terrorist

Acknowledgements

WRITING THIS BOOK HAS BEEN EMOTIVE AND INTENSE AT TIMES AND ONCE AGAIN I FOUND THE NEED FOR COUNSELLING. The adult and mother in me found reliving this journey far more difficult than the child who lived it.

My three children, you inspire me to be a better person, along with my grandchildren, who give my life meaning and joy. You all love me and I love you. I'm grateful to my "real" family for their support and belief in me, which has enabled me to go ahead with this book without judgement.

My closest friends for their unwavering support through the years, in particular, Kent the most honest man I've ever met, and Shaz, so kind and compassionate, whom I have relied on over and over. Frank and Nat… thank you for everything my darlings. I have been fortunate to have crossed paths with many positive people over the years and each of you knows when you impacted on me and that you continue to do so.

My "book" family – Barry, you have been incredibly kind and uplifting throughout this process. This book would not have been possible without you. Lauren, your editing has been invaluable and your sensitivity to my feelings is very much appreciated. Thanks to David and IP for believing in this worthwhile cause and being a publisher with a conscience.

Aside from being readable, there is nothing I would like more than for this book to be empowering to others. It is a saga, my saga, that in my humble opinion and deepest hope is worth sharing with the world.

Names and places, other than major cities in Queensland, have been changed to protect the innocent, especially those that are not ready to face the past or simply were unaware of it and my story did not impact on them.

Thank you all. I'm indeed very blessed and am so humbled by your unwavering love, support and friendship.

– Deborah Kay

Contents

Hope is the thing with feathers that perches in the soul, and sings the tune without words, and never stops at all.

– Emily Dickinson, American poet [1830 – 1886]

I have loved and been loved, not always in the healthiest of ways. I may have seemed splintered at times, even though I'm not quite as polished as I'd like, this sapling has matured and is in no way warped, worn-out or gone to sawdust. Those pockets of sunlight eventually shine through… trust me.

– Deborah Kay

Prelude

I WAS BORN INTO A HARD-WORKING, TIMBER-CUTTING FAMILY IN 1962. MY father, Dan Gallagher had to marry my mother, Julie, because she was pregnant. He told us many years later he "had to get married" as her mum, our Nana, was hitting him over the head with a frying pan and he felt he had no choice. My mother was a stay-at-home mum in those days and already had her hands full with my seventeen-month-old brother, Jim. My conception wasn't planned either, just like my sister, Marge who arrived fifteen months after me, and then my little brother, Sam, thirteen months after that. Mum was overloaded I would say, without help from anyone. So she also became punch happy with us kids.

Life was a struggle on many levels for them. Dad found it difficult to cover costs and it was hard putting food on the table, pay mounting bills, and keep a roof over our heads. The more children they had the harder life became. There were, I suppose as was to be expected, many heated and at times psychological stoushes in those early days. It wasn't until later that the arguments became more physical.

I know the age I was when Dad's abuse began because I clearly remember my brother Sam coming home from the hospital... It wasn't long after that we moved to another house and the abuse started then, when I was three going on four; at any rate, that's my earliest recollection of it.

At first it was only looking and touching but it progressed to far worse, until at fifteen, I couldn't stand it any longer and would have been quite happy when Dad said he could choke me and no one would know. It was difficult enough when Mum would pack all of us up and make a run from Dad over the years, but she always came back to him within a couple of weeks and it would start all over again.

The worst time was when Mum decided to leave Dad, when I was twelve going on thirteen, and only took my sister Marge with her, leaving Jim, Sam and me behind. But again she managed to return after a few months, when things weren't working so well with her new fella.

Having said that, Dad would gladly give the shirt off his back, give his last twenty quid to others, and make sure Mum stretched the family meal to help a struggling nobody off the street. He abhorred violence to other peoples' children, and if he saw them being hurt in any way, would become extremely angry with those parents, sometimes even stepping in to help. He just couldn't see it in himself.

I saw a way to escape all this when Chris came into my life just before I was sixteen... Life has been an amazing ride to get to where I am now. I feel so blessed in so many ways and so glad Dad decided not to kill me as he suggested that night on our way back home from Grandma's...

1.

WE WERE THE ONES IN THE DILAPIDATED HOUSE EVERYONE WONDERED ABOUT, THE FAMILY ON THE BRUCE HIGHWAY, JUST OUTSIDE GLADSTONE. The ones who the passing world, adults and children, wondered what those people did for a livelihood, if they had money, how they could bear living there. While all these people raced by on their way to enjoy school holidays, to clinch deals on business trips, or whizzed by on their way back home from relatives and friends, they probably imagined a scruffy, scraggy family, Mum, Dad, kids, definitely too many kids, struggling to make ends meet. I often wondered, the dirt blowing into my windswept, tiny girl's eyes, what it was they thought, those cars whooshing by our dusty property.

On the best of days, sometimes even the worst, as a child I thought Dad was a good bloke. At six foot and three inches he towered over everyone, and with his square-jawed Ricky Nelson looks and remnant Elvis Presley hairstyle, the larrikin in his sparkly hazel eyes would tell us stories about his youth, how he used to run amuck and get up to all kinds of mischief.

But also he would tell us how in the end he always did the right thing, how he helped out on his own mother and stepfather's property that was in the Anondale district, near Lake Perenjora, not that far from where we lived.

Without boasting, he would tell us children how he was the young lad who carried the Olympic flame as it was heralded through the district for the 1956 Olympic Games in Melbourne. He is even mentioned in a book for it and had a large medal the size of my palm back then, in acknowledgement of the feat. I still have that book and my little brother Sam is the proud owner of Dad's medal these days.

But the thing is, through his stories, through his gregarious and charming ways, he made us feel connected, and with him, or by ourselves, we would pick watermelons off the vine on hot summer days, especially at Christmas time, and the pink juice would pour from our mouths and drizzle through our fingers back to the thirsty soil from which the fruit sipped its nourishment.

On the surface of it, it could be easily gleaned from the highway, we may have been scruffy and scraggy, even scrawny and wanting, but we were children in love with life. On the best of days, sometimes even the worst, I loved Dad. I couldn't help it. He had that sort of "connectedness" about him.

Always phenomenally dark-skinned from his work outside, a tan that continued even through the cold months, on crisp winter mornings he would look out from the back door and seeing the property covered in a layer of white flakiness that looked like someone's sugar-frosted flakes had spilled over the earth, he would tell us Jack Frost had been around and left his tidings.

For us it was a huge mystery, and Jack Frost, although he never gave us anything but a scene of vast ice cold, was no less a figure in our imaginations than Father Christmas.

On those icy winter days, in the early morning cold, all of us kids would sit on the backstairs eating hot white toast covered in thick yellow honey. As the orange sun slowly rose on our expectant faces and over our bodies, the warm honey would slide down our hands and shine golden through our fingers. The image of frosty mornings with warm toast and melting honey shining through little fingers is one that will never leave me.

Inside the house, Mum, forever busy, would always be preparing something, usually meals, but also at times there was the sweet smell of things being baked in the oven. Usually it was biscuits made from no more than flour and sugar, but always hungry, we knew that smell meant there was a treat in store.

Her special treat for us on the odd occasion was a dessert called Roly Poly, which naturally we whooped and carried on about as though it was the best thing since Tim Tams, but in actual fact, personally, I didn't really like Roly Polies. I think it was because of the mixed dried fruit she flavoured it with – it was hard on a kid lacking a sweet tooth. But then again I did look forward to the delicious warm custard that was inevitably served with it. Tim Tams we never had.

Mum had seductive curls of dark brown-red hair and I am told that's where I received my own thick helmet of bushy, rust-brown hair that made my head look like a dramatically curly version of an echidna. In later years Mum would dye her hair black, giving her an Italian look that was apparently very appealing to men.

But she stood a mere five-foot tall and was, so to speak, half Dad's size. She was also never "half" the match for him, either verbally or physically. She worked tirelessly in the kitchen and outside too. All day long, as Dad cut the timber, she would be the one snigging the cut logs with a tractor.

How hard could life have been for them? It's hard to imagine even from my modest home in suburban Ipswich. Everything seemed dry and stoic in those days, everything a tough physical chore. Everything taking a mental toll. While the Beatles may have been starting out on rock and roll's most lucrative career, and most people were beginning to really relish the post-war comforts that flooded into Australia's cities through the fifties and sixties, we may as well have been struggling to survive on Mars.

The first two houses I remember were never our own, the one rented on the right side of the highway as we faced Gladstone, our biggest nearby city, and the other, which we moved into before I was three, on the left-hand side of the highway. Yes, between 1962 and 1965 we moved from one side of the highway to the other, and either way, the terrain was always hot and flat and dusty and people looked into our lives and made aspersions about us from their safe glass windows as they whipped by on the highway.

Dad always told us kids in those days life would have been different if his own father had not been killed in Singapore. In the War. It happened before Dad even had a chance to recognise the word Dad. With gargantuan courage and tears streaming in his eyes, he one day gathered us kids around his knees and told us his story: how his father was shot and killed defending the Commonwealth.

He even showed us a picture in an old magazine of Australian World War Two soldiers boarding a boat for Singapore. He pointed with a badly rasped working man's finger at a tiny blurred head with a slouch hat and duffle bag whose face we could not see, and told us that was his dad.

He was very proud to have in his possession his dad's War medals and carefully unfolded and then refolded the frail, yellowed telegram that his mother had received telling her that her husband, Bennett Gallagher, had died a hero, killed in action.

Also with tears in his eyes, he would tell us kids of his pet kangaroo and its cruel, eventual end, with its guts spilling out. He would sometimes drive us out to his first house, which was a shed with a corrugated tin roof that had no more than hessian bags for walls. It had a dirt floor. If we thought we had it bad, he had it worse.

Dad's stepfather, Uncle Harvey, just happened to be their mother, Grandma Glad's first cousin. There was a whiff of scandal associated with the union, especially in that there never seemed any proof of an official marriage certificate. But to us kids it didn't really make much difference and we were happy to call Grandma's "husband", Grandad Harvey.

In Dad's time, because his sister Dulcie did not get on with her stepdad – actually hated him – and because the small old farmhouse was now overflowing with two younger stepbrothers and four stepsisters, he and Dulcie managed to make a break from the cramped home, and moved in with Dad's grandmother, our Great Grandma Cecily Flanagan

4

and her son who was always known to us merely as Uncle Col. A bit complicated? That's how it was in those days.

Dad, the hardworking timber-cutter, would talk to me more than to any of the other kids, or so it seemed to me. He would talk with me openly and matter-of-factly especially while he constantly sharpened his knives and saws in the old work shed.

When he was out working in the field, no one but no one, not even me, was allowed to come near him. We were only allowed to approach him when he got back to the shed of an evening. I always felt at those times like I was being loved. There was a part of me that trusted him, not just in any ordinary way, but deeply, in the skin.

A true working man and protector, he always warned us about people and how others may harm us, and there was always a profound sense with Dad around that we were safe. He was also very strict, as was Mum, and they almost never allowed us to visit other children or to have other children over.

The only children allowed over, and only at times, belonged to our nearest neighbours, the Groves, who had a couple of kids around me and my older brother Jim's age. Because of the size of the open, dustbowl properties, near wasn't exactly over the fence but was near enough to sometimes even hear the neighbours.

On the negative side, there was a feeling of isolation on the property, on all the properties we lived on, the one on the right side of the Bruce Highway as well as the one on the left – not to forget the property at the centre of my life, the large acreage Dad would eventually buy from the Crannies.

The Crannies were an older couple who thought the world of Dad. He would assist them in every way he could, always helping to cut things as well as hammer and move and fix things, and they treated him like a son. Eventually, at a rock-bottom price, they sold Dad 300 acres of their property on Perenjora Dam Road.

It was this property that we kids really grew up on. It had a border right on the rail line and the noise of tooting and shunting trains became the noise of my childhood. Not only did we have passing trains now, but we were still within a hop of the Bruce Highway. Wherever you looked, there were eyes that could see into our place. Not just from the cars now but from the trains as well.

Just like Dad was to the Crannies, he stood up for everyone who needed help. Always willing to lend a hand, he especially stood up for children.

Nevertheless, there was at times something in the way he treated animals that shook me. He called cows "beasts", and I remember once how he belted the hell out of our one lone cow when it would not move into its milking stall. He was beating the cow so badly with a piece of four-by-two that as the animal went down on its knees and its body curved down to the earth, I was absolutely sure Dad was going to break its back.

No one had the courage to tell him to stop. That poor, old Brindle. On the other hand, if he saw someone else beating an animal, he'd probably get out one of his guns and shoot them. At any rate, threaten to shoot them.

That's another thing, talking of shooting, Dad had lots of guns, and he was a damned good shot.

'Just watch this, Deb,' he'd say to starry-eyed me. I'd turn around and see him throw a bottle top in the air, and – bang! – with a shotgun or his chosen rifle of the moment under his arm, he'd shoot the target out of the sky. He did the same with soft drink cans and old beer bottles, and actually anything that could be hoisted into the air was a good enough target for his eyes.

Sometimes even, he'd turn away and get one of us to throw a small object as high into the air as we could, and then he'd turn back and shoot it spot on. We were awed by his prowess.

'You don't ever want to piss Dan Gallagher off,' he would say.

Maybe it was because of this, but because of other things too, things to come later, as I grew up I developed a very strong dislike of guns, to a ridiculous point where I wouldn't allow any of my children to have toy guns to play with in any form whatsoever.

Dad also had weird theories. He told us how good salt was for you, and that we should have lots of it on our food. At the dinner table, in the smokiness of the woodstove, or while sharpening his saws and knives, he would tell us kids about kings and queens and princes and princesses, and how it was through interbreeding that they maintained their lineage.

Or as he said it, "kept their blood good". He also told us, not quite in this language, but by some sort of child-interpreted association, how there were far-flung tribes in the world where it was perfectly natural for parents to perform fellatio on children and for parents to tickle their children.

But as I said, he was hardworking, helpful to others, and he was there to protect us.

We used to have people coming in and out of our house, relatives and friends in need, and on the acreage on Perenjora Dam Road we would often have people staying in an old caravan.

On one occasion we were helping out Lyn and her husband, John Boetcher, to help "tide them over". They were staying in the house with their four year-old daughter, Grace.

Mum had a Devon luncheon sausage in the fridge, and because we kids always walked around hungry and the sausage looked to me like such an easily obtainable treat in the near empty refrigerator, I couldn't help but eat a massive chunk out of it.

Of course Mum saw the great big bite mark and wanted to know who did it. She was sure it was one of us kids, just not sure which one. I was eight at the time, and as we all lined up and stared at her accusing face with innocence in our eyes, for some reason the Boetchers' little girl, Grace stepped forward from nowhere. It was probably a total misunderstanding on her part, but she said it was her.

Lyn, upset that her child would steal from someone else's fridge, stepped in and began to beat her. As Lyn slapped her daughter across the backside and her daughter ran around screaming, Dad stepped in.

With all six foot and three inches of his awkward, bird-like frame shaking, he began to rage: 'For Christ's bloody sake, Lyn. Stop that, will ya. Just bloody stop it! She's just a little girl, the poor little bugger. She's only hungry, for chrissake!'

I felt like confessing, but something in me told me if I did, Dad would not treat me in quite the same way. So, I kept my lips pursed.

I guess this is my confession now, how guilty I have felt over all these years for poor innocent little Grace. As I grew into adulthood, I vowed never to let another person take the blame for something that I did, whether by choice or inadvertently. I hope that my honesty earns some respect now.

On another occasion, while they were still staying with us, little Grace did something really naughty, something apparently so naughty that it made her mother unstoppably livid, and she began to repeatedly slap her little girl's legs.

'Don't you dare touch that child!' Dad strode towards the action and put an end to the lathering, his head hovering like the world's tallest policeman. He looked at Lyn as though asking how anyone in the world could treat a child like that. 'I never want to see that in my house again,' he ranted.

But I remember mostly from those days the smell of burning dung and mosquito coils; it was always so hot and the soil so dry and dusty, and of a night the mosquitoes would have a field day on our white skins and pink blood.

While we children always shared a room, Mum and Dad slept in their own bedroom. They had a large white net like an ornate regal canopy hanging over their double bed. From a distance they looked like they were very important, like a king and queen.

From that bed would come us, their princes and princesses. It was sacred ground. And yet for Dad... for Dad maybe that bed and its hallowed nature didn't make any difference. Time – and expediency – would be the judge of that.

2.

THE FIRST THING I CAN RECALL REMEMBERING IN MY LIFE WAS MY YOUNGER BROTHER SAM COMING HOME. I know it could be by association of stories of that time, but I can see it so clearly in my head. I was two years and four months old and he was barely a couple of days. I was so excited I thought it was like a new toy or better still a new puppy had been brought home. And it was all for me.

Way back then it was common for family and extended family to have exactly the same first name. You would think we'd get confused but for some strange reason we didn't and knew exactly who was who. Anyway, the point of mentioning this is that Dad's second oldest cousin, Glad, not to be confused with Dad's Mum, Glad, was in our living room standing in her black chunky shoes with their hard square heels.

She was rocking our new little brother backwards and forwards with such vigour that a diminutive two year-old without shoes on like me, eager as a bandicoot to see as much as I could of my adorable little brother, had no chance but to be swallowed under her feet, so to speak. Inevitably, Cousin Glad rocked heartily backwards at one point and one of her big chunky shoes crunched straight down into my teeny, soap-sized foot.

'Ooowwww!' I cried. And then cried some more.

It was so sore I thought my whole foot had been broken. But no one seemed to hear. And that was my first memory of my little brother Sam. It was, in a way, my first memory of all things. Something of a bewilderment, something of a shock, something of a painful scream. Things I could not quite pin together. Things no one would really hear.

Dad should have been "snipped and tucked", as they say,

after Sam because four kids was more than our household could bear. But he refused, believing it was unmanly to do so, and Mum was promptly put on the Pill which she then blamed for a weight gain that was already well and truly beginning to entrench itself. I think she resented Dad ever after that.

Many years later, for some reason he did eventually agree to have it done, but that only brought more arguments to the fore, seeing as poor Mum had to have a hysterectomy not long after the deed was done on him. I remember them fighting over the fact that he believed she had tricked him into getting the despicable "unmanly cut", which was now unnecessary. All I can say is thank God he had the operation when he did.

It may seem strange, but even from the age of two and a half, I had something maternal in me. I always wanted to cuddle and hold little babies; I loved their sweet baby smell and their blubbery softness. It was like warm potato chips to my flesh. And not even Cousin Glad's big chunky shoe on my toe was enough to put me off.

It was the same with Nana's little girl. Yes, Mum's Mum had a little girl, my Auntie Beatrice, who was younger than me! All I ever wanted to do was pick the chubby, little brown-eyed ball of cuteness up. I remember clearly one day leaning over the cot, barely old enough to be walking myself. Somehow I had managed to get the baby in my arms and was trying to figure a way to get her over the sides of the cot.

Nana walked in at that moment and instead of helping me out, as I believed she definitely would, once again my dreams were dashed, this time by a loud Nana voice, shrieking: 'No, no! Silly girl! You just put that child down, now!'

Shocked, I immediately dropped the baby, of course as gently as a small girl could. Nana had one of those looks on her face like it should be the last thing on my mind, wanting to pick up her baby, but the incident never in any way put me off the idea of one day having my own little child to pick up and cuddle.

Dad never seemed to be around much at those times. He was a hard worker, the bills had to be paid and the timber cutting had to be done. Mum was mostly around in the house, telling us kids to keep out of her way as she had so much to do.

But I do remember on occasions her singing around the house, so there were pockets of happiness from her, and love. But the reality was it was never long lasting and it wasn't long after each child was born that she would be back on the tractor behind Dad, doing the snigging.

It was soon after Sam's birth that we also moved to the other side of the highway, which was the left-hand side. It was a slightly bigger house and Dad began to grow crops as well, something that would become a much bigger thing once we moved to the big property on Perenjora Dam Road.

As soon as we were old enough, and that wasn't very old at all, we were all put to helping with jobs and chores around the house. Cleaning floors, feeding the chooks, peeling potatoes, fetching and chopping wood, the older ones helping to look after the younger ones – which was in descending order, Jim looking after me as far as he could, me looking after my little sister Marge as far as I could, and all of us looking after little Sam.

But there were occasions when we obviously didn't do such a good job of looking after Sam. Such as the time when Sam was about two and he decided, come hell or high water, he was going to chop firewood by himself. The only problem was that he was using an adult Tommy axe and it wasn't long before instead of hitting the chunk of wood he was aiming at on the chopping block, he hit his big toe and split the thing right through the middle. Blood pumped and squirted everywhere, something that seemed to be a recurring theme in those days.

Mum thought he'd hacked his toe clean off. She was yelling and screaming, and we kids were yelping and crying even louder than she was. Sam, not to be outdone, and I guess the one feeling the pain, screeched the loudest of anyone.

Eventually Mum must have calmed down a little, because we were all thrown in the car, Mum with the zip of her green pleated dress only half done up, showing her Bombay bloomers and faded torn bra for all the world to see, and off we sped to the hospital in Gladstone.

We were rushed into emergency and, after a flurry of white activity around Sam, the toe was saved. Sam, to this day, still has a dodgy looking big toenail, which gives the grotesque appearance of his nearly succeeding in removing the unsightly digit.

Since we kids were born pretty much within five years of one another, it wasn't long before we were all basically looking after ourselves. There seemed to be no end to the amount of help that was needed around the house. We were busy from almost the second we woke up until the minute we went to bed at night.

By the time we got to school each day we were already pretty well exhausted. Rather than schoolwork, we were ready for sleep. As a young girl, I'd also be responsible for milking our lone cow, Totty. Because of the early hour I had to get up in the mornings, it didn't exactly help me stay awake at school either.

Often on weekends or in the days we were not at school, while Mum and Dad worked in the paddock, we were left somewhere outside the house to fend for ourselves. Just sort of left there, without toys, without games, without anything to stimulate us. So, instead, we created our own games and got up to all sorts of mischief.

One of our main games, something that would become a big thing in my life later on, was sitting inside an old car or truck wreck and pretending we were driving. I just *looooved* to drive, and in fact, to be useful around the property, Dad taught us all to drive by the time we were twelve or thirteen. There was nothing I would not do to get a chance to drive.

But in the very early years, one of the things I remember doing while Mum and Dad toiled away, was building a "cubby" with my older brother Jim. It was really quite an innovative job we performed, a cubby-house built out of new growth saplings and tree branches, and it looked like a real Aboriginal humpy.

There was only one problem: we built the cubby on the banks of a creek that ran through our property, and rather than innovative, a piece of clever if not ingenious handiwork, Dad saw it from another perspective.

We should have known, he lectured, once our cubby had been found out, how dangerous it was to play – let alone build – a cubby on the banks of a creek. A creek that, at times, with heavy rains, swelled to overflowing and flooded the area around it. We could have drowned.

So rather than praise, Dad dished out a hiding for that. On this occasion it was across our backsides and upper legs with a finger-thick ironing cord he often used for the purpose.

But it was better than getting a belting with another weapon he used on us, known as a switchy-stick, a ripe twig cut from a tree that felt like a cat-o-nine tails must have felt to the early convicts. Both instruments of punishment hurt, but a switchy-stick *really* hurt.

Both Dad and Mum were strict, and, in those days, with lots of kids around and no help, control and discipline had to be maintained. I suppose, if nothing else, lacking the know-how, it was practical.

On another occasion, near our old pile of rusted out cars and things, there was this really old wooden caravan that had been there forever. It stunk of dusty cobwebs and mould, and animals like possums and snakes and bats lived in it by night. There was an old electric stove inside, and my brother Jim and I decided to use it – to make glue. We were going to use a recipe we had learned about at school, which was basically heating flour and water and stirring them together.

The first thing we did was carry the heavy stove out of the caravan. Then we put together a series of power leads from Dad's work shed, which was about fifteen metres away. Once the old stove was connected, with plenty of Mum's precious flour, which we had snuck out from the kitchen, we set about boiling our mixture on the stove, in a big rusty pot.

As the potion bubbled and steamed we stirred it with an old plank and stuck our fingers in to feel if the glue was sticky enough. Our hands went red and burnt from the heat, but the pain aside, we thought we were doing a great job.

Just when we thought we were about done and had achieved the beginnings of our new glue factory, Dad arrived. Yet again, while we thought our idea was quite ingenious – and at least did not involve the horrendous cruelty of making glue out of horses hooves which he himself often told us glue was really made of – he had a completely different way of looking at it.

Convinced we were going to set the property alight – something that was, I suppose, quite easy to do in the tinder, dry conditions – and seeing the amount of Mum's flour we had used, he yelled at the top of his voice: 'What the fuck d'ya think you're doin, you little bastards?' He often called us that – 'you little bastards'. And then ranting some more, he yelled to Jim, as the eldest: 'Come here, you little boofhead!'

He gave Jim yet another heavy flogging with the ironing cord. I got it next, but not quite as hard. Years later, retelling the story, he did admit that he always thought it really was quite a clever idea – our glue-making. But at the time that was the end of our "glue business".

The caravan, yes that old wooden caravan, would remain around for other things...

I remember once also, I was just about ten, and with my younger sister Marge and the two Grove kids from next door, we decided to try cigarettes. Since Mum only had the occasional sneak smoke because Dad was dead against smoking, we had to wait for the appropriate time to steal a couple of butts from her new stash of Alpine Menthols which she hid behind the breadbin in the kitchen.

Dad thought smoking was the filthiest, most disgusting thing anyone could ever do, and in retrospect I think Mum smoked mainly to try and prove a single point – that she had some control over her own life. Strangely enough, he never seemed to mind if any of his mates made a "rollie" or a "durrie", as self-rolled cigarettes were known in the day.

Interestingly, too, Grandad and Nana, Mum's Dad and Mum, were chain-smokers. Nana always, even with a baby clasped in her arms, would have a fag dangling from her lips. In her case, a beer in the hand was often the case too. But there was not much Dad could do about that.

Anyway, me, Marge and the two Grove children stole a couple of cigarettes from Mum's stash. We hid ourselves outside the house in a small corrugated iron water tank that was all rusted out with holes in it.

Immediately we lit up and began to puff away. Even though the smoke burned our throats like thick, hot charcoal, the menthol gave a cooling and somewhat weirdly pleasant sensation as we drew in and swallowed down.

Outside the drum we suddenly heard a knocking. We caught a massive fright, only to find it was just Sam. We hadn't allowed him to be with us because he was far too young in our opinion to be smoking. The oldest amongst us was the Grove boy, who was about ten. But there was another thing about Sam and smoking: it was well known that our little five year-old brother had terrible asthma.

Seeing what we were doing, and despite the fact that we were spluttering and coughing away like sizzling, over-heated pork chops, Sam stood defiantly outside the water tank and begged to be let in.

Repeatedly, I yelled at him, 'No, no, you'll get sick! Get the hell outta here, Sam. Leave us alone!'

Obstinate as hell, he cried back, 'I'll dob on yers. I'll dob on yers t' Mum an' Dad if ya don' let me in!'

I could just see that irresistible frown on his little round face. And so with no choice, and rather than face the ironing cord or the switchy-stick again, we gave in.

Sam hauled himself into the tank, and sitting right in the middle of us, in the middle of the little Indian smoke-pyre we had already created, he took a few puffs on one of Mum's Alpine Menthols.

It was only moments and the little bugger's eyes began to water profusely and his throat to close and choke. We were convinced he was going to die. Coughing and scared for his own life, he climbed out of the tank as quickly – and awkwardly – as a baby scrub turkey and we all held our breath and waited.

Next thing there was an enormous racket against the tank that we thought was a storm rolling in from the sky above us. Or World War Three. We all looked up, but the noise continued to give off a sound like the heavens were caving in and our eardrums would burst.

The banging was eventually followed by a deep voice: 'What the bloody hell do you kids think you're doing in there? Get the bloody hell out, this minute! And you, Debbie, you should know damned better!'

I don't remember what happened afterwards, except despising little Sam like hell for many moons to come after betraying his word and dobbing us in.

After that, Sam earned the nickname "Ford Pill", much to his chagrin. Ford Pills were something Mum would take a handful of before going to bed each night so that her bowels would move in the morning. In my view, Sam had the same effect on all of us... he bloody well gave us the shits too.

Those were the good times, the good memories for all their harshness. There were others, many others to come.

3.

WHEN WE MOVED TO THE OTHER SIDE OF THE HIGHWAY I used to wonder if people, the cars passing by, knew that sometimes families moved from one side of the highway to the other. As much as they looked at one house and thought about that particular family, a year or so later they could be looking at the other side of the highway and instead of wondering about another family, they would actually be wondering about the same family.

Maybe they should have known. We always took all of our mess with us. Not that we had a great deal in those early days. The days before Dad started his junk collection, that is. That was yet to come – when we moved to the big property, not that far away either. But what I remember more than anything was Cousin Glad's chunky black shoe landing on my naked foot as I tried to get my first peeks at little Sam.

I remember that because I recall distinctly that it was just a few months after that we moved to our next rented house on the other side of the highway. More precisely, from our local point of view, the move could be thought of as shifting to the other side of the Nebo River, which ran like a big snake through Anondale. Down at its mouth, the river separated Nebo Island from the seaside town of Burrum Sound, a place where I would one day end up too.

Although the new house still had just two main bedrooms, one for us kids and one for their royal highnesses, Mum and Dad, the new house was slightly bigger. Like the old one, it was raised but this one had a whole steep flight of stairs we had to walk down to get to the backyard. The stairs had a view to the paddock where Dad ploughed the dry ground to grow his crops.

I also remember Cousin Glad stepping on my toe at the

time Sam was born because it was not long after, just after we moved to the other side of the highway, that I began to notice the way Dad would gaze at me. He had a way of plucking or flicking with his thumbnail at the gap in his two front teeth when he was distracted or seriously concentrating on something.

Only now it wasn't quite that look I was noticing, it was another, stranger look, like one sometimes sees in a bird gaping down at you from a tree – its head almost but not quite tilting, very inquisitive.

In the event, Dad's gaze lasted even longer than a bird's curious stare and had the feeling of excavating, as though scratching. As though digging at skin with a pick. Unlike a bird, too, his eyes remained absolutely steady, never a blink or even a twitch of alarm. It was like he had become oblivious of everyone and everything around him, and there was absolutely no inclination to fly away. I noticed the look for the first time one day when Dad and I were out in his shed together.

As usual Dad was sharpening his blades, and I had toddled down there with my unbendable curiosity to see what he was up to. The shed at that time, with its open sides, looked more like a gazebo than it did a normal iron shed, and it was big and filled with mysterious things that were like a pile of giant mysterious toys.

They were Dad's toys, of course, but the good thing was he didn't mind Jim and me hanging around him in the shed. In that way he was much better than Mum who used to always shoo us away from all her cooking and baking. As long as his day's work in the paddock was done, he enjoyed our company.

He especially liked mine, and would natter endlessly to me as I sat and crawled at his feet. I enjoyed being among the muck; I enjoyed the smell of grease and petrol and metal, and I enjoyed the proximity to the solid, giant frame that was his.

On this particular occasion I needed to do a pee, and old enough to let adults know when I needed to do so, I told Dad.

'Just do it there,' he flicked with his eyes pointing to the thin grassy scrub outside the shed. So off I went, just outside the shed, and pulled down my knickers under my dress.

All around me, in my immediate vicinity, I saw a heap of old metal timber saws with their huge round cutting wheels that were as tall as me, I saw axes standing against steel frames and heavy metal implements that were used for ploughing. There were also tons of spare and rusted tractor parts that were strewn all over the place like massive brown ants.

It was an environment that excited me. Otherwise it was pretty bare; thin tufts of browning grass here and there and the odd eucalypt tree peeling like snakeskin.

This was my land, the land at my feet – dry and hard like a khaki desert and flat with no place to hide. Whatever we did out there, like my peeing now, was done well and truly in the open. I wonder if anyone saw me from the highway? Too late now.

My wondering head, as I peed, spun out into this endless hot scrub, and after a while I heard a scraping noise. I looked up and saw Dad stepping out of the shed. When he was quite close to me he stopped in his tracks and just stood there, watching me.

He was very quiet and appeared to me like a tall, silent swamp bird. I was not afraid. I had no reason to be. But the look was strange, as I had described, like a probing bird, his head ever so slightly tilted, but unlike a bird his eyes did not blink or look about or flinch.

After a while I could not help but think, 'Why is he looking at me like that? Is he trying to say something?'

Even as my little girl thoughts flew up to his eyes and my urine watered the dry weeds beneath me, he continued to watch me. After a while, he started to pluck with his thumb at his front teeth. He did it until I was well and truly finished peeing.

Then he lumbered up to me, leant down, which was a long way for his tall, lanky body to bend, and placed his hand on my crotch.

'What is he doing?' I thought, convinced he was checking to see if I was finished, if I had indeed done my business. But he did not say anything, and just stayed like that for a while. It passed through my mind again, why are you touching me, but it did not feel wrong or misplaced or scary in the least.

The only thing I do remember being certain of was that his hand rested there, lingered, like one uncertain of a route, like one looking for direction. All the while his eyes looked into mine with that digging feeling, that scratching and picking, as if to say I shouldn't move until he was finished.

Then he jumped up and told me also to get up. He strode away from me, back into his gazebo-shed.

At that time I also used to enjoy being around his mates who would come over now and then to play a whole bunch of musical instruments and sing and drink. Happy, like any little girl, I would run around, feeling warm, feeling affection, feeling like I was being loved. It was the most important time in my life, this fun-making adult world that belonged to Dad.

By comparison, on normal weeknights, sitting near the stove at our dark wooden dining room table, everything at home would be the same.

From the first day outside that shed and in the long nights after that, our family would sit at the dinner table, listening to Dad, listening to him constantly telling us to salt our food – 'You kids must put salt on your food. Eat lots of it. It's good for you.' – And yelling at us to eat all of it, every scrap of our dinner, as we tried to hide our boiled, mushy pumpkin and sometimes other squishy vegetables from sight.

'Eat your goddamned bloody vegies, too,' his wide throat would yowl. 'You're not leaving the table till you've finished every speck. Unless of course you want to get your backsides tanned!'

4.

I SUPPOSE I SHOULD HAVE BEEN ALERTED THAT DAY when Dad touched me after I'd urinated outside the shed? But he did it again and then again as though it were completely normal, eventually telling me with his steely bird-eyes that this was something between us, a father and his daughter. A king and his princess. It wasn't that other people shouldn't know, it was just they would never understand.

What they would never understand, according to Dad, was the way other cultures brought up their children and kings and queens continued their long historical lines. Our own modern royal family not exempt. He said that for some obfuscating reason these days no one wanted to face that part of their history. I was a little girl, and in a strange sort of way glad to be a princess. It gave me a sense of belonging.

There we were stuck out in the middle of nowhere, and there was Dad, a mercurially tall man with strong – in all the ladies' opinions – handsome, square-jawed features, gregarious and funny and helpful to everyone – and there was I, a hopeful little girl, suddenly accessible to him.

Even though I could not always follow the reasoning of his need for my company, I was happy to see the spark in his eye fall on me. A bizarre understanding developed between us that was like clouds melding and becoming one, and I was at times extremely close to him. It felt extra special.

In reality, I was a shy and timid but mostly friendly little bird who liked to see the good in everyone. I would do pretty much anything for others to be friendly back to me. I was the girl with the big fuzz of hair who wanted to be loved. The girl who, with her older brother, Jim, had tried to make glue in the old wooden caravan that was so blemished and dilapidated it had become the accommodations for small animals and reptiles.

But I was also the girl who would go with Dad to the same caravan and do much more than Jim would ever know.

'Come, let's go and see what we can find at the back paddock,' Dad would say to me, and my young five-year-old legs would happily follow him.

There was a mouldy old mattress in the caravan and he would lie me down and take my knickers off. Lying or kneeling next to me he would fiddle with me and touch my privates, then he would take his erect penis and rub himself against me. I never thought there was anything wrong with it, just as on that first day, no more than a three year-old, I had not thought there was anything wrong when he touched me outside his work shed.

With only the slightest sense of trepidation, in all honesty, it felt pleasant.

Strangely, I don't ever remember him ejaculating either. But after a while, after a few minutes – the whole thing would take no more than about ten minutes – he would stand up and tell me to put my knickers back on and then say something as simple and matter of fact as: 'Go and see if the chooks have left any eggs.'

That part was confusing. The cold that came afterwards. The not knowing what had really happened. The only thing I did know for certain as I gazed into Dad's straight worker eyes, which stared back like a wild bird into me, was I should not ever, under any circumstances, discuss it with anyone.

The caravan was "our place", and it wasn't the fact that I was happy to have it between us. More so it was that it was "our secret". A clandestine touching of affections between a father and his naively loving daughter. A place for a king and his princess. It had a feel of more than normal. Of special.

5.

ON MY FIFTH BIRTHDAY I WAS GIVEN A DOG, WIDGET. It was one of the greatest days of my life.

'Go over to that box,' Mum and Dad said to me that afternoon, pointing to the big old tea chest in the living room.

Unsure, I toddled over to the box and heard tiny little yelps. I thought the box was trying to talk to me. I was told to open it, and inside found this minute ball of black and tan fur. My whole heart lifted like the sun had infiltrated every pore in the house. I touched the puppy and felt its fur breathe. I could have cried from joy.

'That's Widget,' Dad said. 'She's yours.'

But like all things in our house, Widget, an Australian terrier, turned out to be mine and not mine. She was in reality all of ours – *the family dog* – even though she was given to me for my birthday.

People were more practical in those days. If there was a need, especially if it was a more nonessential pleasure-giving need, it was saved for an occasion like this, a birthday, and everyone benefited. Although we did not comprehend it then, I guess that's why Dad and Mum called the dog Widget. In the end Widget, like all things in country regions, was expendable: by definition, a mere small gadget, a mechanical contrivance that kept us kids occupied.

Still, for a while I felt a little unique. I was loved and had something smaller than me to love back.

That night there were lots of people in the house, I can't recall exactly who, but typically, as would happen to me, the day would be remembered with some associated pain.

'Deb, it's time for the candles,' Mum called out to me. 'Go on over and get the knife. We'll need it to cut the cake. And then we can all sing happy birthday.'

I walked over to the sink and grabbed a tea towel only to have the butcher's knife – which Dad had sharpened enough to kill a cow – kind of spring out of it and fall directly into my foot. Yes, *into* my foot. The point pierced straight through my flesh and blood spurted everywhere.

At least this time Mum heard me when my cries reached into the heavens. Suddenly a cloud of bodies was swirling around me, and Mum, taking charge, was washing my foot and applying bandages.

Mum... Yes, I remember Mum that night; it was one of the few times when she held me, when I felt the warmth coming from her that was usually reserved for my younger sister, Marge and little brother, Sam. I felt small and wonderful in her arms and wondered why it couldn't always be like this. Why she always had to be so frosty. Why she never heard me.

Come to think of it, Jim, my older brother, was pretty much in the same boat as I was. I don't recall him getting much praise or attention from her either. Maybe us two just didn't fit into the category of cute since the advent of the two younger ones? Now we were looked on in a more earthy, practical way – older and therefore more "workable". It always took something more than just being you to get love in our house. It didn't come of its own accord. You had to have some use.

With my foot bound up, I blew out my five candles and helped Mum cut the cake. Despite the blood and pain, it was a good night, full of happy feelings and caring.

It is the small and simple times like these that abound in my memory. To this day I still have a scar on my foot, a remnant of the event.

And of course there was Widget. She was everybody's dog, the family dog, but on that night and for the next few days at least, she was mine. She licked my face and her tail wagged and I was a little girl in wonderland.

Another thing that was fun at home, especially when we were in this the second house, on the left side of the Bruce

Highway, was walking to meet our older brother Jim as he came home from school. With my little brother Sam wrapped in Mum's arms, and me and my younger sister Marge springing at her side, we'd walk to the wooden gate that led out onto the Bruce Highway. That's where Jim would be dropped off by the school bus.

I recall how I would stand on the old wooden gate like a jittery-winged cicada, jumping up and down and waving my hands furiously at whatever traffic came by. As we walked back to the house, Mum would ask Jim about his day at school and Marge and I would be all ears, wanting to know what school was like.

Once home, Jim would take out his slate board and charcoal and show us younger kids what he had learnt to write and draw at school. In those days, rather than normal exercise books, rather than pens and pencils, we in Queensland still used slate boards and charcoal.

The slate boards went back to Dad's day. And I remember Dad, from time to time, would take out his own old slate board from his time at school. But even better than that, he would show us this perfect wooden pencil case that he had made all by himself at school.

Inside the case were these thin, long pieces of charcoal that Dad used to write with as a child. I was also looking forward to writing on a slate board, eager to learn, but paper and pencil came into our school the year I started and that had its own sense of excitement. Times were changing.

But in those days, fetching Jim at the wooden gate, jumping up and down on it like an agitated cicada, and bouncing next to him until we got back to our house, was warm and exhilarating.

Of course, in the background, also happy and bounding, would be Widget, my, or should I say *our* dog. She would wag her little tail and bark helplessly at the magpies and big black crows that paraded the ground nearby. Like the terrier she was, she would spring with bravado – and the birds, used to it, rather than fly away would merely hop, threaten and glare.

As to Dad, although it is something of a cloudy blur now, or perhaps the truth is I have made it into a cloudy blur, touching me was by this time – at the tender age of five – a part of the daily routine.

Like in the caravan, so on my bed or anywhere else for that matter he found available at the time, he would tell me to lie down or sit at his side and pull down or tell me to pull down my knickers. Always he would rub me first with his fingers and then he would stroke me with his hard, erect penis against my vaginal area.

Was I afraid? Was I afraid of that big adult thing? The truth was it seemed so normal, so run of the mill; I have no memory of it crossing my mind in a bad, immoral or even alarming way. That is the honest truth.

I only ever felt this vague apprehension, a kind of mild anxiety that would increase with time, that I could not really relate to anything.

Now, not even the work shed or even Mum and Dad's bedroom was sacred – he would do it anywhere and everywhere, even in that sanctified bedroom where the king and queen lay under their majestic white mosquito net. Somehow Dad would always find a way to get me alone, somewhere where no one else was around, and he'd lay me down on the bed, or the ground, or wherever, and do his thing.

On one occasion, as I lay there on my bed in my bedroom and Dad leaned over me, a shadow entered the dimness of the room. Something dark, with eyes and yet no eyes. Was it Mum? I don't know. It was a premonition. A feeling. A sense. But it was something dark.

And really, really, maybe I shouldn't have been too worried, because I knew whatever we were doing was *our secret*. Was what kings and queens and exotic tribes did, and the only reason others, including Mum, should not know about it was because they did not know the real story about kings and queens and the way other, happy, far-off tribes lived. They would never quite grasp it. Or even want to grasp it.

6.

AS DAD PUT IT: IT WAS ONE OF THE SAD FACTS OF LIFE THAT OTHER PEOPLE WOULD NEVER "GET IT". With his stiff bird-eyes dug deep into my skin, he would tell me often enough: 'You can't tell anyone, Deb, this is our special secret. They just won't get it. You know how much I love you...'

Yes, our "special secret". 'You know how much I love you...' Dad and me. Cropped from among all of us kids, maybe all the people in the world, Dad loved me in this particular way, which was more than anyone else. Maybe as much as Mum?

I was happy enough with that, to be as important to Dad as Mum and all his mates. If anyone couldn't understand, or wouldn't comprehend it, though, it was Mum. Mum who was so cold and did not really value me.

In the days after that "premonition", after that dark and ghostly shadow above me, strangely, Mum began to ask me if Dad was touching me.

I made immediate connections with what she was saying, but the reality was I still wasn't absolutely sure why she wanted to know or what she really meant by it. What was she really trying to ask? *Why* was she asking? Did she want to know if Dad was being a "king" to me?

I wasn't sure I could trust her either. Dad had warned me. So I simply stood there, and said no, and shook my head. But she didn't let up.

As the days went by she grew more forthright, asking me more and more explicitly: 'Does your father – or anyone else – touch you in your private parts?'

I would peer up at her, this non-understanding woman who wouldn't have a clue, and if anything I began to wonder if Dad had maybe told her something. Let her in on "our secret".

Nevertheless, seeing Dad's hard, square jaw in front of me, his hard bird-eyes telling me not to tell anyone, I continued to dig in, looking down, denying everything with an obstinate silence and a scowl.

I guess, actually I'm sure now, Mum must have been able to see the truth in my face, in my faintly blushing cheeks, in my thicket of dark brown hair that spiralled out and at the same time clung to my head like a ballooning veil of shame, because eventually she wore me down.

Sitting in the sunshine on our back steps one day, she continued to cajole me: 'Come on, Debbie, you can tell me. I won't mind. I promise, I won't get mad at you. Come on, Deb, tell Mum. What does Dad do to you?'

Thinking about it in my little girl head, I was actually beginning to wonder if she was starting to like me because she wanted to know about Dad's and my secret. She wanted to be a part of it. She wanted to be "connected".

Listening to her voice, almost cooing now in that way she spoke to little Sam, finally, finally, which was not really that long after she first began to ask, I broke down.

Looking up into eyes that I saw as moist, compassionate and appealing like a beggar who only wanted friendship, not even money, I went ahead and told her. Not only that, I was sure, seeing the integrity in her eyes, it would only make her love me more.

I began in a timid voice: 'Dad... Dad... he pulls my knickers down and touches me here.' I pointed down to my privates. 'Sometimes he touches me with his fingers... and sometimes with his "thing".'

I looked up and saw Mum's eyes enlarge. They turned dead dry. She stared at me like there was something in me that was... indecipherable? And then she slapped my face. Slapped it so hard my ears rang and my jaw swung and jangled. The tears rolled from my eyes in disbelief.

I remember being so bewildered I could not think or talk. I had thought she liked me again and wanted to know about

Dad's and my special love – about kings and princesses, "our secret" – because she would be proud of me, because she wanted to be a part of it, but now all I could see was how unhappy I had made her.

She grabbed me with eyes like ice-cold hands and yelled at me: 'Stop being such a liar! Your father would never do that! Don't you ever, ever repeat what you have just told me – to anyone!'

Needless to say, I learned a valuable lesson that day... *Never ever* tell anyone what Dad does with you.

Dad was right, he was absolutely right. If Mum wasn't going to believe me, who would? Worse, if Mum didn't really understand, why would anyone else? The world just did not get these things, as Dad had said all along.

There wasn't even a choice any longer; it was our secret and that's how it should remain, between us. Between me and Dad. I also learned another thing: Mum was never going to like me again.

7.

AMONG THE GOOD TIMES THERE WERE THE WEEKENDS, perhaps months in between, of great jollity and merriment. Those weekends when Dad and his mates came together of a night and either in the moist heat of summer or around the old wood stove burning away in the winter, they would sing and chat and play their instruments – and of course drink their beer and rum. Dad always played the harmonica or the spoons, two spoons clicking together in old Australian bush style.

"Click Go the Shears", "Tie Me Kangaroo Down Sport", "The Wild Colonial Boy", "Waltzing Matilda", they would croon and blare. I remember them all, and then there were others too, more modern songs like Elvis Presley's "Wooden Heart". Dad loved that song, his hair was styled a bit like Elvis, and he was always playing it on his harmonica, not just when his mates were around.

Everyone chortling and singing and banging their musical instruments, we loved those evenings, the heat and friendship in the house, the sense of communion they generated. Dad looked so alive, so tall and at the centre of it all, and all his friends appeared like people on a stage around him that we wanted to be with.

They spoke about old times, always the old times, which was like a mysterious ancient time of things hidden under big craggy rocks to a little girl, and the stories grew taller and taller, richer and richer, just as did the fish they caught and the enormous numbers of them they trapped in their nets and on the ends of their pointy hooks.

One of the men there was Davey Dadds. A little older than Dad, he had close-cropped, stand-up hair or a "buzz cut" as it was known. He played the violin. But the amazing thing about Davey Dadds was that he was blind. Yes, completely and utterly blind in both eyes and never wore dark glasses or anything to cover it. His eyes stared forward, a sort of smudgy, grey-pink, opaque like a dead fish, and like a dead fish he would sit there looking at you but not looking at you.

Somehow I was never frightened of Davey Dadds. He was kind and brought us presents and always had a good word for us kids. Of course we loved him for it. Actually, we thought he was great. Once, I remember, he brought my sister and me a pink and blue brush and comb set.

Initially, Davey handed the pink set to me and the blue one to Marge, but Mum came along a few minutes later and changed things around. She gave Marge the pink one and me the blue. I was disappointed, but it wasn't any kind of resentment against my younger sister for getting the colour I wanted. It wasn't her fault. Even at that young age I was aware of that, it was Mum.

On those musical nights, there was also Cec Parsons. He was roughly Dad's age – about thirty – and rather handsome with his deeply tanned skin, dark oily brown hair and thick brows that hung over deep eyes and a thin smile. A fisherman by trade, he also played the harmonica and this stick instrument that had a thick layer of bottle tops nailed to it and made a shimmery, clashing sound when it crashed against a hand or leg. Cec Parsons had a voice, in my opinion, which could be put on a stage. It was a dream being around him.

Truth be told, I loved being around all of them, to be part of the warmth generated by those fun-filled times. The only exception was old Tommy Lubbock, Aunt Sal's father. Much older than all of the others, he played the fiddle and the accordion, and had a face like a big startled fish.

Actually, he looked a lot like Alfred Hitchcock. His big pouting flesh with the hanging jowls was pocked like thick melting wax and his fat, blubbery lips were always wet with spit. He always smelled of alcohol. I guess they all did, but it was worse on him. He smelled like a pub after closing time, three months ago. Like stale hops a hundred times over. In my head, I used to call him "Old Luber Lips".

'Come on up here, lass,' he would call to me, and timid and shy as I was in those days, I would go and sit up on his lap. It is hard to believe how I would even go near him. But I did.

At one time or another on those jolly weekends I would sit on any one of their laps. The men would smile and cuddle me as I hopped up, and with the strength of horses they would bounce me on their thighs or knees. It felt grand. Like at a show park.

It was more than just euphoria rocking that way, it was being right at the very centre of it all. And then... and then, of course... after a while, a hand would slip across my little bony thigh and, with each one of them, at some point or other in the midst of the ruckus, fingers would slip into my undies.

Merrily, while they played their instruments and sang their songs and rocked away, they would let their fingers roam and stroke.

Scary? Abusive? Horrifying? No, no. Believe it or not, at that age, with my sense of the world, to be absolutely honest, it felt nice. I was never scared of any of the men. I loved being around them, and except for Old Luber Lips, didn't really mind the intimate roaming of their hands.

What was scarier than any of them was Mum. Yes, Mum. She was suddenly putting on an enormous amount of weight and could be seen outside in the yard hanging up the washing dressed in a big pink all-in-one plastic weight-loss suit that made her look like an astronaut. Now that was scary.

In those early days, I also rarely remember being given or playing with dolls. My best games were playing with my older brother Jim in the dirt. I remember having a big blue toy truck with a big red shovel on it, and I'd spend the day moving earth with it.

I also remember Jim having this amazing spinning top that was red with a clear plastic cover. It was so cool, the coolest thing ever. It had racing horses jumping over barricades like in a steeplechase. I had to pump the handle like mad at the top to make it spin, and at full tilt it played music like a carousel.

It was great to be allowed to play with my big brother's spinning top like that, and the best part was that Jim didn't mind – well, most of the time.

In honesty, really, really, my best, most fun times were those times when Dad's friends or our rellies came over and there was lots of singing and music, jokes and stories. Dad's friends cared for me – in a way that I never got from Mum or in many ways even from Dad.

Mum was always too busy and Dad, during the week especially, but even on weekends a lot of the time, was out at work in the paddock and never wanted to be disturbed.

So I enjoyed it when Dad's friends were around. I enjoyed the immediacy of it, the release of it. I enjoyed bouncing on whomever's lap was there for me on that particular occasion. I loved being noticed in amongst all the revelry.

Sometimes it was Davey Dadds' lap I sat on of a night and at other times it was Cec Parsons'. Or, yuk-yuk-yuk, sometimes it was even fat Old Luber Lips'. His lap could be terrifying. He was so fat and smelly and old. What was I doing there? Why was I even climbing onto his lap? Why did I let him have his hands down there while his lips drooled moisture and breathed a stale and dry fermented sweetness on me? What made me derive a certain enjoyment from it?

The good thing about blind old Davey Dadds, on the other hand, was that he liked to hug me. Sometimes he would just hold me on his lap with his arms wrapped around me and didn't even put his hands inside.

I guess, whichever way I looked at it, it didn't really matter, being a "big girl" in the middle of all those fun-loving men was somewhere I felt at home and comfortable. This is the truth: I did like it, and being part of the fun was something I craved. I considered myself lucky to have some attention from the grown-ups. It was more than my siblings had, and in my mind it was a privilege and a badge of honour. Almost as good as being grown-up.

How were these men able to do this? It is only in retrospect that I see now, none of them, not one of these men saw anything wrong with it. It was like Dad, who was the man at the centre of my life, gave them permission; and they went ahead.

Dad told me one day, along with his theories about kings and queens and how they "kept their blood good", that it was okay, it was all right, there was nothing wrong in what they were doing.

'That's what men do,' he said by way of confiding, meaningful father-daughter talk.

And somehow it made sense to me. It made everything okay.

He would consider me with knowledgeable eyes, a bird teaching its hatchling how to react to others, and I trusted him in the way a hatchling trusts a mother bird feeding it. Sometimes, of course, it was Dad, even Dad whose lap I was sitting on. In front of all the men, his mates, I would be bouncing there on his thighs while his hand kept me warm under there.

Like an exotic implement they needed to fulfil their carousing, I went from lap to lap at one time or another, and on each of the laps they played me like an instrument. Yes, and yes again, I took pleasure in the sound it made. It gave me camaraderie. It was cosy, it was loving, it showed people cared.

Where was Mum at these times? My brothers and sister? Somehow they were around and not around. I remember my brothers and sister singing and dancing and joining in the fun, and yet in the end it was like I was the only one left in the room in the middle of those men.

Mum? I don't remember other women being there very often, but occasionally when they were, I guess she would be with them and the other kids in the kitchen or downstairs or even somewhere else. In the "girls den", as they called it – and I would be left to happily fend for myself in the great big fun-loving "men's den".

These men, Dad's friends, were my culture, my daily bread, my warm winter blanket. They were my sense of contentment. They were my joy in life. My mates.

8.

MUM'S REACTION TO MY TELLING HER ABOUT DAD – as she put it, 'Your father would never do that!' – told me there was something more to this secret. It beat through Mum's chest, beneath her frail linen dress; and it told me, maybe, just maybe it was not as Dad said.

But I was caught between two hard lumps of gravel, getting love and extra special attention and being scowled at like I was dirty, which only drove the wedge further between me and Mum.

Dad could do bad things too, like threaten and beat the hell out of us kids, but when he was with me in that "secret way", it never felt as cold as Mum.

It was warm while it lasted; it was welcome. Until he told me to go and get on with it, feed the chooks, then it became cold as Old King Frost.

The reality was you grew up fast in the world off the highway. The right side or the left, it didn't really matter.

It was around this time, not long after I got Widget, that we were out one day on the Delaneys' property, just near where we lived. Dad was doing the timber cutting while Mum was snigging the logs and we kids were playing with rocks somewhere in the dirt.

It was a weekend, early afternoon, and we had had our strong Vegemite-tasting Bonox soup, our slice of bread and billy tea, which was our standard lunch cooked over a small fire, when I heard an unfamiliar sound.

It was like a sharp rasping of metal, but with an echo, and I said to Jim, 'What's that? I can hear a funny noise. Can you hear it?'

I remember my heart beating really fast, like it instinctively sensed something wrong, like it sometimes raced when cars collided on the highway or when Dad called me to the bedroom. Only it was racing even harder now.

Jim looked at me, not hearing what I was hearing.

'C'mon, let's just go and have a look,' I urged.

He looked at me, a white boyish fear in his eyes, 'No, we can't. You know we're not allowed to do that. You know what Dad'll do. Anyway, it won't be anything.'

Yes, that was the truth, when Dad and Mum were working on the land we were not allowed anywhere near them. Especially Dad, we were not allowed to approach him until he was well and truly back in his shed. And knowing Dad, we didn't even chance making contact with him before that.

You don't ever want to piss Dan Gallagher off. The words rang in our ears like a constant siren. But in fairness, Mum and Dad were performing hard, heavy work and it was dangerous.

For our own safety, it was better we were nowhere near them – definitely nowhere near Dad's timber-cutting or his hefty chainsaw that sent the sawdust flying off the logs like a circle of angry, humming bees. Even Mum, it was dangerous to be near, twisting her torso backwards and forwards on the tractor snigging the immense logs up to Dad.

Hearing that sound again, I pleaded: 'C'mon, Jim, let's just go have a look.'

My eyes were leaning down to little Sam who was doing useless wind circles with his arms while his large dirty-white nappy dangled like a duck between his knees.

Jim looked down at him too, and then at Marge just sitting there like a yellow anthill in the dirt, and knowing we had to look after the young ones, he said: 'Do we go tell Dad first?' His brows were flickering. It was like his mind had become stuck. That was the degree of fear.

'No,' I said bravely. 'Mum's just down at the creek. Let's go and see for ourselves. We'll be quick.'

In the end, Jim and I left Marge and Sam to fend for themselves, and we raced down to the vicinity of the creek where Mum was working. With stern, adult eyes, we had told the two little ones not to move from where they were or Dad would give them a good bloody belting with a switchy-stick. They just stood there, stared up at us, and understood.

As Jim and I ran closer to the creek, we could hear it more clearly, the noise I was hearing. It was like a rasping, a scratching. Eventually we were close enough to clearly hear: 'Heeelp. Pleeeasse heeelp.'

In front of us we saw the tractor turned upside down and Mum's plump body beneath the back of it, jammed between a huge log and the mudguard covering the wheel.

Seeing us, despite her obvious pain, she began to scream: 'Stay back. Stay back, you two.' I ran forward still, and she called coldly: 'Debbie, do *not* come any closer. Don't even come *one* step closer. Stay back!'

I remember thinking, why? Was this to do with everything else, the ice between us, the distrust? The things I should not tell anyone about? And then I saw it, the petrol spilling out onto the ground; she was protecting me. In the midst of her agony, she was shielding me and Jim from going up in a fireball with her.

'Get your father. Go get your father.' Her breath, like her body, sounded like it had been trapped beneath Ayers Rock.

'Stay with Mum,' Jim suddenly said, and a much faster runner than me, he immediately turned to go and get Dad, who was obviously back at the log stack by now, cutting the timber into rectangular slices, something known as flitching.

He was stopped by Mum's voice, 'No, Jim, no! Take her with you!'

So together we ran for all we were worth, but when we got to the spot where Dad was working, we suddenly halted. We looked at one another. We were both flicking our eyes with panic, our stomachs frozen. We were too scared to even call out to him.

In front of us we had premonitions of a heavy slap across the heads and then very possibly our backsides, and in our heads, even though he was still totally unaware of our presence, we imagined the deep grunt from his throat: 'Piss off, you little bastards!'

Swallowing, Jim slowly bent down and grabbed a stone. I copied him, and then we grabbed a whole bunch of stones. From a distance, rather than call out, seeing Dad sawing away among the swirling, angry dust of bees, we started throwing the stones at him.

In front of his gangly body was a thick brown leather apron that made him look a bit like Ned Kelly or some bushranger, and we aimed the rocks at the apron, knowing they would make an echoey sound when they hit him. We also did it so that the stones would not hurt or enrage him. Whatever we did, we did not ever want to piss Dan Gallagher off.

Eventually he turned around and seeing us, called out: 'Buuuggeeerrr oooff! Buuuggeeerrr oooff, you little buggers!' He was waving an arm wildly in the air to tell us he meant it.

Concentrating, he went on with his sawing. Determined, we carried on with our stone throwing. Finally he stopped his sawing, tore off his leather apron, and with the sawdust settling and globules of fire spitting from his eyes, came up to us like he was going to give us a lathering.

'Mum's hurt! Mum's hurt!' we called out before he could even get near us.

'What d'you mean?' He glared down at us.

Breathing hard, we told him. 'The tractor's rolled away, onto her, and she's stuck.'

I'll never forget the way his face washed from brown to grey to white, seeing a fear I had never seen before flooding into it. And then he ran, his tall, lanky body raging through the khaki scrub like some sort of tall bird, an emu on stilts.

At the scene, he nervously assessed the situation with the sort of calmness I think only people who have lived on a property – or fought fires – could know, and all the time Mum kept shouting out, 'Get the kids away! Get the kids away!'

In the end Dad ran back for a chainsaw and grabbed a sapling from somewhere or other to wedge Mum's leg from under the huge tractor wheel. The wheel had pinned her to the ground at the ankle. He then rolled a large rock close to the tractor to use as leverage for the sapling.

Mum continued to scream at us kids to get away, but Dad kept yelling at us to do the opposite – to stay there, to sit on the very end of the sapling. He wanted some control to raise the tractor enough to give Mum the room to drag herself from under the very possibly ready-to-explode machine. I could see in Dad's ashen face how worried he was, and she just lay there, groaning, while Jim and I enjoyed obeying Dad's more exciting instructions.

She was sweating now, trying to heave her body, and as we sat on the end of the sapling where Dad told us to, we could hear in Mum's alarmed voice the certainty that we were all going to end up in Kingdom Come with her.

Finally, when it seemed all was lost, and Mum might be right about Kingdom Come, Dad just managed to squeeze her out from under the wheel. He then sprinted back to where he was sawing to fetch our old truck so that he could get Mum to the Delaneys' house and call an ambulance.

Mum, at this stage in her life, was almost as round as she was tall, and when Dad returned and parked the truck as near to her as possible, he found it was not as easy as he thought to lift her up onto the back tray. It was one of the many cycles in her life when she would mushroom from petite to a great heaving barrel – making her about five-foot all round.

In the end, Jim and I had to do what our little hands could to help lift Mum and heave her over onto the side-less tray. Once on there, apparently safely rooted to the tray, Dad drove off, leaving Mum bouncing and clutching onto whatever she could for safety. Jim and I, in the back with her, did what we could to hold onto her, keep her steady, and soothe her non-stop yelping and whooping. One thing was for sure, she was in pain.

Even then, Dad first drove to pick up the two younger children, who, true to their fear, had not moved an inch.

They climbed into the front with Dad, and off we drove again, bouncing and rattling along the dusty, gravelled track with Mum, still crying and tossing in pain. At the Delaneys, Dad called an ambulance and when it arrived he travelled with Mum to the hospital. We were told later, they treated her for a badly mangled and sprained ankle.

But while Dad was away, what happened inside the Delaney home was more important to me than anything outside it. It wasn't long before we kids, well, definitely me, forgot about Mum at the hospital and instead concentrated on Mrs Delaney as she made us what I can only describe as heavenly Strawberry Nesquick and handed us gorgeous looking Milk Arrow biscuits. The biscuits had creamy-pink icing on them that she had made herself.

For us it was a real treat, something we never got in as grand a fashion at home, just that smell of thick strawberry milk and the creamy cherry-vanilla flavour of the biscuits. It was so warm in the Delaneys' house, so cosy. They had two children who were adopted, a boy around Jim's age and a girl about my age, and even I could see they were well loved.

Looking at how they lived and conducted their "family business", I felt envy. I could not help it. I think all of us felt it. It was a house we wanted to live in, a house filled with closeness and peace, a house we never wanted to leave. The whole day's tragedy was worth it for this moment of sweetness in the Delaney home, for the lingering warmth of it. I felt like a sugary cocoon, coated in strawberry, had covered my body.

But in the end we had to go back home. To our world of secrets and coldness and deceit. Of playing with stones in the dirt.

Something seemed to shift in Mum and Dad after the accident and in the months it took for Mum to heal.

It was around this time that we moved into our new property on Perenjora Dam Road, but not only that, it seemed for the first time in years there was some happiness in our house as Dad tossed up and tore at the soil of our new acreage so that he could plant things to make an income from.

Dan and Julie Gallagher were making something of their lives, of their new three-hundred acre stake in Australia. We were all very happy.

9.

IT WAS GOOD OF THE CRANNIES TO LET DAD HAVE THE PROPERTY AT A BASE BARGAIN PRICE. It was never too much for him to do anything for them, helping them out when they were having problems on their property and in their house, so I suppose it was only right and proper that they returned the favour to the good-humoured, helpful young man they looked upon as their son.

But the thing about the property is that that was all it was. Just the land to start with, then a short time later Dad put a small shed on it for us to live in. It still had to be built up and turned into something profitable and liveable – a place where we could grow our own vegetables, raise and kill our own cattle for meat, and cultivate the crops of "milo", the drought-resistant grain Dad would sell as feed for cattle and sheep to make a little extra money.

There was no house – and after initially starting in one bare shed we graduated into a shed with wooden sides and a tin roof. Onto this, Dad slowly attached railway huts with fibro walls to make rooms for us kids as well as a spare room. Entering the house, we almost walked straight into Mum and Dad's bedroom. Like in the other places, Mum and Dad had that white mosquito net over their double bed that, of a night, despite the ramshackle nature of the shed, made the two of them look like royalty.

Other kids must have thought we stank, because even though we did bathe each day, there was barely enough water to wash the dirt and grime away. There was no choice. Water was in short supply and we had to be especially frugal with what we had in those days until we were able to connect to the main pipeline.

Our shower was a small, corrugated enclosure that looked like a big drum. We yanked a cord above us to flush water from a small tank, soaped ourselves, and then pulled the cord again to rinse off.

With a bath, which eventually came later, we kids always bathed at the same time. The water was always dark and murky, and at times even Mum and Dad would get into the tub with us.

It may sound intimate and cosy and filled with exaltation, but I can never remember bath-times with Mum and Dad being a particularly happy time. It was more like sitting at the dinner table being told by Dad to eat our vegies – or else. There was something cold and earnest and disciplinarian about it. Also, the bathwater was warmed with pots of heated water from the combustion stove in the kitchen, and the bath was never really that hot or full enough to have a good wash – or play – in.

The house was never painted either and the walls and roof were never lined. As in most old Queensland houses on acreage, the wooden dining room table was part of the kitchen and stood not that far from the combustion stove. Our table was pushed up against a thick wooden beam that in its way seemed to hold the entire structure of the house together. Like Dad.

This was the property that we kids really grew up on, with one border of the property against the railway line, and our house still within a hop of the Bruce Highway.

It was at this time Dad started to gather all his old cars, trucks and junk metal bits, which resulted in our place looking more like a scrap yard than it did a happy man's tidy "selection".

A number of complaints – much to Dad's annoyance and disillusionment – came from the city council to clean the mess up or at least to erect a wooden fence high enough to hide the awful mess from the road, the trains and the passing public.

Dad couldn't see what all the fuss was about. To him everything he saved had a value and eventual use. It was only the rest of the world who considered it as "some messed up stage of never".

As to the trains, we kids got really excited when we heard the older steam trains hooting away as they did their puffing and shunting. We could also still clearly hear the screeching of tyres and the occasional bang of car accidents on the highway.

Having a bigger property did not mean we had more money. And maybe happy was too strong a word in our situation. Because it wasn't long after our move to Perenjora Dam Road, and the initial peace and happiness that came with it, that I really became conscious of Mum and Dad's arguing. Maybe it was just the frequency of it, but after a while they seemed to fight all the time.

There was always this driving need to make ends meet, and no matter the situation it would spark Dad off.

'How we gonna survive if that Davies bugger doesn't pay his bloody bills?' he would constantly rant at Mum as though it were her fault.

Despite the shortage of money, there always seemed to be enough to have alcohol around. Mum hardly ever drank that I can remember, the odd glass of this or that, or a mixed drink like gin and tonic, but Dad and his friends were always downing the glasses, especially rum.

Of a night, there was also always a big plastic container of cheap wine – or plonk – around the house, and Dad would regularly fill his glass from it. I don't think the plonk helped keep the peace at home – although it has to be said, it was seldom that we saw Dad really drunk.

I remember one occasion when Dad's Uncle Col was visiting and they both got quite drunk. Dad was going off in front of us kids that if he had a chance to go to the War he would have. Just like his dad. Just like his dad, he would have shown those "Jap mongrels" a thing or two.

He got so wound up that he got out one of his guns, attached a real bayonet to it, and started charging the "Jap mongrels" all over the lounge floor – until his long, dangly legs somehow managed to wrap around themselves and he fell over and landed on his own "mongrel" behind. Dad didn't think it was half as funny as we kids did or even good old Uncle Col, who, that night, showed off all the gaps in his Chad Morgan mouth.

The arguments were bad and grew worse. Louder and louder. In my head they were like a cloudy mess that brooded above everything and from which every now and then dangerous lightening would strike into our bewildered chests.

Dad was a big man, and at times there were bits of froth and spit, like small flames coming from his mouth. His lips, normally thin, looked terribly narrow at these times, almost twisted. I don't recall Dad ever punching Mum, but more and more, as the fights grew worse, he would take Mum by the shirt or nightie or whatever she was wearing and shake her until her jaws rattled and it looked like her teeth, which were already false at this stage, were going to fall out.

At other times he'd enclose his large, flaking hands around what was becoming her big, thick neck and threaten to throttle her. For us kids it was like our world was about to implode. Our hearts would thud and pound and we would look at one another with frightened eyes.

Sometimes, late at night, we would even wake up to their fighting. Or, as I grew a little older, I'd be pulled out of bed and be made to stand there as they fought. I can't recall why I was woken like that or what their words were, but it was like those fights were often over me.

There was so much pent up rage that I wondered how the shouting would ever end – except by knockout, or death.

Often Dad would threaten to leave, and Mum would call to me on many of those occasions: 'Debbie, Debbie, please, tell your dad not to go. I don't want him to leave me. Get him to stay!'

She would be crying and whimpering and hardly able to breathe. She would rub at her nose in a fidgety, nervous way that always told us when she was distressed.

Why she was making recourse to me, I didn't know. We didn't even get on that well. If anything, I knew I was an irritant to her, like I got in her way. It was obvious, to me anyway, that she much preferred my younger sister Marge. So it was hard to see why it was always me she called on to stop Dad from leaving. I could only conclude, in my young head, it was because of what she knew, that she didn't want anyone else to know about.

What I think she hated most about me was this inordinate attachment I had to Dad; and I think that's why she thought it was through me she could raise the emotional charge for him to stay.

She was in effect using me. Or worse. It sometimes struck me, a little girl with her head buried in storm clouds, all these arguments were over *me*. I felt like a badly carved peg in the middle of a huge tent that could bring the entire structure down.

More often than not, as Mum stood there crying and shaking, the only thing I could feel was a dark choke in the middle of my neck; it represented the utter confusion in my head and a wish that Dad would in fact go.

At other times I just wanted to jump out of a window, but of course I never did. I probably had just sufficient sense to realise I would only break a leg or something worse, and end up bound to our quickly cracking house even more so.

During these wild nights of lightning strikes, furnace and confusion, I didn't want to live at home. I wished I could be adopted, believed it would all make sense if these two people weren't really my parents. But somehow the arguments, the fights, the shaking and screaming and eventual whimpering would just peter out. And then the next thing we saw was Mum and Dad hugging and being all lovey-dovey to one another.

Frightened still, we didn't know what it was at first, but later on we would realise some of the funny noises we heard coming from the sleep-out after their arguments were in fact the soft grunts of them making love.

Making love! It was difficult to work out. It was utterly confounding. The swings from one end of the mood spectrum to the other. We were the car out of control on the famous B Grade horror roller coaster ride. I can only think there must have been a passion there, between Mum and Dad. It was just that it could go either way.

In reality we kids were tired. Tired all the time. So, so tired from doing all our chores, from looking after ourselves, and then at nights hearing their arguments into the early hours of the morning. We never knew if it was ever going to come to an end or if Dad would stick around.

We walked around exhausted at school, always ready to sleep. I suppose the truth was, I was "my father's daughter" and at the end of those arguments he never left the house. That would be left to Mum. Years later, she would be constantly in and out. But that is a story yet to come.

10.

I<small>T WAS HERE IN OUR NEW HOME, TOO, THAT ONE DAY MY DOG</small> W<small>IDGET</small>
<small>WENT MISSING.</small>

I remember the day so clearly; everyone was looking for
her and couldn't find her. It ended up that for two whole
weeks we looked. We even asked neighbours and the locals
to keep an eye out for our little watchdog. But it seemed no
one had seen or heard her. Finally it was Jim who found her
– on the roadside.

Puffing, his face white just like I imagined Jack Frost, he
came up to me and like a real, mature man, said: 'Deb, you
don't want to see this. I've found Widget. But it don't look
good.'

His staring eyes and manly stance told the story. Widget
was found with a big gaping hole in her side and there were
maggots crawling out of her. Dad said it looked like she had
bled to death.

I was devastated. Life was full of cruel blows. It upset me
how easily life could be turned upside down. The cause of
her death appeared to be connected to a large petrol tank we
had on the property. It was known that some misfits in the
area would come around at times and try to steal the fuel.
On this particular occasion, it seems, Widget had caught
them red-handed, made a noise to ward them off, and got a
bullet in her side for her troubles.

Mum was around then, but I don't remember feeling
a great deal from her... there was no hugging or words of
comfort. But that's not to say she wasn't upset, because she
was, so was Dad. We all were.

Perhaps they were all affected in their own way by their
own grief? They just didn't show it like we kids did. Then
again, that was life on a farm. Mum saw another emptiness,

a gap around the place, and Dad thought if only he could catch those bloody mongrels... Yes, if only he could. If he had, they would have felt one of his bullets in their butts for sure. But the incident reminded me of a story much worse than mine. It was the story Dad told us around the same time, about his pet kangaroo.

When Dad was a boy growing up he had this pet kangaroo that he loved and which followed him everywhere around the paddock. It was at the time when he was still very young and staying with his real mum, Grandma Glad and his stepfather, Uncle Harvey.

It was a time of massive rainfall and flash flooding and Dad was frantic about where Joey, his pet kangaroo had got to. The kangaroo was nowhere to be seen. Sometime during one of those days, it was Uncle Harvey, a man Dad mostly looked up to, who with a smile told Dad to go down to the back of the paddock – because Joey was around there -- "hanging out against the black stump".

Relieved and excited, Dad raced through the muddy paddock to the black stump. As expected, Dad found Joey there, only his pet kangaroo was lying up against the stump with its stomach cut and hanging out. Its underbelly was like a neon pink jellyfish, its insides half-eaten out by dogs.

Without having to tell us, from the red in his eyes, we could see how Dad must have cried and wondered about the random punishments the world dished out. In the background, Uncle Harvey was laughing, telling him he was *such a boofhead*. I knew from my own experience how it felt.

Yes, there was always something to tarnish the good times.

To be honest, if I wasn't exactly happy, I can't say I was exactly unhappy. What I was getting now on the new property as Dad built the house, was a lot of attention. And not just from Dad or from his mates when they came around to play their musical instruments and sing and make merry.

I was getting extra special attention from Cec Parsons.

Cec was always around on the nights of the merrymaking but he would also be around at other times too.

A fisherman by trade, like Dad, he was also in the timber industry, and would help Dad with the felled trees. He also did the ringbarking, which was a way of poisoning those that needed to be culled to let new growth come on. Because of this work, sometimes he would stay overnight at our house.

Somehow, and I can't recall why or even how, everyone would manage to traipse off to bed, and I would be left out there, in the woody living room with handsome Cec, the man with dark, mesmerising eyes, a subtle smile, and a voice fit for a stage.

What I especially liked about him was that he was a much softer and gentler man than Dad. He would call me over to him in a smooth and kind voice, his dark brow almost begging, and then when I was comfortable he would do what Dad used to do, only much more gently.

Sitting or even kneeling, he would take down my knickers and rub himself on me. On occasion, he would be lying on the daybed in the lounge where he would sleep of a night, and he'd call me to come over and stand by him.

Out would come that extra tense and it would seem unmanageable part of his anatomy, and, just like Dad, while I stood there, he would rub himself against my vaginal region, in the clitoral area, like he knew exactly where the right spot was. I would stand there, a little girl who should be in bed fast asleep, feeling tingly and soft like velvet.

Sometimes, and again don't ask me how this was possible, when I was sent to bed early he would later come into the bedroom, which we kids all shared, and he would climb into my bed. He would lie close to me and rub himself against me. It was fleshy and comforting and so intimate, in some ways almost sacred. I would feel needed, a child in a church choir looking up at angels.

It was good to be noticed by Cec Parsons. It made me feel different to the others. It made me feel like a wanted human being. And yet I can't say I remember there ever being a single conversation between him and me, not even any of that "adult to sweet little kid" talk between us. Strange, but I can't even remember him asking me how I was or even how school was.

But he was handsome and charming and gentler than Dad, and that was enough. He never felt like he was hurting me or forcing himself on me. I was a little girl, and in my eyes, seeing how well he sang and played his stick of bottle tops, and how friendly he was with Dad, the unbreakable pole that was at the centre of our house, it was hard not to feel special.

Unlike Dad, he never said things like: "You! Get yourself over here!" No, he never ever talked like that, never got all cranky when I wanted to do other things. He only ever called me in that wet and generous voice that sounded like an archangel.

Late one night, after Cec Parsons had been with me, Mum and Dad appeared in the bedroom and hauled me out of bed. I could tell Dad was acting at the behest of Mum, because she was standing behind him like an overfed ship commander, raging and ordering: 'Get her on the kitchen table, dammit, and let's have a look. Then we'll see what's going on here.' And Dad, strangely, like a gawky cadet sailor unsure how to proceed, was obeying her.

Half asleep, I was led through the darkness of the house into the kitchen. There, in the complete black of night, I was lifted onto the kitchen table and told to lie on my back. The ceiling felt so close to my head and everything around me was so dark and threatening that my head felt like a flock of migrating birds lost in a jungle of squalling clouds.

Above me, Dad's menacing bird-eyes were looking grey and frozen while Mum's dark eyes blazed so intently and seriously I thought they were going to jump out of her head and beat me. It was like her eyes were a surgeon's knife cutting through my skin.

And in the end, like surgeons, it was like the two of them, Mum and Dad, knew exactly what they were doing and where they were going with it. Only to me as a person, as a little girl alone on a dark wooden kitchen table, their eyes didn't speak. They just barked orders and sliced. My body was writhing with the heat of small yet hugely painful incisions.

As I lay there like that, confused, self-conscious and embarrassed beyond belief, Mum was only about to make it worse. She ordered me to take my flannelette pyjama pants off. When I had done that, one of them, I think it was Mum this time, pulled down my knickers.

She growled to Dad to fetch a torch, and I completely believed, even without my pants on, they were going to examine my eyes. The birds in my head were whorling like a big and dusty whirly-whirly and I could not help but wonder if this was some new ritual Dad had not shown me that kings and queens performed.

Finally, a yellow light shone into my face. Behind it stood Dad. They both gathered at my side and Mum stood there, the short and plump commander, the Lord Admiral, giving orders. She was looking into my eyes but yelling something completely unfathomable.

'Open your legs, Debbie!'

'No, no. Why?' I was sleepy and befuddled.

'Just do it. Open them! *Now!*'

Looking up into Dad's eyes, I saw stone. Looking up into Mum's eyes I saw desperation – that urgent, sharp-gashing surgeon's blade. Neither of them were giving an inch. I opened my legs.

All I remember was it was cold, and I sort of peered back with my head into the darkness behind me as they shone the torch between my legs.

In another world, in another era, it could have looked like a witches coven or like a Medieval torture chamber; in this world it was a torch held by two adult people, called parents, searching between my little girl legs for I did not know what. It was an investigation, a close and brutal interrogation. I was their prisoner and I held all their enemy's secret truths.

Staring intently down there, the torch waving just slightly, Mum was the first to put her verdict on it.

'It's red,' she said. 'You can see it. He's been touching her.'

Dad beckoned down with his eyes but stopped at the top of Mum's head, like he was avoiding her. In a sense, without saying a word, I could see by the way he fidgeted and looked about Mum, that what Mum had said was his verdict too. He was just not prepared to openly say a word about it.

For me, the word "touching" was my clue. I knew from experience what Mum was on about. Only I couldn't tell her, I couldn't say anything. And quietly I knew it wasn't just Cec, it was Dad. It was Dad, too.

Eventually, it sounded like eventually because Dad was silent for a long time, but finally he breathed: 'I'll have a word with him, Julie. He had better not be doing anything like this. Else he won't be allowed back again. I'll make sure he knows.'

After that I was allowed to go back to bed. There was no *goodnight*. No *can we help you in any way?* No *my poor darling, we need to talk about this.* I was simply ordered back to my room. There was no word of sorrow, or explanation.

11.

THAT NIGHT I PEED MYSELF. THAT IS TO SAY I PEED MY BED. It was something I had started to do, pee my pants, whenever anyone put too much pressure on me. Whenever I felt locked into a corner. It happened too whenever Dad was going to give me a belting, or did give me a belting, or shouted at me. It also happened when Mum was about to attack me, verbally or physically, or did attack me, I did that thing. I peed myself as if I had no control over my own bladder. I remember having lots of urinary infections; but a kidney X-ray didn't show up anything. Something else pushed to the background; something that would last into mid teenagehood.

Leaving my wet bed behind and out early into the dry cold of the paddock the next day after the events of the night before, I heard a train tooting its head of steam and I wondered what the day was going to bring. I could not help it. I was expecting some kind of thrashing from Dad. For, I don't know, being "caught"?

But seeing me, Dad, in a very friendly manner, like everything in the world was exactly as it should be, like the night before hadn't happened, took me aside and took me into his confidence.

Around us the magpies were yelling through the dry autumn air, and with firm bird-eyes bearing down on me, he told me not to tell anyone about what Cec had done to me. He was very strong about it, and trilling resolutely like one of the birds he repeated what he said. In fact, this time adding: *'And do not tell anyone about anyone.* Least of all Mum.'

His hazel eyes really softened now, beginning to explain, to mentor, to lecture me with almost chirpy retinae: 'This is what men do, Deb. There's no need to worry, it's just the men having a bit of fun, hey. Nothin, absolutely nothin wrong in it. Cec's a good man.'

Dad, my guide, my teacher, was so tall his head sometimes looked like the sun. Like the hot sun, he stood at the centre of the earth and he knew what he was talking about. He knew much, much more than Mum, who slapped me for the truth, who had me on a table with a torch shining up my privates with my legs drawn up and wide open like an upside down beetle. As Dad said, she should never know because the truth was she would never "get it".

What I do remember very well about that time, young as I was, is feeling completely isolated on the property. Even when I eventually started primary school at age six I felt isolated.

We siblings had one another, but we were ninety percent of the time not allowed to have friends over or allowed to visit friends. Other people, we were told, were bad; we should never trust them. Mum and Dad warned us constantly. They were concerned, they said, they were doing it for our own sakes. For our safety.

Which is probably why I never told Mum – or Dad – about Uncle Barney and what happened on the way back from Mum's younger sister, Aunty Lorraine's twenty-first birthday party in Gladstone.

I was about six years old and it was very late at night. All us kids were told to lie in the back of the ute and go to sleep until we got home. With us in the back of the ute was Uncle Barney, Mum's older brother. The ute was Cec Parsons', and he and Mum and Dad were huddled in the front cabin, with Mum doing the driving. The back of the ute had a high frame that was covered with a tarpaulin. On the floor of the ute was Cec's thick fishing nets which made everything feel comfy and warm.

Bumping happily along in sleep, I was awoken by something pressing on my lips. I opened my eyes and had to blink. I blinked again. It took a while of blinking but eventually I realised what was going on. I may have only been six but I was no idiot. I had already seen a good couple of things.

So I knew after a while what it was. It was Uncle Barney forcing his stiff penis into my sleeping mouth. He was holding the back of my head and pushing me onto him. I don't know what it was, but maybe confused with sleep something jarred in me. Everything stood still. It was like there was a concrete post in the middle of me and I remember biting my teeth so hard together it felt like they were going to crack.

Persistent, Uncle Barney kept pressing himself on me. Beneath me, the car was wobbling and the road felt like small stones jumping into my ears and head. Around me, I became aware of the awful smell of dead fish. A piece of large cork on the net beneath me bit uncomfortably into my side. Inside my head, clouds were gathering. It felt familiar and yet unfamiliar, everything so dark, frightening, cold, just like that night on the kitchen table with Mum and Dad examining me. Birds were swirling in a cloud behind my eyes.

I didn't know exactly what was going on. No one had ever done this to me before. There was a taste of humidity and salt on the tip of my tongue. I continued to clench my teeth as hard as I could. And Uncle Barney continued to press as hard as he could. The taste of salt grew in my mouth.

'It's good for you, Debbie. You must eat lots and lots of salt if you want to grow big and strong like me.' Dad's mentoring voice groaned inside me. But it wasn't that kind of salt. It was what men do kind of salt. Only this wasn't what any man had done before. Caught up in the fishing nets, it felt dirty. And yet maybe it was all right? And yet maybe it was normal? What men did? My tongue pressed against my teeth and tasted it. The salt. It slid into my mouth. I felt like I was going to be sick.

'Deb, Deb, are you all right? Is everything okay back there?' The ute ground to a halt and Mum's voice was calling from the front like a siren. It was like her voice intuited an emergency.

There was silence. She called again.

Eventually someone – it must've been my older brother Jim – called back that everything was okay, and at last Uncle Barney withdrew.

The ute continued on. Uncle Barney turned away from me.

That taste in my mouth. That thing on my tongue. There was a lot happening in those days, but that was the thing that didn't sit right. I didn't tell anyone about it. Like Dad said I shouldn't. *Don't tell anyone about anyone, Deb. No one will understand anyway.*

And Mum...? I don't know how, but it was like she had sensed something. But if I told her she would only tell me not to ever mention these things again. She would slap my face. Put a yellow torch in me. Only this time it would be down my throat.

In the end, I didn't have anyone to tell. But the feeling of something being wrong only grew worse.

And was made worse, quite a long time after, when Dad began kissing me. Yes, Dad began kissing me like an adult. Real French kisses that made me feel sick and yet at the same time tingly and loved.

There was something in the closeness of it, its exoticness, which once again told me Dad had chosen me above anyone else. I was being singled out for sure. Dad had taught me another lesson in how to be a person and how, maturely, to show affection for others.

In fact, I learnt the lesson so well that one day at a birthday party for our next door neighbour, Mr Grove, I would do just that – show I knew how to give affection like an adult.

Mr and Mrs Grove were the only ones whose children were sometimes allowed to come over to our place, and so when Mr Grove came up to me for his happy birthday kiss, I slipped my tongue into his mouth.

I'll never forget how the very staid, very steady, very genteel man reeled back. His head, half bald, looked like grey ice. He glared at me, his usually ruddy cheeks whiter than a flicker of light. He looked afraid, even more afraid than I was.

Taking a deep, considered breath, and then another, his chubby cheeks bloating and narrowing, finally he seemed to collect himself. Like they were searching for a familiar pathway, his eyes gazed deeply into mine. I could see he was lost.

In response, my eyes blinked back into his. But painfully. I felt my tongue sucking into my cheeks, and as best I could, if that were at all possible, I tried to hide my shameful eyes behind my big bushes of curly brown hair.

Finally, tongue twisting for words, he told me that what I had done was absolutely not appropriate. Not for a little girl barely eleven years old! Not for anyone.

I looked back into his eyes, saw the earnestness in them, the uncanny gravity of concern, and I suppose I should have been alerted then. I should have. But all I can remember is feeling ashamed. So very, very deeply ashamed.

In the end, he also didn't understand. Like Mum, he was one of those who didn't realise what happened in the real world. The world of men.

And yet there was something in that kiss with Mr Grove, something in that sick, overt reaction that told me something was amiss. And it was useful knowing what I did, because one day with that knowing I saved my sister Marge.

I was walking into our bedroom and saw Dad already in there. He was standing there with my sister, leaning over her like a big dark shadow, and I could tell it was like she did not understand. She was backed up into a corner of the room, wanting to get out of there. I could sense in the stiffness of her straight dark hair, she was dead afraid of the advancing bird in front of her.

She was unwilling. I could tell that a mile away.

She needed protection, she needed a shield, so I went up to Dad, took him by the hand, and started kissing him, kissing him in that way I had tried to kiss Mr Grove. Like a lover, I smooched him and led him to the other side of the bedroom. And like a big puppy he followed me, and my sister slipped away.

A gallant soldier, with my knowledge I had stood up in the line of battle and shielded her path from my black world of love and affection and the ways of men.

To this day Marge doesn't like to remember that incident, not anything like that with Dad. For her it didn't happen. And maybe to this day that is why the most important part of my body is my lips. Never mind what they say about protecting your privates, it is in the lips where the lies and deceit can be seen and felt. Even if I don't see it, I will feel it through the lips when people are being dishonest. Nowadays, I do not readily accept lips – or anything else – on mine... And when I do, I devour them.

Maybe it is also why I can tell when someone has been abused. I just have to look at them and I can see it not only in the eyes and cheekbones but on their lips. Did I have a face like that? Men seemed to think so. They seemed to recognise it in me. Men have a way of knowing these things.

But with Aunty Bev and Uncle Max it was different... without people like them I would never have survived.

12.

I THINK THE DIFFERENCE BETWEEN AUNTY BEV AND OTHERS IS THAT SHE NEVER REALLY LOOKED INTO MY FACE. Even when she was looking there, she was really looking into my heart. She saw only goodness and dished it back from her own heart.

Even if she did see in my eyes, in my hair, on my lips, what was really there, the secrets, the deception, the hidden truths, she spooned back with her heart in heaps and knolls. It was as though, intuitively, she was making up for it. The damage. The scratches and dents people around me did not even know was happening.

Aunty Bev and Uncle Max were Dad's aunt and uncle, and all my life I think what saved me was having people like them around, people who counter-balanced the darkness, the iniquity, who showed me that what I saw as light and life and a part of the everyday, was really dark and dank compared with the open windows, the lit Christmas tree that potentially stood beside it.

Dad's Mum's older sister, in some ways Aunty Bev even looked like Dad. She had the same square jaw and prominent cheekbones, but unlike Dad, although she was nearly twice his age, her hazel eyes glowed and her features were soft as snow.

There was nothing at all accusing on her pallid skin. Her hands were always so warm and calm. Unforgettably so. They comforted me, they held me, and always they radiated with heat against my skin. They say cold hands mean a warm heart. It is not so. Warm hands mean a warm heart and cold hands, like Dad's, and come to think of it, like Mum's, mean a cold heart. I know. I have experienced them.

This did not mean Aunty Bev could not be stern. A no-nonsense woman, she was upright and firm, but this was the point, she was also playful. I learnt how to behave around her and I was amply rewarded with rays of warm colours and enchantment.

I loved being around her – in ways that were different to those men and their drunken fun and musical whooping. I knew I could fall backwards and she'd always be there. I did not have to do anything for her.

Her feelings were genuine and sincere, but then again at that time so did I think Dad's mates' were. But unlike them, Aunty Bev talked constantly to me. I can't even remember about what, but with her short wavy-brown hair that was peppered with specks of grey and with her eyes that shone, it was always like a Noisy Minor twittering away next to me. *Pipipipipee, pipipipipee, pee, pee,* her voice was a steady song – and unlike the others she couldn't give a damn if I did pee her bed, but because I felt safe and calm there, I never did. I just loved the sound of her voice.

It was probably my one bit of luck. When Mum and Dad needed us to be looked after in school holidays, I'd be taken to sleep over at Aunty Bev and Uncle Max rather than any of the other relatives. My older brother Jim, on the other hand, usually went to my Aunt Dulcie, Dad's older sister. The younger two, Marge and Sam, would be kept at home.

While it was good for Mum to have me and Jim off her hands, the truth was she didn't much like having us around in any event. In me, she saw too much of Dad, and this thing that she saw would only grow worse as I grew older.

'Wake up to yourself!' she would scream over and over at me. Like I knew what it was I was meant to be waking up into. Like she had shown me another self I could be. Like she had given me directions. The only things I saw in front of me at home were inside out. And no one gave any real pointers. So it was a great relief whenever I could get out of her sight.

Aunty Bev... she would take me to a hall in Gladstone where they played Hoy. It was a game like Bingo – only the idea was to match all the cards on your sheet to the cards the dealer turned over. And when all their cards came up, the ladies playing the game would call out 'Hoy!' to show they had finished.

When Aunt Bev's cards came up, she always shouted it with a smile that stretched across the hall and then looked into my eyes like *I* had won. I remember her winning all these cans of fruit and vegetables and jams and I would feel so proud as we walked out of the hall with our packages of goods.

At other times, I would follow her around at home as she fed the chooks or hung up the washing in her backyard. Unlike Mum, she'd let me help with her constant baking and cooking. And in the background, Uncle Max, a man with full and ruddy, freshly shaved cheeks and an almost bald-looking head of spiky white hair, would always be pottering around the house.

I remember always hearing tinkering and hammering from somewhere in or under their old wooden Queenslander that was right in the middle of Gladstone. To me, old as they appeared, they were people who were at ease with life, who always looked at home in their own skin, people fresh in their age. They were anchored and it made me feel calm and wanted. It was like having a long warm shower whenever I went there. It was reviving and cleansing and reassuring.

And yet... and yet... I never found I could ever confide in Aunty Bev. More like, it was probably that I was too scared. There was absolutely no one I ever wanted to tell about anything. I couldn't. I could hardly comprehend my own life.

What hurt me more than anything was the constant cold that drifted through the doors at home, the voices that were raised, the isolation and the uncertainty. Removed from that, it was the closeness, the touching by Aunty Bev, that was such longed-for relief, but still I did not have it in me to tell her about home.

The evenness that I experienced at her and Uncle Max's place was enough for me; it gave me hope. It was like walking into the sun after a shuddering storm.

I remember the lawn at Aunty Bev's. Actually, I could never forget that lawn. Compared to our stony, dry, wispy-grassed acreage with Dad's dead old trucks, spare parts and bits of metal and machinery strewn all over the place, their lawn, sitting below the lofty gaze of their Queenslander, was like a bowling green. Only it was even softer, more like a velvet trampoline.

I loved to roll on it. The garden sloped down to the road and I loved to roll and roll all the way down it. Just me on that lawn, rolling, watching the grass and the sky and the clouds wrap around me.

The alternative to go to when Mum and Dad needed to get rid of me and Jim during school holidays, was Aunty Dulcie, Dad's older sister. She also lived in Gladstone, was much younger and more modern than Aunty Bev, but I didn't like going there at all. She was a real boss in boots. Even when she was being nice she didn't have a patch on the cosy feel of Aunty Bev.

I recall Dad saying how "hen-picked" her husband Len was and that Len was a better man than him for putting up with her. Like Aunty Bev, though, Aunty Dulcie was straight up the line – unfortunately with her it was a cold and spiky line. Step out of that line – which she drew any way she liked in the moment – and she let you have it.

She slapped me more than once and I'm sure Jim got it a few times too. A gossipy sort of person, always having a go at others, I recall being at her place once when she was telling a friend how she had done some or other particular thing and how she had said this and that.

Only it was not the way I remembered the particular thing happening. Being keen to be part of the grown up conversation, I piped up and said, 'But that's not what you said to Uncle Dave... You said...'

Well, one-two not even three, just like that, she sprung up from her chair and slapped my face. 'Don't you ever talk like that again!' She slapped me so hard I found it difficult to talk in her company ever again.

On one occasion, I also peed the bed. She glared at me next morning with a loathing and distaste like I was worse than a baby or rather a baby animal. I was already about six, and the way she looked at me made me feel less than six weeks. Then, of course, she slapped my face. I can't say I hated her, but I certainly didn't like her and never quite forgave her for that.

The slaps from Aunty Dulcie reminded me of home. Whenever Dad or Mum gave me a hiding the pee would just come trickling down my legs. I wished it would never happen but it did.

'You're disgusting. Go clean yourself up!' Mum would grunt after giving me a slap across the legs or a punch in the chest. And both Mum and Dad, sometimes together, sometimes individually, would glare at me like I was a dirty, grubby little girl who had no control over her privates. Dad should know.

But not only that, Mum would refuse to wash my underwear. It was like I had a disease, like every time I peed myself it showed there was something radically and insanely wrong with me. Whatever I did, whatever mental acrobatics I tried to perform, I could not cure it.

I was a girl without control. I would never have control. The way Mum looked at me, it had to be true.

So, I felt more than blessed when more often than not it was my older brother Jim who would be dropped off at Aunty Dulcie's and me who would go to my steady-hearted and very, very warm-handed Aunty Bev.

When I went to Aunty Bev it was like the entire world was a different planet. She was forever hugging me and telling me that my thicket of dirty brown hair that bushed out like an overgrown Roman helmet on my head, was the most beautiful mop of hair she'd ever known. She would brush my hair, over and over, and I felt like I was a prize-winning doll.

'Annie Get Your Gun,' she called me, something I liked. It sounded intimate and grown up. I enjoyed the sound of it, even though it wasn't until I was much older, an adult, that I realised she was calling me that because of the uncontrollable mop on my head and the similarities with the famous Annie Oakley of American musical fame.

What's more, at nights, unlike at home, Aunty Bev and Uncle Max would allow me to sit with them around the dining room table in the large kitchen where we'd talk and laugh and watch TV.

They had a real modern gas stove, which was so completely different to our big, wood-burning, smelly combustion stove. Aunty Bev would also give me ginger nut biscuits and make me cups of Milo on powdered milk. I loved spooning out the creamy lumps that formed on the top and which were covered in chocolate.

It was so refreshing with Aunty Bev and Uncle Max and everything was so positive at their place. Seen through a child's eyes, there was no yukkiness that clung like dusty cobwebs to the skin; I often wished I never had to go home.

13.

THERE COULD BE GOOD TIMES AT OUR PLACE TOO. Even with Mum and Dad. Christmas at our place on the acreage at Anondale was like that sometimes. It wasn't that we received huge presents or toys, it was just that everyone was so free and easy, so balmily jolly and full of high spirits, and not even drunk.

I remember one time we had all these big tents in our back paddock, well it seemed like a lot of big tents to small eyes, and there were lots of people because Dad had all his family over.

On the property there were acres of watermelons that we grew, and we kids were told to run off and choose the largest one we could find. Dad chopped it in half and then cut it into huge slices and we ran around in the hot sun like dots of dry dust blowing about the place, pink juice running freely down our faces and fingers and arms.

Hot and grubby from the watermelon eating, out came the water-hose and we ran around in our togs, having water fights. I guess Mum thought at least we were getting clean, and on account of that didn't mind. The hose-water shimmered in the sunlight and it was good to feel free, just to whirl in the sun and eat and drink and play with no demands.

Dad's family were also pretty sober, so these occasions never went overboard, and I guess Dad, under their watchful eye, didn't want to show them the rough side of our existence either.

Dad's brothers, unlike Dad, were very much gentlemen. Maybe it was because they had a different dad? Dad's Dad, the one who died in the War, had a reputation for having a fiery, quick-sparking temper. He also, apparently, had a bent for the plonk. The sort of bloke you didn't mess with. Just like Dad.

Dad's grandma, who brought him up, Grandma Cecily Flanagan would also be there on those occasions. Grandma, as we called her, could be quite loving too. She and her son, Uncle Col lived in this large, standout Queenslander, not very far away from us.

It was the house everyone from all around could see on the banks of the Nebo River. The house may have been old and ramshackle, but it always felt convivial, well, compared to ours, and I could always remember there being other people there: aunts and uncles, friends and workers; and we would all sit around the long wooden table in the kitchen near the stove having cups of tea.

She and Uncle Col were hardworking people, farming people, as they say; they grew pumpkins and peas and beans and other vegetables for sale to the market. There was no slouching with them. They would always be out in the fields doing their work, coming in for smoko, a good quick chat and a cup or two of tea, and then back out into the fields.

Not a huggy type, Grandma Cecily Flanagan would also never push us kids away, and it has to be said we felt completely safe with her and Uncle Col. She always wore a grey bun on her head and we kids didn't know how long her hair really was – until one night she undid it and we saw these thin reedy wisps falling right down to her bum.

I also remember she kept a chamber pot under her bed, which seemed terribly old fashioned and a mystery to me. *Yukky*, it used to pass through my head. Her head also was a wonder. I think she had Parkinson's disease or something, because it always shook. But at the time, I guessed that's what happened when you grew old.

Dad adored her, and he used to tell us high-drama stories that occurred at Grandma's place, like the time he had this enormous boil on his nose and he was experimenting with making gunpowder. The gunpowder blew up in his face, nearly making him blind, but it burst the boil. So from bad came good.

And that – even maybe as a result of that small story – is what I have always thought about life. As bad as things get, life is never all doom. From even the worst explosions comes some good. In my past, there were the good times mixed in with the dark and inexplicable ones, but always in the black corners of life I managed to find spots of light.

And yet... knowing what I did, I had to ask myself: How did they come from the same family – Dad and Grandma Cecily Flanagan? Was there something more than met the eye? Did it all just start with Dad, or his mum, Grandma Glad? Or did it start with Dad's Dad who no one ever knew? There was gossip, always plenty of gossip, but no one ever spoke. The only stories Dad ever told us were the ones about his Dad, the hero, who took a bullet for the Commonwealth in Singapore.

I guess the important thing at that age was that being at Grandma's place and having Christmas days there or at our place, were the good times, the good memories... the things that made me realise how, even in the bleakness of my own immediate family, life could be worthwhile.

Both my uncles, Dad's half-brothers, used to play guitar and sing beautifully; it was another way to feel connected with everyone and there was a sense of belonging. They were also sober, and the fun was always clean.

But inevitably reality would swoop like an enormous black crow or come pecking like an angry magpie right into the back of my head. Christmas would end, the sober cheer would fizzle, the rellies would go, and with all the arguments and fights Mum and Dad used to have, I had to wonder how life could ever be so good.

In many ways, the only release at home was the "touching". On the one hand it was a release, and on the other, it never stopped. Neither from Dad nor from his mates. In the gloom of the fights at home, the hoary uncertainty, it was at least a love I got.

I wished those Christmas days would never end. The sun stood still in the sky, the hose-water cooled us down from the extreme, moist heat, and the day rolled into the night with such ease I could not think where all the problems could possibly come from.

14.

MUM'S FAMILY WERE QUITE DIFFERENT... Aside from Uncle Barney, Mum's older brother who did that unforgettable thing in the back of the ute, the most memorable person on her side of the family was her own Mum. We called her Nana, but she was actually Nana Milly Murphy. I loved her, but I tell you what, to be perfectly honest, she was drunk a lot of the time. The truth was Nana loved her beer as much as did Mum's Dad, our Grandad Phil.

Grandad Phil only had one leg and he used to get around on crutches. I'm sure it was not so pleasant for Nana, but as a day of drinking would get on, and the sun began to set, so, more often than not, they would begin to fight.

From soft-sounding niggly words, their voices would grow to grunts and taunts, and before anyone knew it, Grandad was grabbing for one of his crutches and beating Nana with it.

To us kids it was a laugh, but I'm sure to Nana, it really got her goat up, or so to speak. I think it actually made her feel quite humiliated. To be fair, although there were these negative moments between them, they were never rough-handed or unkind to us kids. They were in the true sense of the word, real characters.

It happened quite a few times that Nana and Grandad would come up from Bundaberg, where they lived, and stay with us for a while. They would stay in the little flatlet Dad had built downstairs.

I remember once they came upstairs – it must have been a summer weekend because the sun was streaming into the lounge – and there were records playing. As the day and the beer and the plonk wore on, everyone began to dance. Nana loved Bing Crosby and Mum loved Dean Martin and the crooners like Frank Sinatra. Bing Crosby was playing at the time, and we kids as well as Nana were dancing and skipping around like the floor was one huge trampoline.

Because we were hopping up and down so much the needle inevitably jumped and the record scratched. It didn't take a lot to get Nana and Mum fired up – and the jumping, scratching record did just that.

Mum was standing in one corner of the room – a slim woman once again at this time – and Nana, even tinier than Mum's five-foot, with skin so wrinkly her face was like the leg of an aged elephant, only much thinner and more gaunt of course, was standing puffing at the other end of the room.

They were facing off, stepping closer and closer to one another.

A wet fag as usual dangled from Nana's lips and a drink wobbled in her hand. With rounded shoulders she was trudging forwards as though emerging from some dark alley in a Dickens novel. She was screaming at Mum for ruining her record, and Mum was screaming back: 'Why the hell don't you stop jumping like a bloody kangaroo if you don't want the record to scratch!'

Chewing on her cigarette, Nana puffed a cloud of grey smoke into the air: 'What the hell does it matter to you anyway, Julie? It's *my* record!' Her voice sounded just like a parrot squawking. Only louder. It always sounded like that, like something was stuck in the back of her throat, only it sounded even more so when she was drunk or angry. Now she was both.

I think Mum must have bought the record as a gift for Nana, because the next thing Mum was lifting the record and throwing it like a Frisbee across the room at Nana, howling: 'I gave you that record for Christmas and you don't even care...'

That was followed, as they continued to close in on one another, with a parade of spitting and cursing. Finally, nose to nose, a fountain of tears flooding from both old and not so old pairs of red eyes, they clashed with swinging arms. A second later they crashed in a bear-hug to the floor, where they thrashed and flailed about some more. It looked like a circus, and we kids could not help but continue to spring around and laugh.

This time the episode ended in amusement for us children, and even the scratching mamma bears on the floor seemed to manage to sort something out. But it wasn't always like that. On many occasions, rather than laughing, I remember feeling uneasy and unsettled at the anger, at the sheer extremity of it. It amazed me that there could be such resentment between a mother and her daughter. And mostly, like the record, it wasn't even over that much.

Something inside me would freeze during these episodes, and I could not help but think, Where does it come from? Such bitterness and rage? One minute everyone having a good time and the next, this cursing and fighting and almost irredeemable ire.

Dad, towering over everyone, was no different. In fact, he seemed to set the example. From sitting there playing his musical instruments and singing like he was on top of the universe, the next moment he could be as angry as the devil. And not just at the people around him but at the world.

He would stand up and rant whatever came to his mouth, but often it would be things like: 'The War took my father. Those bloody fuckin Japs! I would've knocked them bloody over. I would've killed all those bloody bastards.' Just like that it would happen. Like he was hallucinating or something.

It left me feeling cold, numb and confused.

But back to Nana, I loved her, such a character, but I guess that was easier said when I didn't have to be brought up by her or Grandad Phil, like Mum was.

Unlike Dad's Mum – Grandma Glad – who always called me 'love', as in "Come and give your Grandma a hug, love," Nana Milly Murphy would always call me 'dahl'.

'What ya doin, dahl?' was the way Nana spoke. And then she'd say to me, 'Deb, have ya got yesself a fella, dahl?'

'Naaa,' I'd say shyly.

'Well... ya need t' get yourself an old one,' she'd look at me, shoulders curving, skin wrinkling, smoke blaring out of the sides of her nose, '... an make sure his rich, one foot in the grave, an then kick im in there.' And then she would laugh.

She eventually divorced Grandad when she was sixty-five. 'I'm not putting up with that old bastard any longer,' she declared. And that was that.

The truth was, much as I liked Nana, I'm surprised, thinking of her, that Mum never drank. But she didn't. I suppose I had to at least be thankful for that. Things could have been worse, far, far worse.

15.

ALTHOUGH THEY OWNED THE PROPERTY IN ANONDALE, ON PERENJORA DAM ROAD, THE REALITY WAS MUM AND DAD WERE PAYING OFF A SUBSTANTIAL MORTGAGE and the arguments between them about money and where it was all going to come from, only increased. We kids also walked around feeling continually hungry. There were no snack foods to speak of, Mum's biscuits or jam drops were a rare exception and we always felt when dinner came around we were lucky to be eating.

On the other hand, it has to be said, while breakfasts and lunches could be pretty scanty – lunch was more often than not bread dipped into hot Bonox followed by a mug of billy tea – we never missed a meal. One had to be a little amazed, with all the work Mum did with all of us kids around and with all the fighting and general disorganisation that seemed to define our house, that she managed to have something on the table for us at all.

Cups of tea were like our snack food. Even from a young age, the tea Mum and Dad gave us was so strong we could stick a spoon up in it. Coffee, on the other hand, was considered an adult drink, bad for us, and we were never allowed to have it.

More than anything, I remember Dad was always out working. Even most weekends he'd be out there doing something, ploughing or planting, harvesting or busy with his saws and timber cutting. If we were always hungry, he was like a ravenous beast by the time dinner came around. And he expected his food, especially his dinner – pre-salted and peppered by Mum – to be ready and served up to him as he sat down.

Mum made sure there was always enough salt on Dad's food not just so that he could taste it but so that there could be no doubt there was enough to start a salt mine. And then he added some! Every night he would keep urging us kids: 'Put salt on your food. It's good for you. Your bodies need salt.'

I'm amazed we survived, but hungrily we ate and salted our food, one eye on what we were doing and the other on Dad shovelling mounds of meat and vegies into his ravenous lips. Hiding leftovers, or food we didn't like, was an impossibility. Not under Dad's eagle gaze. It would be suicidal.

Always taken together as a family, mealtimes were the complete opposite of Christmas time, and although we all, for better or worse, looked forward to our dinner, we didn't look forward to sitting at the table. Inevitably, Dad would groan to Mum about where the money was coming from, and if he wasn't doing that he would be shouting at us to finish everything on our plates.

At times, his mood was so bleak we used to literally shiver in our boots. On a bad day, he could suddenly lash out with a slap across the cheeks or over the back of our heads, and we soon learnt it was better to keep clear, remain silent, eat all our food, and at all costs, obey.

I remember once being out in the paddock by the tractor and seeing Jim act a bit brave in his mischievous way when Dad called him to move away from the thing. Defiantly, he just giggled and continued to stand there. Dad asked him again, and again Jim just stood and giggled.

'OK then, you little bastard,' Dad fired up, his face dark and swelling with blood. He grabbed a hammer from nearby, held it shaking in the air like an Indian warrior, and we kids, seeing the mad glaze in Dad's eyes, were sure it was going to be the end of our poor brother Jim.

As it happened, when the blow came, the hammer just missed Jim's head, but it slammed into the tractor mudguard, so hard and furiously that it left a massive dent in the machine. Jim, quivering, moved away from the vehicle. I actually don't think Dad meant to hit Jim, but he sure had a way of making it look like he did.

Also, by the time we got to the Perenjora Dam Road property, Dad was slaughtering our own cattle, or "beasts". So there were times when the food was even quite rich and tasty and full of meaty protein. But as the meat was stretched further and further through the days, so the stews it was added to would become more and more perilous until our meals had that vomitable blend of soft vegetables and grains, especially incorporating barley and pumpkin, which I hated.

'You kids finish your frigging dinner. You're not leaving this bleeding table until you do!'

Dad would growl the words as I felt the food coming up to the top of my throat, threatening to explode back onto my plate. Which, of course, would have only made everything worse.

Salt. Salt. Salt. Thank heavens for salt – and Dad's absolute, unflinchingly strong belief in it. Because without salt, most of my food would have come straight back up onto my plate.

'Put some salt on your hand, Deb, and just lick it off,' he would say to me of the condiment now considered by medical experts as a killer. And to this day, I still add salt to everything.

On occasion, we did get a real treat for dinner. My favourite, I cringe a bit now, was when Dad used to go out and shoot the little wood ducks that gathered at our two dams, and we would have them for dinner.

When they weren't being eaten, the little ducks were wonderful to watch. We kids would spend hours observing them swimming and waddling around our dams like the very small geese they resembled.

Strong flavoured, I'm afraid they were "good tucker" in those days, and because of their small size we would pretty much each get a whole duck to ourselves. The wood ducks didn't stand a chance against Dad's shooting skills. They would have heard him coming a mile away, mumbling things to himself like, 'You don't ever mess with Dan Gallagher.' And hearing that they should have run for their lives.

But on those nights when we had the wood ducks for dinner, Dad was a hero.

Another meal that I used to love was cabbage stew. It was made up of cabbage, onions and chunks of meat, boiled up and served with rice. There is not a lot I like to emulate in my parents, but this is one of the things. Cabbage stew. It was a cheap, easy meal, made with our own cabbages and meat from our own beasts. I loved it and love it still.

But back at the ranch, such as it was, the fights continued, only they were growing worse. When Dad didn't like his food he would simply shove it back at Mum until she returned with something better tasting.

The whole house, even in mid-summer, would freeze on those nights. There were some foods he refused to eat, and threw them back at her – yes, right over the table. But we kids were never allowed to turn our noses up to anything.

'Don't you ever put tomato sauce on my dinner again,' he would rage at Mum. 'I'm not putting up with that bloody fucking rubbish!'

Dad would swear like a storm trooper. Everything was effing this and effing that. And many, many other words too.

I remember once being out in the paddock with my younger sister Marge. We were pulling out some crops from the ground, just generally of a weekend helping Mum and Dad. Only Marge couldn't get one of the plants she was tugging at out of the ground and my innocent little sister, doing her best to emulate Dad, yelled as loud as she could: 'Come out, you cunt!'

You can imagine.

'Get up here now!' Dad screamed like the earth was caving in at his feet, and an instant flogging was dished out for the dirty word. We kids knew not to swear. Goodness, no. We weren't even allowed the word "damn" in our house. Like everything else in our house, only Dad was allowed to say what he liked and in the language he liked.

The Ten Commandments – *and more* – applied to everybody

and everything but him. There were two standards in our house, and the one we had to obey, was Dad's.

To this day I find it hard to swear and there is one word that rankles more than any other, it is that word c-u-n-t. I find it totally debasing of women. I remember once my daughter Sarah coming home from school, she was only nine, and she repeated that word.

'Do you know what it means?' I instantly sprung at her, probably overreacting. She shook her head. 'It's a disgusting word for vagina. That's what it is! It's a word *men* use!' And then seeing her eyes close to crying, I softened and explained, 'That's exactly how we women should *not* see ourselves. The most sacred part of us, like a dirty, demeaning swear word.'

Still standing there a bit white, blinking her eyes, I am sure the message got through.

Funnily enough, Mum never swore, or very rarely, only when she was extra, extra furious. I guess it wasn't considered ladylike in the day – or Dad didn't allow it. But that was another thing I had to be grateful for. Imagine if they both swore like Dad. Our home would have been like a slop-house.

There were other kinds of arguments too in the house now. They could fight over just about anything, but now Dad was beginning to accuse Mum of things. Of fancying other men, of having affairs. He was also becoming violent.

I was about ten when we heard Mum arriving home one day, skidding the car to a halt on the gravel outside the front of the house. All of us kids ran outside to see what was going on. We found Mum, plump as a watermelon once again, hauling herself out of her car, puffing and shouting: 'C'mon hurry, hurry. Get upstairs! Your father's coming!'

We all ran inside the house and up the internal stairs, only to hear Dad a split second later, in his truck, skidding up behind Mum's parked car. It was almost incredible that the loud screeching of tyres wasn't followed by a bang. We could smell his fury burning in the rubber on the stones.

Behind us, we heard Dad's heavy worker boots bounding up the stairs. I have no idea where Mum was by this time, but the four of us kids were standing huddled together, shuddering with fear. We saw Dad's big square head appearing and suddenly Mum was running across the lounge and Dad was chasing after her.

He was spitting fire: 'What the fuck were you doing with that fella? D'you think I never saw you with that cunt? Don't think ya gonna fucking get away with this!'

Mum, her neck thick and bloating red, was turning around as best she could, screaming back: 'I wasn't doing anything wrong. I wasn't doing anything wrong.'

She was running to the phone, I don't know, probably to call the police, to get some help, but as she picked up the phone, Dad, in one of his quick army style manoeuvres, had the cord wrapped around her throat and was squeezing it. Mum was standing there shrieking and puffing. She was unable to move, unable to gasp breath. Her face looked so red it was beginning to turn blue.

The four of us kids were standing in front of them like white ghosts; we did not have to say it to each other, we thought this was the end of Mum. Perhaps us too? Dad, all six foot and three inches of his lanky, iron body was shaking with rage and thunder. It looked like he was going to choke Mum to death right there in front of us and then come for us.

Just when we thought she had taken her last pant of air, we watched as he breathed out heavily and sharply and suddenly, unexpectedly, let go of her. Instead, he leapt across the lounge to his gun cupboard.

Inside the cupboard, you could see even from where we were standing, he had any one of about twenty guns to choose from. It flicked in our minds, this was even worse than the strangulation was going to be. Our hearts were racing again. We saw bullets in our heads and guts. No one was going to escape.

Unable to take our eyes off him, we held our breath and watched. He was standing in front of the cupboard with the slow determination of a cowboy. And like that cowboy he took his time in choosing his weapon. When he turned around we saw he had chosen his carbine.

It seemed strange, because of all his guns he always kept the carbine in pieces – each piece wrapped in cloth like some sacred metal scroll.

Even more slowly now, a cowboy reconnoitring and planning his high-noon strategy, meticulously, he put the gun together, one piece at a time. He did it with the purpose of a world champion chess player, breathing deeply, thinking every step of the way, and out of the corners of our eyes we watched as Mum's body shook and sweated.

She was free from the telephone cord now, but she was standing dead still, like she could be a spear of metal stuck into the floor. Her eyes, dark and dry, stared back at Dad with the certainty of death.

Finally, screwing the stock into the barrel, he began yowling: 'I'm gonna kill you! I'm gonna fucking kill you, Julie! You'll never do anything like that again!'

Sam, my little brother, couldn't take it any longer. He broke from us and ran up to Dad. He was clutching at Dad's knees. 'Dad, Dad. Please, please! Don't! Please don't kill Mum!'

Foam firing from his lips, his eyes spinning like a wild boar, Dad looked down at Sam hovering around him, and we thought that was the end of Sam. Moments later, something in Dad's entire being froze over. It was like a beer out of the freezer meeting fresh air and suddenly going to ice; it seemed to crack something in him.

He breathed in as though about to squeeze the trigger, only instead of pulling the trigger or even bludgeoning Sam with the gun, as we expected he was going to do, Dad took the gun and placed it, his prized possession, carefully on the lounge floor.

He pushed Sam aside like he was an annoying fly and stepped up to Mum. He grabbed her by the top of her dress and shook her. They were both screaming and shouting at one another, and all of us kids, as though one, ran for our lives.

We ran to the outside patio, which had a waist-high railing but no security rails. The boys instantly half jumped and half slithered down the long, two-storey-high posts and scurried into the backyard. But Marge and I, unable to make the jump so easily, were still slowly climbing down the posts when we heard Dad breathing just above us.

We were so frightened that we were ready to jump, but as we did so, we felt Dad's big hands around our hair. He literally had us both by the locks of our hair and was heaving us up like an elevator back onto the patio.

Once back up, still holding us tightly by the hair, he dragged us across the floorboards back into the house.

We believed we were going to be gathered together and die with Mum. It was the only thought shooting across our foreheads. Our eyes crying with a kind of sharp, serrated pain, he launched at Mum with a vocal tirade, and Mum, as though beyond afraid, somehow launched back with her own tirade. The shouting and howling and Mum's tears were so loud that anyone outside would have thought the wood from the house was splintering to pieces.

I don't know how the phone arrived back on the hook, but at that moment when Marge and I thought we had seen our last, the phone started to ring. Almost astounded, Dad looked at it like he was going to kick it, like it was some kind of beast he could murder, and then, on second thoughts, eyeing Mum like a prison guard, he picked it up and answered it. He stared forward like he was seeing an unexpected mirror.

It turned out to be our elderly neighbour, Grace. Someone not so far away who had heard the damage going on in our home, who knew there could only be something wrong. She was checking to see if the house wasn't falling down or that we weren't being attacked by some murderous, drug-infused bikie gang.

Holding the phone, seeing it shake like a frightened rat in Dad's hand, we thought Dad was going rip it from the wall or at the least growl as loud as he could at whoever it was on the other side to go and get whatever'd. And then, of course, he was going to continue his attack, first on Mum and then us two girls. Or maybe even the other way round.

But somehow, almost like the sun had poked out in the middle off a storm, Dad's upper lip began to quiver, and then silent and pliant, almost like a reborn gentleman, we heard him say thanks to our elderly neighbour for her concern. He then quietly replaced the receiver. A different man, he looked away from Mum and released me and Marge. He began to heave in oxygen.

Standing there, stock still, breathing in deep breaths, it was like he was unsure what to do. We knew, inside of us we knew, out neighbour Grace had saved us. Knowing someone was hearing him had somehow diminished him. Had taken the fight out of him. It was a kind of lesson, something I learnt as life progressed, never to be silent. Always tell someone.

At the time, never mind speak, I could hardly catch my own breath. I was too scared to take in oxygen.

But what I also remember thinking is that I did not want to die. As bad and rough as it looked on that day, I did not want to die. Life was too precious. For all that was going wrong, for all that was upside down, life still held too much. It is difficult to know why.

16.

WHEN I WAS NEARLY TWELVE, MUM STARTED GOING AWAY A LOT. Really, I suppose, it was running away a lot. And always she would take my little sister Marge with her. Never me. I got used to it. I longed for her to take me but I got used to her leaving me behind. I also got used to, as I guess did everybody, including Dad, that it could be anywhere from a couple of weeks to a couple of months and then Mum would be back.

And then it would all start over again. The fights, the arguments, the accusations, the slowly winding one another up until Mum had to leave again.

Each time she ran, I was left to fend for myself, in the "men's den", the lair. I was left all alone for Dad. It was open slather. In the background, as he knelt beside me with his fingers stimulating my clitoris, while he rubbed his hammer-like penis against my smooth little girl legs, I would hear the trains rattling and tooting by and the cars on the highway rustling the wind, knowing they were wondering what was going on inside that messy, disorganised, metal-heap place.

I was really starting to resent being left with him and didn't like what he was doing to me. My body was changing and the sound of screeching wheels on tar would remind me the cars were looking more than they should. Or not enough.

And then, as I said, Mum would be back. But it didn't make any difference anymore, because Dad had become bolder. It was like he didn't care anymore. He would just send me up to my room, tell me to wait up there, and then follow calmly behind.

Even with Mum there, he would simply bolt the door and do what he always did. It was always short and quick and yet intensely intimate, and all I knew was that Mum would never understand. Or would she? I was getting older, kids were talking at school, but I never heard even in the ignorant language of children one mention of anything like the love I was getting from Dad.

Around this time Dad called out his usual, and while Mum was downstairs busy with the washing, he told me to go up to their bedroom. For some reason on this day I wanted to do other things, girl things. My own things. I didn't want to do what he wanted to do.

I said, 'No, I don't want to. Not now.'

And he said: 'Just get in there!'

He smiled thinly and I knew there was no choice. I had to drop what I was doing and go into their bedroom.

As usual, I lay on their double bed and he lifted my dress and then pulled down my knickers. He knelt like a tall bird in front of me, and with my legs open and my feet dangling off the side of the bed, he began rubbing himself on me.

Only it happened again, what had not happened for a long time. I saw a shadow above me. Felt it looking right over Dad's shoulder. I knew Dad had locked the door, but the shadow was there and this time it followed what was a kind of jangling, at any rate a loud tinging noise at the door. And then the shadow was there. Above me. Above us. This small, overbearing shadow, and Dad immediately, ruthlessly, was up.

He was standing there looking down at me like I was sick and he was in there checking if I was okay. He stood like that still bird when he was ruminating, flicking his front teeth with his tongue.

I sat up on the bed, feeling exposed, ready for I wasn't sure what. I felt guilty. Deeply culpable. Mum walked up to me. Right up close to me. She had the wild but steady gaze of a flustered old schoolmarm who a child had tried to trick. She glared into my eyes like she was drawing something from them, something that she wanted to see pour, confess, vomit, and when it did not come, she slapped me. And slapped me again, and I peed myself and then Dad left the room.

I could not define it then, but that look she gave me, I felt denigrated, soiled. I didn't or rather couldn't comprehend the depth of her loathing for me.

'You slut,' she shouted. 'You bloody little slut. No wonder stuff happens to you! You bring it on yourself. You're pathetic!'

She was howling the taunts into the backs of my eyes. I sat there, feeling the pee trickling. I knew, beyond doubt, that whatever I did was my fault. I was to blame. I was the cause of Mum's anger; I was the one "taking" Dad away from her. It was true. I was a slut. It was the absolute and complete and honest truth; I had created everything, this whole ugly bloody mess.

Still staring into my grotesque throat, Mum turned in a huff and left the room. After a while, hearing little yelping sounds, I came out of the room and went into the lounge. In the lounge, I saw them standing together, Mum and Dad. He was holding her and she was clenched onto his arm. He looked large like an ever-growing silhouette, like the wooden structure that loomed over the house, and she, small like a humming bird, was leaning into him, crying into his chest.

'Get downstairs and hang up the washing,' her voice managed to break through the tears. And like the sky was blue and the sun was still as it always was up above, I went downstairs and began to do my chores.

I never told anyone what was happening to me. I am sure my brother Jim knew what was going on, I could see it in his eyes, but I could also see in his little darkening hazel eyes that he was simply too afraid to say anything. Other than that, no one knew, not even my sister or younger brother. Not even my lovely Aunty Bev. In any event, as far as I knew, no one ever even hinted at it.

Inside me there was something biting, an anxiety, and when for my twelfth birthday I received a diary from Aunty Bev, yes, I'm sure it was from Aunty Bev, I took to it like one does to running once you realise you can walk.

Every day I would write on a page my day's activities. Furiously, I would log it all – well, to be honest, not absolutely all. There was one thing I knew *not* to write in it. But I did occasionally write, 'He hurt me again today.' Yes, I used that word "hurt".

The truth was I was getting older; I was beginning to see things differently. With my diary, somehow, by having to think about things, to frame them, to look for words and *at* the words I used, I felt something in me beginning to wake up. It was a secret I hid from Mum and Dad; the secret I locked up in my diary and hid in a drawer.

And then Mum found it one day; well actually it was Marge who showed it to Mum. All my secrets. I remember feeling completely betrayed and dishonoured as I sat on my bed and Mum slowly took the little key and unlocked the book in front of me.

After reading a few pages, she began to sniff and then snort and then rub her nose in that fidgety way that was common with her. Suddenly her voice pitched, and then dipped, and she just said: 'Get out of my sight. I can't stand looking at you.'

Her voice was colder than metal that has stood out of a night in the winter; it was so cold it was rusted. It made me feel not only unwanted but grimy. Unwashable. Wherever that dirt had come from – I saw it in the pinned look in her eyes – it had nothing to do with her. It came from other sources, other elements. Other genes.

And then, as if having second thoughts, she turned and set upon me. As I sat there, she began shaking and then punching me, yelling into my eyes: 'Wake up to yourself, Debbie! Don't be so bloody stupid!'

The strange thing was, despite everything, despite what I well knew, when I thought of the searing ice in Mum's voice, my mind turned to my father and I felt that by him at least I was protected.

She hurt and knew how to hurt. How to isolate. He hurt, but I felt like he was there for me. There was safety in his shadow. In the shade of his bearing I felt connected. It is a strange thought how those who hurt us the most are often those we feel closest to. It is like, through familiarity, we know them better. We have seen inside them. We know what to expect. We know if there are true feelings there.

But in the end the reality was I was nearly in high school by this time, and not only was I beginning to develop little breasts and menstruate, I was beginning to feel like my body was *my* body. Like it contained mysteries that all belonged to me.

Of its own accord, my body was telling me something was wrong. But it would be Mum who finally did something about it.

And, of course, in the strangest of ways.

17.

NOT LONG AFTER DAD NEARLY STRANGLED MUM TO DEATH AND SHOT ALL OF US, well in our eyes nearly shot all of us, the imbalances in our home must have shifted right out of control, because for a while we found ourselves in a motel room in Rockhampton. That is *all* of us, except Dad. Even my older brother Jim and I were included this time.

Then the phone call came. Dad could not live without Mum. He needed her. He needed us. We were his life, the people he loved and cherished. And Mum, teary-eyed, gave in and we were trekking back home again.

Things seemed to calm for a long while after that, well what seemed in a young girl's eyes for a long while, because the reality was after only a few months Mum started with her questions again – well, that's what I link it to – and things went all curved in the house again.

'Is Dad touching you?' she asked one day, and then asked again and again. And again and again, I said no. Emphatically *NO*. There was not a single way in the world I was going to risk being slapped and slandered by her again.

She took it further. One night, with all of us kids sitting at the dining room table, it must have been before Dad got in from work, because he was definitely not there, Mum asked me if Dad was doing things to me. That was a pretty nerve-wracking thing in itself, given that none of us kids even hinted at such behaviour among ourselves.

Now Mum was laying it out bare, for all to see. I remember looking at that solid wooden beam that the dining room table leaned against and going red and flushing. I was so shy and passive at that time in my life, all I could do was sit and feel guilty. That beam... it was lording over me. Once again, rather than being wrapped in Mum's arms and consoled and reassured, I felt like I was being accused.

But as clear as day, as though trying to protect me, as though knowing and understanding what I never thought he knew or would ever understand, my older brother Jim, his short brown hair neatly side-parted, began to prod me: 'Well, c'mon Deb. C'mon. Tell her. Tell her the truth.'

Of course I looked the other way, or rather down to the floor, and pinching in my cheeks with all my breath, once again I denied it all. But what is important and sticks out about this event for me, is the realisation that others must have known about me and Dad. It confirmed that my older brother Jim knew. But who else? Who else? We kids never discussed it, never said anything among ourselves.

The word sex was banned in our house. We never even joked about it among ourselves. We were too afraid. Anything to do with sex was dirty, filthy, unmentionable. Afraid that the switchy-stick might come down on us, we never breathed anything to do with that word. And yet there were these people – like Jim and Mum – who knew. For me, it was enough that Mum knew.

She was rubbing her nose, agitated. 'Well, I'm telling you now,' her eyes were sharp and hard as pins, 'tomorrow I'm going to the police.'

It didn't change my mind about saying anything to her. The police were always a threat – like boarding school – that made us scared and think our world was about to collapse, or that we were going to get severely punished, but personally I would rather take my chances with the unknown than tell Mum anything.

Amazingly, the next day, true to her word, after Dad had gone out bush to do his work, Mum gathered us together and drove us to the police station in Gladstone. And then everything in our house did change.

Whether Mum had had prior conversations with them or not, I don't know. I just remember some detectives – all of them male – saying to me, 'Can you tell us what's going on? Does your dad touch you? Does he interfere with you in any way? In any way at all?'

Feeling pinned and cornered, I was blood-frozen scared, not just of them but also of Mum and Dad, the centre-bolt of our universe, and I said, no, no and no again.

'It's all right, you're not in any trouble,' they kept repeating to me, but still my answer remained the same.

Then they had a new idea. They took me away from Mum and walked me to a room downstairs.

Cut off from Mum, one of the detectives peered down into the bending eyes that were mine, and I saw something in those police eyes, a moist strength, something I didn't experience every day, a sense I could trust. It was a kind of fatherliness that said I was safe. My stories mattered.

I blinked, breathed in, looked up, and all of a sudden I was telling them everything.

Strangest thing of all was I was enjoying it. I actually grew excited by my own words. I felt important like I was at the centre of the earth and was actually being appreciated for it. It was like I had just won a running race at school and everyone wanted to hang their arms around me.

At bottom, the honest truth was that telling them all these stories wasn't like it was a great release off my chest. The facts were still confusing for me. Beyond me. But what was good about it was that there was not the slightest feeling that these people were going to suddenly lash out or slap me or call me a little ratbag bloody liar.

I told them everything honestly and without shame. How Dad undressed me and touched me with his hands; how Dad rubbed his penis against my vagina and how he put his fingers inside me.

I called everything by their proper names, all the secret parts of my body, using words like penis and vagina. They were writing everything down and the "interview" seemed to go on forever. But I never grew tired of it. It was daytime when we went into the station and we were still there by nightfall.

I don't know where my brothers and sister were kept during this time, but soon after night fell we were all together again, sitting at the entrance to the station.

This very tall man was scuffled into the place with his hands cuffed. He looked like he was resisting, did not want to be there. I was looking right into his rocking eyes and then had to flicker my eyes a couple of times. It was Dad.

Not one of us was happy to see him. We were shocked. We each felt guilty in our own way. I, like I had broken a Holy Commandment. Like I had blasphemed, which in his eyes, I knew, I had done of course. I had taken my dad's name in vain.

The only thing worse than our shock was seeing the way Dad glared at Mum: it was like a bird choosing its prey, letting it know it was swooping down ready at some time soon to smash with its beak and scrunch with its claws.

I could see Mum sitting there with her heart beating rapidly. It was like she knew she was gone. When we saw those same eyes swoop on us, we shivered too, knowing we were equally done for. All we could do was look away; the colour draining from our faces.

'Don't worry, it's all right,' one of the policemen at last beckoned to us. 'Really. I promise. You won't be hurt.' It was said with such assurance, such authority, and seeing Dad in handcuffs, we felt somewhat better.

But looking back at Dad, I don't know about the others, there was in me such a strong surge of heat from the back of my neck down to my ankles, such an extreme dizziness in my skull from breaking the family code of never dobbing one another in, that I thought I was going to faint.

When I looked into his face I saw the sharp ice of being double-crossed. I saw in his chest the deflation of being let down. There was one person even more than Mum who had done it: and that person was me. 'How can you do this to me, Deb?' His eyes were grunting into my forehead.

Thank heavens Dad was soon tucked away through a door somewhere and we went home. In the car, even in the darkness of it, as we drove, you would think all we could talk about was our experience at the station. Instead we said nothing. Yes, nothing.

Even when we finally got home and unwound, Mum said not a word about Dad or what happened at the station. She didn't even ask how we felt or what was going through our heads. Not even did she ask that most basic of all questions that a parent is meant to encourage in a troubled child: Do you want to ask any questions?

No, no, and emphatically no again. Incredible as it may seem, not a word about what happened at the police station or even a word about the actual abuse or even what might happen to our dad was said. It was all zipped behind tired eyes and our mystified skulls.

Interestingly, though, on the way home we stopped over for a while at our neighbours, the Groves. Yes, Mr Grove, the man I had kissed so *maturely*, so *differently*. But even there, nothing was said directly to us kids. There was a lot of talk, I remember a lot of talk, but it was not about me or any of my siblings, it was about Mum, about her life, about how everything was affecting her. We kids were left to the side to sit and play and get on with our lives in all the simple ways we did.

The next day, though, something of a newly revived bird was put among the worms, because Mum received a call from the police that they were no longer able to hold Dad. He was on his way home. Their advice: she was to get us out of there as fast as she could.

None of us were breathing easy now.

But Mum obviously had some support. Maybe more than we were ever aware of. Because not long after the call from the police, a man we had never seen, a man almost as tall as Dad, only bristling with a sense of urgency and fear, was getting Mum and us kids together and bustling us into a car.

'C'mon, let's get out of here,' he kept saying as Mum wept her story to him and he looked at her – rather than us – like the world was coming to an end.

Once we were all packed in the car, from memory, my brother Jim – I think it had something to do with school (he was in high school now) – was dropped off at the Groves, while the rest of us were driven up to Rockhampton. There, at some point, we were deposited into the keeping of Aunty Sylvie and Uncle Barney.

Yes, Mum's older brother, Uncle Barney, the one who had tried to put his dirty, salty penis in my mouth. I still felt the gross taste of it on my tongue and wouldn't trust him even as far as a child could chuck a sheep.

But in the event, even though we were staying under his roof, he left well away from me and in fact never ever tried anything again. For the time being we were all safe at Uncle Barney and Aunty Sylvie's.

We must have stayed there for quite a long time because we even went to school there – a little bush school for kids from Year One to Year Ten. I was in Year Seven, which in Ogmore, the town where we were living, was Year Six because there were no Year Seven students at the school.

It's a bit unclear to me now, and I have never been able to settle the detail with my reluctant family, but after a while we had to leave Ogmore to come back for Dad's trial. He had been released but he still had charges to face. What really is bizarre in my memory is that when we came back, we came back to our house on Perenjora Dam Road, and stayed in the house *with* Dad.

I still cannot get my head around that, but ahead of us lay the biggest occasion of our lives, definitely of my life and probably Mum's too. It was Dad's trial. Just the thought of it was heart-thrashing and spine-breaking, and yet there was something intrinsically exciting about it.

To suit the occasion of going to court, I wore the best dress I had. It was a frock that was blue and white-spotted at the top with a narrow shoulder sleeve that bottomed out into a little yellow skirt. The outfit had specially been bought for me for some big occasion, a wedding, I think.

And that is the way we arrived in court. The scariest day of our lives, all of us dressed like we were going to a huge celebration.

18.

Sitting there in our best outfits, I remember noting a sparse crowd in the court, people I did not recognise, people probably waiting for the appearance of their own relatives and friends. There was also a policeman, some officials in black, and then came the moment we had been waiting for.

Dad was brought in.

We kids were sitting in a row, and what I saw was Dad standing there shaking his big square head like a man who had never done anything wrong in his life. In his long black pants and smart white shirt, it was like he could not understand why the universe had chosen him of all the people in the world to make an example of.

His head just hung, but it was not with the shame of a man who had done anything wrong; it was with the shame of a man bitterly disappointed that he had been caught. A man who had let himself – and perhaps all other men on the planet – down.

He looked up and you could see the questions in his eyes: Who were these people to judge him? What did they know of hard work and family? What did they know of his relationship with his own kin? Before him he saw stupid police and a law that did not *get it*. And *these* people were pointing fingers *at him*.

Dad was asked if we were the children, and he nodded his head. At least he agreed about that. Eventually he was asked if he did it, the things he was accused of, and all I can remember is Dad, like a bird after a bath, rustling his neck and shivering his head, a man looking deeply offended.

'No, I did not.' He called out, confident, strong.

I saw a dry swelling in his eyes; it was coming in my direction. It hit beneath my dress and stabbed into my chest, saying: 'Why the hell am I here?'

He was accusing me. Again, like at the police station, I felt a deep and painful heat reach from my throat and swell in my shoes.

In the end, at the conclusion of the examination, Dad was given a non-custodial sentence with an undertaking to do time in a rehabilitation centre. And so, believe it or not, after the hearing we all climbed into the car and went home together. Mum, Dad and all us kids.

The entire journey, which was about twenty minutes from Gladstone, all Dad could gripe about was why Mum had dressed me the way she had. He said I looked so young – implying it was because of my youth, because of my appearance, that made them believe there was something wrong with him. I was the reason, the way Mum dressed me, that he had to go and spend time in a rehabilitation centre. For my part, it was difficult to see how he was not sitting there threatening to punish us all for standing in court against him.

In the end, the relief to all of us was that he was not home for long. It was almost like he only came home to change, pack his bags and then he was off again, in fact the very next day – to the rehab detention centre, which was down the coast in Bundaberg.

For us left behind, there was no victory celebrations, no special drinks or feasts, everything remained just like it was, no questions asked, no questions answered.

If Mum was making a song of Dad's going, it certainly wasn't to us kids. From memory, she made a point of telling everyone she could about it. All her adult friends. How she had nabbed the bugger, our father who just happened to be her husband, and he was now in rehab detention. We kids only ever heard the natter at the margins. Never the detail. So it was hard to be sure exactly what she said.

For us kids it was just like any other day. It didn't even matter that Dad wasn't there. The world went round, and just like when Dad was there, our only concern was eating all our vegies or risking a beating if we didn't.

On the real point at hand, the one we had been to the police and now all the way to the courts about, nothing was said, taught or learnt. The world was silent on the subject, the world out there, as well as the one inside.

If there was a lesson in it, it was one that came despite our own thoughts; it came through seeing most of our relatives and friends withdrawing from us.

Somehow, after the court case, the rellies seemed to find a way to avoid us – and I can't even remember Dad's friends like Cec Parsons or the other men being around after that. Even Aunty Bev, even my warm-handed Aunty Bev, much as it hurts to remember it, withdrew from us.

People also started to stare at us. I became acutely aware of being looked at and regarded by others in a particular way. The worst were the kids at school. Suddenly they were not friendly, and even the couple of close friends I had, began to keep a distance.

After a couple of weeks, we went to visit Dad one day, all of us, off to Bundaberg to see the man who was supposed to be our protector. He was in a ward full of other men, and all I remember is feeling deeply sorry for him.

Peering up at us from his bed, the tall, proud man with the square chin and the deliberating gap between his front teeth, who once stood solid like wood among us, was so doped up he could hardly keep his eyes open.

It was like, quite literally, he wasn't even a quarter the man he used to be. Like a withered tree, he heaved in shallow breaths, and all he could mumble was: 'I have to get out of here. I have to get out of here.'

The worst part was I was convinced I had destroyed him. The extraordinarily long, half-live figure in the bed was breathing its last. No longer could he be where he needed to be or who he was meant to be: at home, with his kin, the hardwood frame of his family.

Dad was away for months. Two things stick out in my

memory about this time. The first is that the longer Dad was away the sadder Mum became. I guess, a bit like me, without saying anything, she blamed herself. The second, which should have been a benefit but nobody seemed to remark about it, was that with Dad away, instead of Mum becoming more agitated and more frustrated with having us kids on her hands as well as everything else she needed to do on the property, life actually calmed down.

During the time of Dad's absence, I can hardly even remember Mum shouting at us – well, other than to eat our vegies. And since she shouted at me and slapped me around the most, there definitely had to be something to be said for that.

And yet we missed Dad. And I discovered an unfortunate truth: we get used to a certain way of living and no matter how bad, how poisoned that way might be, once the destructive element is removed, we actually miss it.

In the same way now, calm as our world had become, without Dad it felt uncomfortable, like there was a niggling gap. Madness? Masochism? Yes, madness and masochism. But there it was. We were living on earth, but it was a different earth. It felt different without our Lord Protector around.

Outside our house it really was different. Everyone had taken to treating us like we had the plague. I was barely a teenager, Mum was living through hell, and people were lifting their noses at us.

If the absence of the relatives was visible, it was the absence of Aunty Bev that hurt the most. It is still difficult to work out, to get my head around, but I suppose that's how it is, even if it isn't your fault, it's like you are tainted.

Abuse doesn't just taint the abuser, it taints what the abuser has touched. I felt like I had been soiled with a tarnished brush and could never wash the grime from my skin. It was literally like I had an incurable disease.

As though to prove it, even though we were already bigger kids by now, well Jim and me, I remember clearly standing outside the sandpit at school one day and asking a school friend if I could hop in and play with her.

'No,' she looked at me with a distinct curl on her lips. 'I can't play with you anymore. You've been manhandled.'

Another girl, even more blatantly told me, 'I can't play with you, you're dirty.'

On a more positive note, a very good friend at school broke down in tears one day and confessed, 'I want to play with you, Deb. I do. But I'm not allowed to.'

The reality was we had all been discoloured with the shoddy strokes of a single bad brush. The bristles on Dad's brush were not even shoddy they were contagious; but it appeared he was definitely right about one thing: no one but no one would understand.

For all the negativity, there was something that came out of the episode. And it was this: the more the kids at school told me I was dirty, soiled, rotten, and had been *manhandled*, the more, oh yes the more I felt degraded – *but also* – the more it made me look at myself, at the reality of my life.

I was beginning to develop as a woman and the message was beginning to come home: what was going on with Dad was not right.

All these accusers, cruel and demeaning as they were, had a point. What I was doing was, yes, filthy and dirty – but maybe, despite what Dad said, it was also wrong. Their words were just so hard to shake off, and they would follow me from primary school into high school. There would always be a batch of kids who "knew".

At home, something else was happening. The hard reality was that after months in rehab detention, and with Dad supposedly healthy and cured from his wild royal fantasies, he was back ensconced in the house again.

No matter what I did or thought, my being was still inexorably bound to this tall, unbreakable shaft that stood at the centre of my life and taught me all its irreversible lessons.

19.

AROUND THIS TIME THERE WAS A NEW PROGRESSION: when Dad took me aside, he would read to me. Well, maybe it was more like, would read to me and show me pictures. He had these little magazines that he would take out. I don't know what they were called or where they came from, but they were small in shape and contained both pictures and drawings. Not of Snow White or Cinderella like most children would want to see, but of men and women in various fantastic poses. The text too was also not exactly Noddy or even The Secret Seven.

Dad loved reading to me from these magazines. It was about as close as he ever got to reading anything to me.

So, while most children were just developing out of fairy stories and into young teen reading, and while my dad was meant to be back from detention a rehabilitated man, I was viewing the breathless stories of people explaining in easy to understand, very straight and plain English how fucking felt to them. How it always felt so incredibly delightful, clean and scrumptious.

Everyone in the pictures, it cannot be denied, looked so unbelievably pleased with their acrobatics and the positions they assumed, that it was impossible, even for me, not to take my eyes off them.

(An aside: I also remember at this time having a couple of large black encyclopaedia-size hard cover books in my bedroom that were called The Brothers Grimm Fairy Tales. Of course, they were books owned and borrowed by many kids around the world at the time, but how they came to be in our house, I don't know. I would like to imagine it was Aunty Bev, but really I do not know. Probably they were some of the richer neighbours' throw-outs. In any event, once I started reading them, I loved to lose myself in the make-believe fantasy of them. If only Dad was the sort of man who was capable of reading those books to us, how different life may have been? How different life may have been for all of us kids?)

'Get over here, Deb,' Dad would call out with that playful manly roughness of his. 'I want to show you a magazine.' Alone with Dad, I cannot deny, the magazines had an effect on me. In fact, there were times when I asked Dad *not* to read to me from them for one simple reason: they turned me on – so much so that I could not fully comprehend my own thinking. I was beginning to distrust what I would do.

But more usually than not, as I lay back on the bed, my dress flipped up and my legs wide open, he would read to me from the pages and show me the pictures. At the same time, of course, he would rub himself against my vagina, something he knew by now how to do with amazing ease and expertise. It happened time and time and time again.

On one of these occasions, aged thirteen, yes, just barely a teenager, I was so agitated, so frantic, or to put it more bluntly, so moist with excitement and arousal, that something could not stop my little girl hands from... pulling him into me.

Christ. Christ. And Christ again. I cringe, I cry, I beat my breasts; even to this day, at fifty years old, I cannot get the image out of my head – that it was *my* fault. Well, it was me who pulled him into me, wasn't it? If I didn't do that, despite everything, despite everything he had done in the past, he may never have gone *that far*.

In later years, I would begin to see how it is that our bodies respond instinctively and betray us, yes betray. It's not like we want to encourage or even plan for it to happen but betrayal, it seems, is something innate in our bodies. How could I blame anyone – including myself – for that?

I cry from inside my chest, but the strange thing is after that first encounter I felt like I had matured and grown up. I felt like I had become a woman. I felt like I was now a knowledgeable young person of the world. I was *advanced* for my age. It was amazing to actually know what people meant when they said that word sex. More than that, I knew now what it meant to lose one's virginity. It was pleasurable, it was dizzying, and, yes, yes, it was intoxicating to feel and be felt like a woman.

There is one emotion I still feel more than any other: guilt. It is my life-sentence.

But for me there were to be other occasions. On one of those occasions – Mum gone again, yes, Mum away again – and Dad kept me home from school. We were going to some event late that afternoon, it could have even been a funeral, from memory, and Dad pulled me into his bedroom and made me have sex with him before we left.

I remember this particular occasion because afterwards I wore a pad in my underwear, a sanitary pad to stop the leakage. To keep from spotting my panties with what my father had left inside me. I felt so grown up wearing that pad, to find a solution that prevented that awful leakage from being noticed.

20.

DAD ALSO PROTECTED ME. AND BY THE TIME I WAS IN HIGH SCHOOL HIS PROTECTION BECAME PARAMOUNT. It was more than evident one day in the way he dealt with a man who tried to get his son to approach me.

I was about fourteen going on fifteen, and we had this man, Davo and his sixteen or seventeen year-old son, Grant staying at our place for a while. They were staying in the flat under our house. As we became more friendly with them, Davo, the dad, a short, very slightly built man, whose mentality seemed no bigger than his build, thought I would be a "good catch" for his overgrown, stick-like son.

Both father and son were happy, gregarious types in many ways, heavy smokers who didn't mind a beer or two. Lacking in subtlety, Davo started making open assertions about his son being interested in me. It was almost like I wasn't there, like I didn't count, but Davo kept pushing Grant on me, and at one point asked me outright if I was on the Pill.

Frightened, I went and told Dad. He stared into my eyes as though to confirm, and, boy, I was not expecting to see the way his face burned. It went blood red and then blue, and he acted immediately. Lumbering two steps at a time like some fairy tale giant, he ran downstairs and bailed Davo up against a wall.

With fists raging like mighty rocks in the air, he threatened to take Davo's head off with his bare hands. He said he would do so if Davo so much as brought his son near me. Dad was roaring and raving and spinning his hands about. Davo caught such a fright that he and his son left our place not long after.

Dad had proved himself: he was both Lord and Protector. He could bring people in or toss them out at will. He had complete power over his offspring and everything in his house.

Mum, on the other hand, wasn't happy that I'd gone to Dad about it. As I was about to find out, she was rather fond of Davo. Before they left for good, after Dad's outburst I was forbidden by Mum from stepping a foot in the flat downstairs – even though she was in there regularly herself, having her afternoon cuppa with Davo.

Just the way they looked at me, Mum and Davo, the corners of their eyes like pin-pricks, it was obvious that neither of them forgave me for telling Dad. (Another aside: Mum was devastated one day, about a year later, when Davo died of a heart attack. She heard the news after she'd returned home from one of her "excursions"... Strangely, I remember Dad comforting her like he was genuinely sorry for her loss. I didn't quite follow at the time, but I think Mum and Davo were closer than they looked.)

In any event, Dad had proved he was my knight in white satin (and I suppose Mum's as well). There definitely was something a daughter felt when, under threat, her father acts with such an indelibly hard step of the heel. It wasn't just impressive, it made my imperfect chest bloat a little. It bound me further to him.

Dad's power was omnipresent. Sometimes, as my sister Marge and I grew older, Dad would allow us to go to dances. They were held in a large hall and were really community dances, which meant they were actually whole-family affairs, from the littlies right up to grandparents. Nevertheless, Dad made sure we girls knew his eye was on us at all times; that our King was watching. Known as "barn dances", the dances were a definite highlight on the social calendar for me and my sister.

A set of rules was put in place for us girls. One of them was that we should never go outside of "the barn" by ourselves and another was that we should let Dad know even when we were going to the toilet. He said this was so that he could watch out for us, which, one had to suppose, was just like any good country father would do.

But probably the main rule was this: Dad said a girl, and that included Mum, should never refuse an offer of a dance from a bloke. The rule seemed bent around an unwritten kinship with every bloke in town, that we girls should never in any way make a guy feel bad, ugly, unwanted, or in any way embarrassed.

Yet as in all events in our lives, Dad would lord over me and my sister, and with a nod or shake of his head, he would let us know exactly who we could dance with and who we should say no to.

On the other hand, standing there next to Dad at those dances, all six foot and three inches of Dan Gallagher, made me feel pretty special too, like no one was going to step out of line or try anything.

That, of course, was Dad's terrain.

21.

BEING AT HIGH SCHOOL DIDN'T MEAN THE SLANDER STOPPED. The good thing was not everyone at high school knew about the court case, but among those who did, the slander only grew worse, more sophisticated, more venomous.

On one occasion some girls phoned me up from an afternoon birthday party. I wasn't invited, of course, but they took the time to call me up to giggle into the phone and tell me I was a dirty little girl who slept with her father.

"Slut", was the word they used. How they knew *that* much about me, I don't know. But even though it was meant to be just pure poisonous gossip, it was like they *did* know. And all it did once again was confirm how soiled I was.

I also actually had a classmate as a boyfriend at this time. I was pretty happy with this newfound boyfriend and he was pretty happy with me. We spoke and kissed a couple of times, all rather innocently, as kids of fourteen might.

But even he, not that long after we were together, phoned me one day and said, 'Deb, I'm sorry. I know about you and your dad. I can't go out with you anymore.'

And that was the end of that. Silence. I cried and cried, now knowing another type of hurt. Strangely, though, it was Dad who comforted me. I didn't tell him the real reason why I no longer had that innocent boyfriend, only that I didn't anymore and I was heartbroken.

The truth was, as was happening more and more, while I felt denigrated and mucky, the taunts also galvanised me. I wanted to fight back, I wanted to do something for myself, not only against these kids – but also against Dad. Somehow, some time, I had to face him.

More and more I was seeing everything through the eyes of the kids around me, and ill conceived and badly spat out as their logic was, they were right. The fact was, although they thought they knew everything but were being no more than "bitches", the kids at school were so right they didn't even know the half of it.

If they knew it... I don't know... a public hanging in the middle of the town square wouldn't have been beyond them. And of course their parents would have applauded them.

There was one teacher at this time – actually the principal of my school – who turned out to be unexpectedly good to me. Good may even be far too soft a word for her. It was like she knew there was something not quite right with me, or at any rate had a knowledge of what was going on in my home, and whenever I was not feeling well at school, which seemed to be an increasing amount of time these days, she would allow me to come into her office area and lie down on a big, comfy cushion.

She would let me just rest my head and sleep there. It was warm and calming, with no pressure or expectations even of a thanks. In my mind it built a certain faith that even in a place like school there could be delicateness. As bad as things got, there were always little corners of light.

To me, especially at that time, it seemed almost unnatural that I would find it in a school principal's office, but there I was, safe and secure and under no strain with her. Despite what she knew, or heard, she never asked me anything and I also never told her anything.

Whenever the thought of telling her anything so much as entered my brain, I saw in front of me Mum galloping into the schoolyard and there, right in front of everyone, giving me a crack or two across the face. Dad, I knew, would go utterly ballistic.

I imagine, in her soft and comforting way, the principal was hoping eventually something in me would crack open and I would want to spout the secrets from my buggered up brain. It never happened. My fears were too great.

Sometimes, though, I wished she may have prodded a bit more. Because if she knew the following story she definitely would have done something. No one knew about it. That is to say, there were some who did know, or possibly knew, but in effect they didn't, because nobody was saying anything.

It was the height of summer, the air hot and indecently thick with humidity, and we were all out at this swimming place in the Nebo River, that is to say, us kids, Dad and a woman friend of the family, Doris and her two young children.

Mum wasn't there. She was away somewhere – with my younger sister Marge. Yes, Mum away again, and it was obvious even to my very young teen head that Dad had eyes for Doris, at any rate he was continually swimming pretty close to her. It was also obvious she didn't mind. Was in fact enjoying the proximity of him.

We kids were splashing one another and jumping into the river from the bank.

But Dad was also full of fun on that day. He was taking time out from Doris to play with us, and when Dad played with us it was like there were two suns blistering in the sky. We loved his towering strength and boyishness.

'One, two, three,' he would shout and we would jump off his clasped hands like it was a springboard into the water. Sometimes we would even dive from his shoulders. He was so tall it was like double the height of a normal springboard.

Then he would swim back to Doris and they would stay close for long periods. But, inevitably, he would come back to us kids and splash and throw us about.

At one point, I'm not sure where everyone else got to, but it was just me and Dad; that is to say he had me alone and I was loving it as he did the things normal dads do, splashing and chucking me into the water. But then he started paying me that special attention, that is to say, doing what *my* dad did that was special, rubbing himself against me.

It was not long before he had all his fingers down there.

It was not what I wanted to do right then and began to swim away. He pulled me back, struggled with me, considered me with those sharp bird eyes of his, and then the strangest thing happened. Well, it seemed so strange to me because it happened so fast, so frenetically, almost impossibly.

While I put my awkward girl resistance up to his hands, he heaved me under the water. In fact he pulled me down so hard into the water it felt like I was about to be fired back up into the air with the power of a canon. Only he kept me under the water, and I felt this blunt skewer-like thing thud into my behind.

With my togs pulled to one side, what he did right then hurt like someone was sending a spike right up my spine. Like I imagine a lumber puncture feels. I could not help but send out a kind of shrill animal shriek that came right from deep inside my lower back and speared back up through the air.

Hearing my agony, and seeing everyone turn around, Dad let me go, and the first thing he whispered into my ear, was, 'Sorry. I'm sorry, Deb. I didn't mean to do that.'

Do what? I didn't even know what he meant, except that I was in extraordinary pain and had to drag myself to the banks of the river where I lay hurting like never before, blood streaming from my rectum.

How? How did he do it? That jab that was like a torpedo entering me? I thought I was going to need stitches, that I was going to faint or maybe even die. For two days after that I bled and had diarrhoea and thought I would never recover. To this day I still don't know how a man – any man – could do that.

I wonder if that kind and compassionate school principal would have remained silent if she knew that story.

22.

ONE THING I HAVE TO SAY ABOUT DAD IS THAT AT LEAST HE WASN'T A PREACHER, well, not in the strict sense of the word. In fact, if anything, he was anti-religion. 'A load of croc-shit,' was the way he put it.

With a wry smile, sometimes with a bird-like laugh, he called believers "God-botherers". And so although we did go to church once or twice for special occasions, and even to Sunday School once or twice, it was never a fixture of our lives.

Maybe Dad was right on this one. But the taste of Sunday School we kids had, made us want it, made us hang out for it. Just the idea of being with a bunch of other kids on a Sunday seemed like a great idea. It was a whole heap better than just hanging out by ourselves on the property.

But of course with Dad, and even Mum, that was never going to happen, regular Sunday school. Still, just about the age of starting high school, when things were looking pretty dismal at home with Dad and Mum, and the kids who knew about our family saga were running me ragged because of the court case, we started going to a Sunday school of sorts.

It was at a new family at the school, the Ogilvys. They were very religious and encouraged a Sunday school group at their home. Even Dad and Mum managed to get roped in. For us kids it was not just a change, it was like a holiday: everything at the Ogilvys was positive and sun-filled and non-judgemental. We loved it. But there was no way Dad was going to allow us to continue going there on a consistent basis – not to those "bunch'a God-botherers".

Nevertheless, in the few times we did go there it was enough time for me to take in one of Mr Ogilvy's foremost messages, which was this: 'If you really want something and you pray to the Lord, you will get it.'

That really appealed to me, the idea that I could ask for something in my heart and I would get it. I can't remember there being anything major at that time that I wanted, so with Dad's "croc-shit" stance and our not being taken back to the Ogilvys' Sunday School after a short while, I didn't try very hard with my prayers.

But one day, not that long after, that was to change with strange effect. It happened on the day when our teacher, Miss Lovestone announced that she had lost her very expensive, very sentimental, absolutely irreplaceable diamond and sapphire engagement ring.

She was convinced the ring had become lost somewhere on the school oval. The whole school even had an "Emu Parade" around the oval the next day to try and find her precious ring. But after more than an hour of looking there seemed to be no luck there.

When I saw the distraught look on Miss Lovestone's face, the way it seemed to have lost its colour, the way her eyes stared as though lifeless, with all my heart I wanted to find that engagement ring and bring back the ruddiness to her cheeks. So I got down on my knees, as I'd seen the Ogilvys do it at Sunday School, closed my eyes, and began to pray: '*Please God, pleeease* help me find Miss Lovestone's ring.'

Kneeling there, I opened my eyes, and no word of a lie, I looked down and there it was. My heart leapt, I picked up the ring and ran over to give it to her. The colour immediately shot back to her face, even a couple of tears filled her eyes. The smile that took over her wasn't just for the sake of a good child – it was like I had wrought a miracle. In her excitement she said I could have anything, absolutely anything I wanted in the world.

My heart racing, I stood beside her and thought, and then thought some more. But the amazing thing was I could think of nothing. Well, there was this one thing – stop my parents from fighting and arguing and make them into better people

– but of course that was not something I could talk about. So, in truth, when I thought about it there really wasn't a lot I wanted.

'How's about a lolly?' she eventually said.

'Mmm, yeah, okay,' I said, rummaging, not really expecting to hold her to it.

As kids we hardly had lollies, and much as we loved Nesquick and biscuits the only lollies we were ever given, and infrequently, were those old boiled lollies. So when I told Ms Lovestone those were the lollies I loved, she ended up giving me a whole bottle of them. I was so happy when she actually placed the bottle in my hand the next day, I couldn't wait to get home and share the sweets with my family.

But the ring incident proved much more important than that.

It was weird, but finding that ring after calling out to the heavens, gave me a sense of peace in myself, a kind of solace. I guess it was a kind of peace and comfort in the idea that there really was something out there, some force, some energy bigger and more knowing than us. Not necessarily "God", or a god, but some Unknown Force that was actually listening and watching over everything. There was a connection between me and the great "out there".

To this day I feel no guilt in saying in my heart, *'Please God. Pleeeease...'* I believe it is good to ask, I believe it is good to pray – because it is a way of clarifying in ourselves what we really want.

It is a test: the more we want something, the more we internalise and pray for it. It is a way to see if we really want that thing. I don't know of anybody who prays deep in their heart for things they don't want.

Did it help my situation? Did it release me from Dad? The short answer is no, but it did give me a sense of the *power* of belief. Which was really, I came to realise, belief in oneself.

I found that ring. I also found, just in time, books like The Brothers Grimm that saved me from dipping into hell.

That is the important thing. Knowing it is there. Something always to scoop us up from the floor. We don't have to be religious to believe that. Just believing in ourselves and knowing someone is in a worse situation than we are is like a big, thick glass of strawberry Nesquick. It is, believe me. I've been there.

For me, it should have been a time for belief and hope.

23.

As always, without even being allowed to go out, I was growing up fast. But my father, my teacher, my Lord Protector remained relentless, and back at school, the taunts only grew worse.

Did they have spies out there? Or just very intuitive gossips? Because as far as other boys went, despite their sometimes quite arduous endeavours, I was far less active, far less of a "hunter" or even a "gatherer" or even an "experimenter" than ninety-five percent of the other girls.

Yet everyday on my way to school I would feel it. The pinch of accusation and smear. By the time the school bus arrived at our stop on the Bruce Highway, almost always the bus was already more than halfway full and there would be no empty double seats left. I would have to sit next to someone. Only no one wanted to sit next to me. So I had to stand. But even when I did manage to rush into a seat next to someone, they would slide themselves right up against the side panel of the bus in order to get as far as possible from me.

Often even, the particular kid I sat next to would get up and go and sit somewhere else. Crowded places, believe me, can be pretty bloody isolating. Every day on that bus, to and from school, I experienced it.

And the mocking only grew.

There was this one brave boy at the school – he had to be brave if he was openly talking to me in the schoolyard – who asked me to be his girlfriend. It was as simple as that at school. The way kids sometimes became boyfriend and girlfriend. We'd spoken a few times and there was no two ways about it, Simm was quite a handsome lad.

So, I said yes, and we became boyfriend and girlfriend. After a couple of weeks an old friend, Laura, who definitely knew the family history from primary school, started to lay claims on Simm. I guess she was pretty upfront, because she asked me outright if Simm could be her boyfriend instead of mine.

'No, no, don't be silly.' I looked at her like she was out of her tree. 'He's my boyfriend. You can't do that.'

'Well then I'll tell everyone about you and your father!' She yelled it out without the slightest sense of privacy or decorum, for the entire playground to hear.

It stung. Oh God, it stung. As if most weren't in on the gossip already. But it stung so bad with Laura that I capitulated. 'Okay then, you can have him if you really want him. I don't care.'

I walked away, only to hear her behind me, 'Naaa-naaa-nanna-na-naaa... I got your boyfriend.'

'Leave me alone,' I mumbled back.

She continued... 'Naaa-naaa-nanna-na-naaa... I got your boyfriend.'

'Okay, so tell me more!' I wished for a moment I could actually be like Dad, and tell her to bugger off or I'd rip her head off. I felt the blood in me whistling like a rattling kettle.

She started to push me.

I pushed her back. 'I don't want to fight with you. I've given you my boyfriend. What more do you want?'

She pushed me back again, this time adding: 'Yeah, yeah, but you let your father fuck you. You're a father-fucker... Father-fucker! Father-fucker!' She sung it; she actually sung it, like a nursery rhyme, only so loud that even kids who knew nothing about me now suddenly knew everything. I felt so beaten, so, so degraded I could die.

The whistle in the kettle steamed over; it burnt through my eyes and into my chest and out through my badly maturing breasts, and suddenly my fists were flying. I laid into her with everything I had. And it must have been pretty hard – all that cow milking and working out in the paddock, I guess – because instead of fighting back she was raising her arms to protect herself and crying for me to stop.

Finally, I cannot remember how or by whom, the fight was ended. But my once friend was taken to hospital and sometime later returned to school with a plaster cast. I had broken her arm!

I was confused and afraid and at the same time amazed that I could hurt another human being like that. Everybody knew about me now, not only how perverse I was but how wild and crazy; I felt like jumping off the planet.

The next day when I climbed on the school bus and went to sit next to one of the kids, I was expecting the usual treatment. Only worse. Maybe even to get a belting. I put my head down like I couldn't see anyone. I definitely did not want to see any of them.

Nervously, shifting in next to one of the boys, I found he did not even move. Not an inch. No word said. Not on the entire bus. It was like in that silence, in that lack of movement, everything had been returned to normal.

I remember it as "returned to normal" because there was this one big difference in that motionless silence. With the sky outside its usual thin, metallic blue and the sun busily making its way across that dry central Queensland heaven, suddenly an empty seat was an empty seat again. Not a word said, not a movement made.

I am sure I even saw a smile as I sat down. I think so. It really was quite bizarre – to go from villain one day to hero the next, or at any rate just to a plain, simple "normal" kid. I was someone people would sit next to again.

If I had lost that fight, I have no doubts, the insults would have continued, even more pronounced. Everyone, not just Laura, would have been singing that taunt: *'Naaa-naaa-nanna-na-naaa... Father-fucker! Father-fucker!'* It's not the way I would like the world to be because there are too many weak people out there who cannot defend themselves.

Nevertheless, I felt like I had achieved something. I had broken a deadlock on my own weakness. My own fears. I had confirmed the belief I was finding in myself. I had shown

I could, at the very least, put up a fight. That was important. Not only had I seen I had more muscle in me than I thought, I had proven I could use that strength to win. Talk about law of the jungle.

I guess I could have had friends then, at least chosen a couple, but I was beginning to enjoy my isolation, and the best part was, as bad as things got, I found this one thing that I was beginning to see more and more clearly in me: I may have been a loser, I may have been shy and introverted, I may have been badly used, but I never saw myself as a victim.

No, I am absolutely sure of that. I am not sure how it came about, given my childhood, given the isolation of the properties we lived on; but, given that fight and the resistance I put up, it is the reality. And it is one I am grateful for.

To try and bring some logic to it, when I was at primary school, I guess it was all innocence and I was like a tadpole trying to find my way, thinking all the frogs around me knew exactly who they were and what was right and wrong for me. Whereas at high school, as I developed into a young woman, the derision and slander showed me there was something definitely not right with me. It built in me an inner strength – maybe even brought out an innate wisdom – to never allow myself the lethargic, self-destructive luxury of saying: 'O, woe is me. I am going to sink and drown in my hardships.'

Always I had the feeling I was going to survive. I wanted to survive. Life, for all it had handed out, was, it is hard to find other words, too precious.

By this time, at lower high school, the terrible reality was I already had a "steady" sexual partner – yes, the girls were right – *my Dad*. Father-fucker! Father-fucker! But it never felt bad, well *that* depressingly bad – that I wanted to kill myself or cry away my days until I faded into anorexia or bulimia or suicide.

One of the things I also had to thank for saving me was… the school library. To get away from the other kids, the taunts and teasing, I used to go to the school library during my breaks and read. Just read and read and read.

My speciality was books of woe, tales of tragedy, tales of other people's loss. They were books written by authors like Eleanor Hibbert along with her pseudonyms, Jean Plaidy, Philippa Carr and Victoria Holt, and others like Susan Griffin who wrote about true-life rape and brutal assaults on women in the 1970s. All of the people in these books had these sad, tragic stories to tell that made mine look, well... like fluff.

Yep, as bad as things got for me, there was always someone worse off. It was in black and white, right here in these books.

The idea of books started coming to me not long after Dad started having sex with me. I'm not sure who suggested I start reading, or if it was the delight I got from discovering The Brothers Grimm, those famous fairy tale volumes that seemed to have no place in our ramshackle, uneducated house, or if it was from the diary Aunty Bev gave me and that I wrote in fastidiously... but one day I went to the school library and these books simply gushed out at me like a rush of cool hose-water.

Some of the books must have been standing up on a table, the librarian's small way of marketing reading, any reading among us "couldn't-give-a-damn-about-books" kids. But when I think about it, what may have actually helped me into reading too was a time when Dad actually did read to me from a genuine book.

I had menstruated before I was ten. It was a one-off, and the cycle never returned until I was twelve. Nevertheless, at age ten, I caught such a fright at what I saw that I told Mum and Dad. They must have decided they had to do something about it, because they quickly went out and bought me a book – on sex.

Yes, Mum and Dad bought me an educational book on the female body and sex. Not only that, but they would read to me from it. Dad, who until then had never read to me in his life, whose attitude to reading was – *Put those bloody books away, there's no need to be doing that. Get your frigging arse down here* – read to me from that book... on menstruation, sex and womanhood.

But the fantasy, the human compassion, the eternal relief I gained from the books in the library at high school lay in this amazing discovery: I was not the only person having it tough on the planet. There was a whole club of people out there, particularly women, who were being so badly brutalised and even destroyed that I probably couldn't even gain membership to their club if I tried.

Particularly, though, what appealed were the historical novels of Victoria Holt. I could drift into another universe and the world I was taken to always appeared so real to me. More real than my own world. There was other reading material too that were my favourites: booklets about *True Life Crimes and Confessions of Serial Killers* and also Mum's *Lonely Hearts Club* magazines that made me cry with their stories of heartbreak and pain.

Dad also had this series of "True Crime" booklets. They were given to him by a cousin of his who was some big shot real-life detective in Brisbane. Dad was very proud to know Jonny, as he called him, and would often ask him for advice on things. Though you can bet your life he never whispered a word of what was going on in his own family. Anyway, the thing with these booklets was that they made my experiences with Dad seem like some kind of merely wrong-minded "puppy-love". A kind of mistakenly soiled rag that could be left behind.

One of the stories I read at the time of Dad's intrusion into my body, was of a girl around my age who had been raped by her father. Yes, *raped*. My story was so different. So, so much softer. I had wanted Dad, well I wanted *something*, so technically I left him with no choice. I had pulled him into me. It was a part of my world, my culture.

There was another book that helped me at the time: Alex Haley's *Roots*. I mean, if I thought I had it rough, just look at the poor slaves in that book. Black folk kidnapped from Africa, raped, treated worse than shit, and murdered by whites in one of the world's most civilised societies.

The year I first slept with Dad, oblivious to me, to Dad, to Mum, probably to everyone we knew, it was International Women's Year and untold millions were dying of cruelty and starvation.

I was one of the lucky ones.

24.

THE REAL START OF MY "FIGHT-BACK" AGAINST DAD BEGAN ONE DAY WHEN I WAS ABOUT THIRTEEN GOING ON FOURTEEN AND IN THE CAR WITH HIM. I was in the front seat next to him, and my older brother Jim and younger brother Sam were in the back. We were on our way to Childers, about 200 kilometres away, to visit family friends. And yes, guess what? Neither Mum nor my sister Marge were in the car. Because Mum had gone away again.

Dad, so much the pragmatist, taught us to drive at an early age, and by the time we were barely teenagers we could all drive cars, trucks, even to some extent tractors. One of the ways Dad taught us to drive – and to practice our driving – was by getting us to sit on his lap while he showed us how to steer and how to operate the gears and foot pedals.

I loved driving. It was to me like what going to the movies was for other kids. I loved it, loved it, loved it. There was nothing I would not do to drive.

Dad knew that. And of course one of the conditions under which I could drive, was that while I sat on his lap he could touch me. I didn't care. I was so used to it anyway. As long as I could drive, that was the main thing. Dad got what he wanted and I got what I wanted.

Only as the hiss of my school friends had taught me, the sex, the touching, the everything that went alongside it, was not what Dad made it out to be. More and more, like the swimming incident in the Nebo River, which left me with a split rectum, I was beginning to let Dad know that I didn't feel like it.

On this occasion, going to visit friends, with Jim and Sam sitting in the back was no different. Dad asked if I wanted to drive. I knew what that meant. Even with my love for driving, it wasn't an easy decision. But I decided to stick my neck out and say no. I told him I wasn't in the mood. Dad knew what I really meant: I wanted to drive all right; I just didn't want his fingers up my crotch.

'Get here, now. Come and have a drive,' he growled at me.

'No,' I looked the other away.

'Get over here now,' he repeated, and this time pulled at me with his hand.

I shook my head and pulled back.

It was obvious, even to a drunken wombat, I was saying no. Next thing I knew Dad was pulling the car off the road, stopping, and with his long body and brute strength was leaning over, grabbing at my thick wavy hair and smashing my head against the car door-jam. On and on he went, smashing my head like I had committed a heinous crime, like it was the death penalty he was dishing out.

There was no stopping him. He was a man out of control. If it felt bad, it must have looked like murder, because for the first time in my life I heard my brother Jim, usually terrified of Dad, begin to yell with a loud and shaky voice, 'Stop it! Stop it now! Please, Dad, stop it!'

The amazing thing was, after a few seconds, after Jim's defiant screams, Dad actually stopped. He let go of my head.

In one way, it was already too late. I had already peed myself. Yes, I sat there and peed right down my legs, but Jim had saved me and Dad didn't say a word more. I am forever thankful to my older brother for that particular time, when for a moment it seemed like Dad, in front of my brothers, could have rearranged the brain cells in my head, even taking into account that they were already so badly damaged.

But more than that, I saw something else that was happening in me. At the least, I was beginning to let him know I wasn't always going to be at his beck and call.

I just don't think they, the kids at school, or anyone really, realised how much courage it took. It was not easy against a man like Dad. Have you ever fought off a lion? Well, that was Dad, in our house, King of the Jungle.

They say men break things and they don't even know they're doing it. But I tell you, bad men break things twice as badly. And from where I was sitting on that day, frightened as hell, Dad was looking like a pretty bad man.

25.

I WAS BEGINNING TO FIGHT THEM BACK ON BOTH FRONTS NOW: Mum as well as Dad.

I remember once, in one of her rampages against me – which could be for anything, like not hanging up the washing or not hanging it up properly – she was calling me a slut and a bitch and saying what she usually did in those moods: 'No wonder things happen to you!'

This time, age fourteen going on fifteen, I turned around and slapped her. Yes, I slapped my mum. That word "bitch" struck a chord in me. It locked right into my solar plexus.

Unfortunately, good as the slap felt in the moment, it didn't stop Mum. Once she'd recovered from the shock, I saw that look coming into her face, that severe, pointy look, that snort of the nose that said: *Retaliation*.

I ran through the house to get away from her and she chased me around and around until I finally made it into to my bedroom where I jumped like a falling parachute onto the first bed in the room. It was my sister's bed, and as I jumped I pushed my head into my shoulders and face into the bed, knowing I would need to protect myself so that Mum could not see my face to slap it or perhaps even punch it.

What I didn't see on the bed was the old metal laundry basket, which was filled to the brim. As I jumped, trying to flip onto my back, I smashed my backbone up against the edge of it. I was stunned and in pain and turned around to Mum in agony.

It was too late. She was already slapping me. Only in all honesty, on this occasion, I think she was slapping me to bring me around because I was crying but no sound was coming out of my mouth; it had taken my breath away.

I don't know. It's hard to say; in those days, when I did something wrong, Mum had taken to chucking me on the ground and then pinning her knees into my shoulders and punching me with a boxer's fury in my back. So, I don't know. To this day, I'm still unsure.

But in truth, could I blame her? It was obvious she was not just reacting to me, she was reacting to everything, to the people and pressures and inexplicable events around her. With her soft-glowing brown eyes, her full "c'mon lips", and attractive round face, she was still married to Dan Gallagher, had four kids, lived on an intensely dry and needy property, and in effect, without much support, her life was a misery.

No wonder she sometimes blew out to a hundred kilos. Which was no joke when she was pinning me down on the floor and smashing her fists into my back. But I can see it now, the frustration, the anger, the fury that was aimed at her own life.

In the background, other things were happening at that time.

I was starting to make my own clothes, and full-on fifteen now Dad was starting to make sure I was wearing the appropriate clothing for the dances we were allowed to go to. I know one would expect Dad was ensuring I sew my way into long dresses and tight-collared shirts or, at the least, considering the times, close to knee-length skirts and near completely done-up tops.

Well that was almost true – with the exception of one pair of blue satin hibiscus print shorts which were very skimpy and showed all my legs almost right up to my bottom – and the black dress he bought me for the "Miss Anondale" dance which presented my small breasts like they were the centrepiece of my body.

I guess he thought whatever happened, I had him there to protect me from any prying eyes, well at least ones that he hadn't given permission to.

At the time my older brother Jim, now a lad of sixteen going on seventeen, was at technical college in Rockhampton and there was this one kid he became really friendly with who he would bring back down with him over weekends.

Brad, only seventeen, was taller than Dad. Yes, only seventeen, and taller than Dad. What he was not, was as physically imposing or strong looking. It took a lot to achieve that. But fair in colour and modest in build, he was pretty handsome. Fresh-faced in a blokey sort of way, he had wavy, longish dark blonde hair, and his biggest flaw was that he had this squashed-in nose. It came, I learnt later, from playing footy – rugby league.

His nose looked like it had been tackled into his face, and made his face always look a little "out of focus". Somehow it managed even to "squash" his giant height. On the other hand, the asphyxiated nostrils gave to a certain generosity in his surprised-looking blue eyes.

Lips, yes the lips. Brad had these slight yet generous lips that gave me an instant belief in him, and soon, instead of just Jim's friend, he became my friend. In fact, more often than not, he started to come over just to visit me.

Dad and Mum must have known about the relationship, or figured it out, because they often saw us together. They never said anything, well, not until later. The truth was the friendship between Brad and I was perfectly innocent. All we ever did was kiss and hug and kiss some more. But it never got further than that.

Until Dad interceded.

Dad had obviously put two and two together, but on the positive front, and to my surprise, there was no anger, no questioning, no jealousy, and it was like he had smiled on Brad, deciding he was the one.

What I did not realise was what was going on in that twisted mind of his. Dad had obviously escalated everything in his head, because one night, late at night, when I had stayed up with Brad, after Brad had gone to bed, Dad called me into his and Mum's bedroom.

It was the weirdest moment of my life, even weirder, I would say, than the night I was investigated with a torch between my legs on the kitchen table. It definitely ran close. In the event, I was wearing a short skirt and while Mum quietly slept on the one side of the bed, both of them beneath their royal veil, Dad told me to come and stand at his side of the bed.

He looked me in the eyes, jutting the gap in his front teeth with his tongue, and with full confidence, perhaps I should say the usual confidence, told me to open my legs.

Confused, standing there, I shivered but did as he ordered. Then he leaned down with his head and looked up my skirt, but like a doctor or a forensic scientist, and with his one hand he pulled my knickers aside. I stood there, blinking, unsure what to expect, wondering why he wanted to do something now – with Mum right there on the other side of the bed.

A moment later he had a finger in me, right up my vagina. He was pushing something up me. It felt small like a little round tablet, and then suddenly it went fizzy.

A second or two later, like a backstreet abortionist he pulled his hand and eyes away from under my skirt, and said: 'That's for you and Brad, so you don't get pregnant.'

I have never investigated it, but to this day I still don't know what Dad shoved up me. I can only suspect it was some kind of spermicide.

My mind was racing and whirring at a million miles per hour and I didn't quite know what to do – what Dad expected me to do. But as I walked out of Mum and Dad's royal bedroom it slowly started to sink in that this is what Dad wanted for me: he was giving me permission to have sex with Brad.

In an unsure, spinning-head sort of way, I felt thrilled and elated. Dad was finally opening the curtain to something real for me. He was giving me permission to become a woman. A real woman. I was fifteen – still not sixteen – and he obviously seemed to think the time – and the fella – was right.

I went to Brad, where he was sleeping in a room with my brother, and led him, all six foot and four or five inches of him, into my bedroom, and there for the first time I had sex with another male. While my sister slept soundly in the bed next to mine.

I suppose in any normal household that would have been my first real sexual encounter. Brad never asked and I never said anything. Officially now, I suppose, I was no longer a virgin.

26.

UNLIKE WITH DAD, I REALLY DID GROW UP THAT NIGHT. I had a boyfriend now. A real boyfriend. We became entwined, looking with the same eyes into a similar future, both of us sure... and a little unsure. Much more importantly in the weeks ahead, as our relationship grew, so the more I did not want Dad near me.

This isn't to say that he didn't stop *wanting* me, or to *have his way* with me, as they put it in some of the books I read – but more and more now, in my eyes, he was becoming just plain old Dad, definitely not "my boyfriend", not "my lover", not even "my mentor". I was beginning to see it clearer than ever now. What he had been doing was worse than perverted. It was just plain bloody wrong.

As far as I was concerned my loyalty belonged to Brad. I probably shouldn't have been surprised, this caused problems between Dad and me. He was getting cranky and impatient because he wasn't getting what he wanted. Threats of sending me away to boarding school or a "girls home" began at this time.

It still haunts in the mind the way he "gave me away" that night. Like a horse he owned. Like a cow at a showground. Happy as I was with Brad, Dad was still somehow managing to get in the way. I just wanted to be a normal teenager, just a normal young girl, free to live and love and breathe. But somehow I was still chained to Dad's clunking shackles.

It came to a head one night when he asked me to go with him to visit his mum, my Grandma Glad. We drove silently together to Grandma's house, which was only about ten minutes away, on the other side of Perenjora Dam.

What stands out, is that Grandma Glad looked totally surprised to see us. Normally we would drop by in the day or always call first. Nevertheless, on this night, it was obvious Dad had arrived without calling first. Once Grandma had gotten over her surprise, we stayed for a while and Dad nattered with her and did whatever it was he told me he had to go out there for. And then we left again.

It seemed particularly dark on the way back and on top of that Dad took one of the many sidetracks he knew well from his timber cutting. On one of these tracks he stopped the car and offered me the keys. Even at my age, fifteen, and in my relationship with a fella Dad had given his approval to, I knew what that meant.

He wanted to sit beside me, and while he watched me drive he wanted to put his fingers inside me. He was still doing that. The only difference now was that I was no longer sitting on his lap.

What he was asking was the last thing I wanted to do. The very, very last. Not only was the road dark and dusty, so was my mind. Everything in there was like a storm full of windswept dirt.

I shook my head but Dad insisted. He started pouring out eyes to me like he was astounded, disappointed, that knew I loved to drive. That knew I would do anything to drive. He was considering me like a wise father who knew I was only defying my own best interests. I still said no. He kept insisting, now pricking those "seeing" bird-eyes into me, maybe more honestly now, like not only was I defying my own best interests but his as well.

Eventually, I relented. I had to. Dad smiled, a thin, curled worm, and walked around the car. I shifted over into the driver's seat.

I started the car and the first thing he did, naturally enough – it was like a cow in season to a worked up bull – was put his hand under my dress. I pushed his hand away. He put his hand back again, and again I pushed it away. I looked to my side and saw the bull, nostrils snorting, lips dry and stiff, tongue sitting against front teeth ready to charge. The hand came back, and affirmatively, almost aggressively. I shouted that most disallowed of all words: No.

The bull bucked and then kicked. That is to say, Dad freaked. He actually freaked so much that he leaned over and took me by the neck and started throttling me. Just like we had seen him do to Mum with the telephone cord. Only this time he was throttling me with his tough, bare hands. His eyes were lit with blue-white heat and everything in my head and in the car was shaking and smouldering.

'You know I could strangle you and throw your body in the creek and no one would ever know!' He stared at me like he was capable of anything. *Anything.*

'I don't care. I don't care.' Eyes wet and burning, I stared back at him. 'Do what you like. I don't care if I die!' The words squeezed from my throat and the reality was, right then, I really didn't give a damn. For the first time in my life I really didn't care. He could do what he wanted with me. The only thing I knew was it was over. I wanted it to be over. And I didn't care one iota if I died in the process. At that point in my life I was willing to die. I was trying to be independent, my own person, and if he didn't like it he could kill me.

I don't know what it was Dad saw in me then. What he saw in the outrage of my wet eyes; I really don't know, but as I struggled for my last dying breaths before I passed out, suddenly he released his grip on my neck and sat back in his seat.

He breathed out heavily, a bull confused and deflated, like all the wind had been taken out of him. He turned away from me, to the darkness outside, sitting there, despite his height, crinkled looking and dispirited. Finally he half turned back to me and mumbled something about starting the car.

Coughing, my neck shrieking in pain, I turned away from him like I did not ever want to see him again, did not ever want to be duped by his sorrow and dejection. I started the car without a single word further – from him or me.

My throat was steaming, my head was stormy, my hair felt stiff, still so full of muck and dark cloud. The car took off, and although I was sitting there with him I kept having this flash of somehow driving all by myself, in isolated safety, aware he would not dare come near me. And yet still I wanted to die.

In the end, we got home safely that night, safer in many ways than I had been in my entire life, and in many ways blessed, blessed Dad decided not to strangle me as he had said he so easily could on that dark road back from Grandma's...

Unfortunately this was no Jean Plaidy or Victoria Holt tale, because there was still more to come, lots, lots more.

27.

IF THERE WAS ONE THING I HAD ACHIEVED WITH DAD THAT NIGHT IN THE CAR, it was an end to any sexual relationship between us. Not that he didn't try again, he did. But by now I had become forceful, and I was saying that word NO with power and confidence. It was rattling him, it was shaking the whole house. Our world was changing.

And yet still Dad would continue his advances. A jilted father? A jilted lover? The last I can remember was him coming into my bedroom one night, turning me onto my back and straddling me. 'No!' I yelled at him. 'No!'

In the dark night I shouted it into his face in that assured way I was becoming used to. It rose from my gut and bellowed through my throat. He reared back like a horse and grabbed me with all his strength in his rough hands and squeezed my brittle shoulders. Then he shook me and shook me and shook me some more.

But in the end he trotted out of the room, empty-handed.

The next day my neck was in such agony that even he could see I needed help. He drove me to the doctor and told the physician it had happened while riding with me on his motorbike. He had suddenly jerked the bike to avoid something on the road, and my head had lurched forwards. In front of the doctor, I did not have it in me to defy Dad. I listened in silence, nodded, and let Dad have his lie.

On some indefinable level in my head, he had the decency to take me to a professional person for help and I appreciated that. By doing so he had made amends and a connection on that mysteriously close father-daughter level had somewhat been re-established.

But it was over now, the sex and abuse was all over now. Or was it? Can it ever be? Like my sore neck, he would live in my head, daily, nightly, weekly, forever, and at this time he would still loom large. So very, very large. The things he had done and their effect would carry over into my everyday life. Into every second of my life.

The things he did – the things he and Mum did.

While Mum and Marge had been away around this time, they were back now, and I was feeling generally contented. But Mum, seeing my close relationship with my boyfriend, Brad, the steadiness of it, the sheer fun and enjoyment of it, had other ideas.

One day when I was not around, she made a point of giving Brad some clues about my past. About my relationship with Dad. About why I may even have had a sore neck. She did it like it was her duty as a mother to do so, to let her daughter's boyfriend, perhaps a future son-in-law know I may not be all that met the eye. That maybe I belonged to someone else and he should watch it. He should at any rate be aware of it.

I learnt about what Mum had told him on a weekend not long after she had spilled all these sordid, so-called family beans. We were sitting on the shores of the Nebo River together, doing the things we used to do when we were alone: fishing in Dad's tinnie, swimming and watching the birds, talking about other people and the future, and, well, smooching, yes, lots and lots of smooching.

Sitting there like that, Brad turned to me and suddenly became very serious. So serious I thought his tackled-in face was going to fracture.

His voice was pinching through that squashed nose: 'Why didn't you tell me, Deb? About your dad? How could you not say anything?'

'What! I don't know what you're on about,' I replied in a small voice.

His nose began to flare, becoming braver. 'Don't bullshit me, Deb. I know all about it. I know about you. You let your dad touch you. You let your father... fuck you.' The noise in his nose was like an off-key saxophone.

133

I was shocked. I felt my face caving inwards. It was like a hurricane had blown right through me. I felt my breasts literally cowering. My neck was crimping into my shoulders and still somehow I managed to find faltering words: 'How... would you know anything?'

'Your Mum told me. She showed me everything. All the papers from the court case.'

Game over! I knew it was over. Yes, thank you, Mum. Thank you very much indeed. From your cold, never-there bosom, you had yet again allowed my entire world to disintegrate around me. And yet really, I knew somewhere, somewhere deep down in me, it was really, 'Yes, Dad. *Yes, Dad.* Thank you very much, Dad. Once again you have destroyed my world.'

I was at a loss. I could only look down, into the brown of the snake river.

And then he said something that would hurt more than anything else. Even worse maybe than Dad's abuse.

'No wonder you were so easy.'

I sat there like I had taken a police bullet in the stomach. Like I had been caught on the run like a violent criminal. I felt so dirty, unclean, like a slut. Like my life was prostitution. Like yet again I was the guilty one. Everything was my fault. I recalled Dad sticking that pill up me and thought how easily I had allowed him to do it. How excited I had become by it.

And yet, and yet... with my new strength, with my renewed belief in myself, I had the sense of mind to feel totally disappointed in Brad too. Tearing with my eyes into his chest, I collected myself and saw that in this young man, my ever so tall and now shredded friend, there was yet an immature boy, not the strong guy I had come to believe in, the one I thought would stick by me no matter what.

I saw in his youth, in that naive squashed nose of his, that, like Dad said, he was yet another of those who would never "get it". Only he would never get it on the levels I wanted him to get it, the levels that were more than Dad's twisted mind set the rules upon. Levels that existed on the simple plains of civilised human morality and decency.

And so, in the end, in the upshot, sitting there crying and dismayed on the banks of the river, it was me who had to soothe him. To be the one to do the comforting. I did it in a way I did not expect it to come out: by confessing. By spilling all those poisoned family worms from my mouth.

I faced up to the hardening skin of my young lover, and told him how it was true, it was all true, and then pleaded to him to forgive me and try to understand. It wasn't my fault. If he could just understand, not every bit of it.

I told him how I hated my father now. Hated him in a way that it was hard even for Brad to breathe in. But I think that did it, more than anything that did it, seeing that I could hate another man so much – the man I was meant to have made love to.

Suddenly he saw, or was willing to believe, I didn't want any more of "that stuff". It belonged to another universe. Another girl who wasn't me. He accepted we were a couple. Dad, my father, my abuser, my mentor, my lover, my friend, was over. Completely done! I hated the man with a passion.

It restored faith. It reconnected us, and we remained close, Brad and me, boyfriend and girlfriend, real young lovers after that, but I always knew from then, from that time of accusation and confession, there was something missing.

It would end with Mum on the run again. She needed help and Brad was the one who could supply it. On this occasion it was so bad, apparently, she was even taking me along.

Yes, despicable, despised me. I was over the moon excited, being included in Mum's plans with Marge and Sam, and we were all, all of us together running away from that man, her husband, our father.

28.

I WAS ALMOST UNNATURALLY ENTHUSIASTIC ABOUT THE WHOLE RUNNING AWAY THING THIS TIME. It actually made me warm towards Mum, like she was on my side, like she was putting herself out for me – only to realise not long after we had sped away that the real reason she had included me was because of Brad. Because Brad had a car. A vehicle big enough to get her and everything she needed out of town.

What Brad had was a pale yellow Holden HR sedan that roared louder than a tiger, but it was exactly what she needed to get her and her ample things to Bundaberg, where we were headed.

Aside from Jim, we were all included this time because Mum was going for good. There was even a bird cage with Marge's pet cockatiel, Joey stashed in the car.

It all came to a head when Mum as usual, but in this instance after a few months rather than weeks, called Dad to say she was sorry, she was missing him – and we were all hauled back home again.

But Brad, who on weekends used to specially drive all the way from Rockhampton to Bundaberg to visit me, was suddenly not included in the transportation home. And of course I wondered why. In fact, he would not be seen again for a long time.

I learnt later, as these things always turned out, that sometime after the run to Bundaberg, Dad found out Brad had helped in the get-away. And Dad – *You don't ever piss Dan Gallagher off, Dad* – came out all guns firing. Not quite literally in this instance, but with that square-stone face of his, he got hold of Brad somehow and told him to leave off'a his daughter – quicker the better – and never step back on the Anondale property again. Or he would tear him apart with his bare teeth.

The real words he screamed and ranted, I also learnt later, were ones that went something like this: 'Come near my property again, you fucking little mongrel dog, and I'll have you up for carnal knowledge. Now keep the fuck away, little mongrel pisshead!' I could just see the tip of Dad's tongue blazing like a gun.

Scared as a rabbit, Brad, even with all his rugby league height and strength, didn't ask any questions, waited to hear no replies, and ran for his life.

Feeling absolutely and completely left in the lurch, utterly confused and ready to blame myself yet again, I wrote a number of letters, pouring out my heart to him but he never answered them. I even rang his brother trying to find out what had happened. But no one had any answers for me. His brother said he would pass on my message.

Then one day, out of the blue, Brad rang. He said he wasn't supposed to call me but just wanted to say he was sorry that he wouldn't be able to speak to me again and couldn't explain why. He sounded upset but that was that, no more to be said.

It wouldn't be until much later that he finally got up the courage to visit the property one last time and admit the reason he wasn't able to call or come to see me again. Even though it was well and truly over now – thanks to tough old Dan Gallagher – my dad – it gave a sense of relief to learn it wasn't that Brad had simply had enough of me – or found that unspeakable father-daughter "thing" too hard to live with.

Trembling, I could hear the truth in his voice: he never returned because he was dead scared of Dad. He apologised and confessed what others already knew, *Piss off Dan Gallagher and prepare for the next world.*

Brad should have known it already from the fear on men's faces who had looked into the whites of Dad's eyes as he told them he was going to rip their heads from their shoulders.

Like the story of the time Dad made Jacko Johns dance. Yes, Dad actually made a man dance. Known for his warmth and open-heartedness, people in the pub would say, *If you need a bed, go and see big-yarning, get the plonk out, "have-a-chat" Dan Gallagher.* This same man, Dad, one night made a man dance.

It happened when Dad's cousin Ruby and her partner were staying at our place. Ruby was pregnant but she and her partner Jacko Johns weren't hitting it off all that well. Dad, very protective of his cousin, heard that Jacko had hit Ruby. He went straight to Jacko's room and told him in plain language to bugger off and not come back for a while.

Seeing Dad's fury, Jacko heeded the advice but headed straight for the nearest pub. He came home much later that night, full of bravery.

Hearing him scuffing up the drive, Dad opened the front door and yelled out: 'You need to bugger off, mate. You're not comin in here.'

Jacko called back, 'I just want to see Ruby. It's got bugger all to do with you, mate. She's my partner.'

'Not the way you're acting,' Dad hollered, and warned him again.

Instead, Jacko walked straight towards the front door, and the next thing, what nobody had seen coming, Dad's shotgun came out from his side and he started blazing away. Rocks and sand and stone were flying everywhere, but Dad was shooting with such pinpoint accuracy around Jacko's feet that the man actually began to dance. He was wriggling his body and jumping with such dexterity he looked like a famous Irish stage performer.

'I'm sorry. I'm sorry,' he eventually howled until Dad finally shot the last bullet and held the gun up against his shoulder. Jacko Johns, sobered up and frightened like a rabbit, ears stiff and beaming up to the sky, ran all the way down our dusty driveway and off the property. Not to return again.

And so with Brad, he had been warned, and all six foot and four or five inches of him, took the warning like it had come down from the Judge in the Sky himself.

Even after his apology to me, I never saw Brad again. I even met with his new girlfriend once, the girl he was going to marry, and who was already pregnant, and she admitted this to me: she was his second choice.

Without any bitterness, Shalene, Brad's fiancée, pulled out from the glove box of her car the lovelorn letters I had written to Brad. The very ones I had thought he hadn't received when I was waiting for him to contact me once we were all ensconced back in Anondale.

She said Brad had always cared for me more than any other and would always have a place for me in his heart. But he was her family now, she smiled faintly, pointing to her enlarged baby-filled belly. Yes, the deed was done. Dad had done his work. Work nobody else in the world had the capacity to understand.

I may no longer have been afraid of Dad, but at the time I was still in need, needy.

Basically, I was still just a Year Eleven schoolgirl going on sixteen and still badly in need of love and direction. Mum would also divorce Dad not long after this, yes finally, eventually, walk out on him forever, but that didn't necessarily make life easier.

I had some strength by this time, even reached a certain peace with Mum for a while, but love and a known path to walk along were another thing altogether.

To put it another way, physically I may have loosened Dad from around my neck, shoulders and everywhere else he had laid his bare hands on, but mentally I was still seeking understanding, solace, still wanting the world around me to spin on its known axis, not some parallel, distorted one.

And like the high school principal in those hard times had allowed me to lay my head down on a big comfy cushion and thereby show me there were always warm little corners of light in the world, I was soon to find someone else in my life. Another teacher, of a different ilk, who would also bring a kind of solace.

29.

SOME TIME JUST BEFORE MUM'S DIVORCE FROM DAD, she hauled us all off to the nearby beach town of Burrum Sound where we rented a house to live.

It was over there, midway through Year Eleven, after the split from Brad, that I fell in love with someone else. My teacher. Well, one of them. And maybe love was too strong a word. Let's just say I became infatuated. Totally and completely. But then again, who wasn't infatuated with Mr Dreamboat Doherty?

The thing about Mr Doherty was that he was young, handsome and always ready with an open-minded laugh that felt like he was on your level. There were few who could resist the twenty-five year old teacher's charms.

What I think I liked most about him was that he was always so rational and calm. He listened. And not only did he listen, he was interested. In fact he listened and was interested just like he was one of us.

When I met Mr Doherty, that is to say when I moved into his class, it was around the time Mum and Dad began divorce proceedings, so it was obvious the move to Burrum Sound was going to be for a long time. All of us girls thought Mr Doherty was drop-dead gorgeous.

Dark and tallish with long curly hair, Mr Doherty stood out in a crowd. And yet, our teacher was so much like one of the lads that some at the school even mixed in the same circles as him.

Burrum, as we called it, was a small community, and everyone knew everyone. But there were some people who were so worthwhile knowing you would always find a way to meet them. Mr Dreamboat – Luke Doherty – was one of them. And I was one of the girls who would.

Well, in my case, really, there was no choice but to plot and plan a way in which Mum would allow me to mix with my newfound friends. If I told Mum I was going out with a group of girlfriends, and on top of that we were going to be at a party where Mr Dreamboat was, I knew what the answer would be.

So, not being totally honest about what our plans were, the girls came up with the idea of saying we were just going to "hang out" with some other friends from school at Peter's Play Park, a place where kids often congregated. It was really the only way I could get out. Mum actually agreed, so I was over the moon.

One particular Saturday night was special though, when a group of boys and girls from school were at Mr Doherty's house. Yes, on this occasion, the party was at our teacher, Luke Doherty's house. Best of all, there were no parents whatsoever around. I guess, being a young independent professional man, an educator of children, it was only obvious Luke Doherty would have a house with no parents around. But it seemed like a massive adult leap forward to us kids at the time.

Not only were we at out teacher's house, not only was he handsome as hell, there was absolutely no nasty threats of the cane or punishing judgemental repercussions staring into our foreheads.

I am not quite sure how it happened, but Luke Doherty actually singled me out and we got talking. I mean he was actually talking to less than mediocre, dim-witted me! He was so easy to talk with, it was not long after we began to chat that I was calling him Luke.

There was definitely something different about him, because he so obviously enjoyed hearing what we girls and boys had to prattle on about and had such a patient ear – if not a smile – for every whinge and whine we had about school and school teachers.

In the background, there was music, The Moody Blues from memory and Dire Straits, or even Elvis Presley, my all time favourite – and Luke and I danced together.

It was fun. Straight out fun. And soon – I'm not sure how it happened – we were secretly touching hands. Just the gentle feel of him, his warm, smooth fingers and the idea that he was touching me and none of the other girls was more than enough to have the brittle bones all down my spine tingling and shivering. My skin felt alive like a wave of little electrical shocks.

He loved his music and wanted to show me his collection of favourite records. And then we were in a bedroom together, laughing and talking. He was gentle, ever, ever so gentle. He had these long, tender hands, pink, unworked and warm; that's what I think I liked most about him. Hands that reminded me of Aunty Bev. Breathing heavily, it was not long before our faces came together and we were kissing. And then… and then… we were having sex. He was even mindful to make sure we were protected, another thing I wasn't used to, protected sex, no chance of an unwanted pregnancy for him.

More important than anything, I was having sex with my school teacher! The handsome, caring, Mr Doherty.

Afterwards, I felt guilty. But it was in my opinion – and I knew, in most other girls' opinion at the time – no great sin. The guilt was simply that of a young girl feeling the inevitable tinge of conscience – for doing something grown up. Something beyond her years.

In reality, I felt my head spinning and the whole episode felt like nothing short of… heaven. The only thing that mystified was that he'd chosen me. Me, out of all the girls. Me, Deb, Debbie, Deborah, above everyone else. *I* was the one who had slept with our drop-dead gorgeous teacher.

Despite my being directionless, dysfunctional, bred upside down, for me our teacher was no longer the authority, Mr Doherty, who stood in front of the class but plain and simple Luke. That didn't just happen. It was like something ordained.

Did it ever cross my mind that he had overstepped, that he had led me into some misguided hallway, that maybe what he had done was not really that different, really, really to what Dad and his mates had done to me in their men's den? The answer to that is, no, no, and no again.

Maybe I was an idiot. But then half the girls were idiots. We all wanted Mr Doherty to notice us. And in the event, it felt closer to floating, to a comforting, abundantly rolling cloud than anything I had experienced in my entire life.

Everything about Luke Doherty was as it appeared: gentle, slow, kind and genteel. It was like Dad in reverse. And definitely a lot less awkward than Brad with his six-foot four or five inches, who was still really a kid, who freaked out as soon as Dad stared him down.

Dad. Yes, Dad. By comparison, this was Valhalla, the Elysian fields. The other kids knew it too. It was like sleeping with a rock star. Only, I felt strongly I was not just a groupie. Luke Doherty really meant something. Meant it when he hugged and held and did all manner of things with me.

Or did he?

The next day when I saw him at school, obviously a bit embarrassed, I still managed to give him a shy hello and a tentative smile. It was during break, in the playground, and he walked right past me with only the slightest of nods and a tight little rat's quiver on his lips. I looked back at him. I was mystified. He stopped. I walked up to him, a young puppy, not sure how to proceed.

'Don't ever, *ever* indicate there is anything between us,' he said below those once warm lips that I had so voraciously kissed the night before. 'I could lose my job.' Then, with that tight little smile of his, stiff as a ball pen, he walked on.

Was I destroyed? Confounded? Lost for words? Yes, maybe lost for words, but in my barely sixteen year-old mind I understood or did my best to understand. Mr Doherty was protecting himself, that was all. Anyone in a similar position would do the same.

Inside my heart, I knew he was still the same Luke Doherty, the same gentle, friendly, kissable Luke Doherty as he had been the night before. I was a grown up and this wasn't exactly my first time. Just the first time with a real, gentle man. I had to be careful. For both our sakes.

It was worth the effort: our teacher, Luke Doherty had no intentions of ditching me, and after school everything would change. In fact, on weekends to come he made sure he was there for me and we continued to see each other. Even if it was not exactly openly – he had of course already explained why – it was always, in all seriousness, affectionate and intimate. Often, nothing happened, it was just hangout type fun with the rest of the gang.

Luke even came to my house a couple of times to help me with my homework. Mum didn't mind him being there because she thought he was simply my teacher and helping me with subjects I was not really fond of. She obviously trusted him enough to agree and didn't think anything was amiss.

To be fair, he did help me with my homework. But one of those nights after Mum had gone to bed and we'd finished my schoolwork, he climbed into my bed.

My relationship with Mr Doherty seemed like aeons, moons, many, many turns of the universe. I loved everything about him, the way he listened and laughed and thought what I had to say was mature and important. Time was infinite. I loved even the silences at school, in the classroom, as long as I could be in the same place as him. I loved the fact that I was spending a great deal of time at his house now. That we were like adults.

I also loved the other, more exotic times. Like the times we spent together on the beach. Just the two of us, lying there, on the nude white sand, the day waning and the moonlight rising, the soft beams of silver moonlight tickling on our naked backs and sunburnt faces as we made love.

I thought those days were forever. They seemed an eternity.

Not only was there this genuine communication between me and Mr Doherty, but here I was with this man who everyone looked up to and adored, a guy, a fella, an adult fella who could have clicked his fingers at any girl he wanted. Or so it seemed to me. But guess what? It was me having sex with him. It was me, Deb, Debbie, Deborah, of all the kids, who was Mr Doherty's special girl.

Did it have my head wobbling and my grades spiralling down? It had my head wobbling all right, but actually I was so inspired my grades went up.

I was a young girl lost but ready to believe, and yes, yes, absolutely infatuated. But because I wanted to be.

The only thing I had ever been taught by Dad and Mum was not to trust anyone, not ever to go to other peoples' homes or parties, and then, on the other hand, Dad would trust me with whomsoever he saw fit.

Dad's world, an obscure, parallel universe, and now I was slipping into this seemingly real world. Where love and sex were intermingled, and true. Where my feelings pulsed freely on my flesh. Where I was grateful to feel love without fear.

30.

WHAT I REALLY NEEDED WAS LOVE AND STABILITY AND SOME KIND OF EMOTIONAL ANCHOR. I wanted, I suppose like any girl my age, to be seen and noticed and desired. But I also wanted to be desired for what I was, for what I now thought I was: an empathetic young person with some innate wisdom and sensibility. And the fantastic thing was Mr Doherty saw all of that. Saw the young woman in me. The line of beauty that stretched from the tip of my head down to the soft flesh beneath my toenails. Who saw the unsure, raw wisdom in my breast.

In retrospect, I now realise he probably saw even much more than I could have ever thought he saw. Also heard more. When he very first laid eyes on me in his classroom he would have known things about me, known I was the "problem girl" from Perenjora Dam with more bad experiences than you could chuck a half broken house at. He probably would have been told, or in some way advised, about the abuse, about the almost reformatory-strict upbringing of my parents mixed in with all the drinking and merriment and running away craziness.

He would, anyway, have been able to see it all over my face. In the way my hair fell so thick and shamelessly to my shoulders, like a hussy, like a girl lusty. In need.

And yet... he probably was the kindest, most caring man I had ever met. I already used that word gentle, yes, several times, but he was the most gentle too. He was the father, the older brother, the lover, the mother I needed all my life. I think it was the hands, so much in the long, tender hands, like Aunty Bev.

Unlike other men, well the two tall ones I had known until then, Dad and the other one, Brad a mere boy, Luke

Doherty was never rough; it was never just about him. He was the first man who bent between my legs – not to shove it in like a tent peg and then run off like a satisfied boy scout – but who put his mouth there to pleasure me. Who did not always end our nights together with sex, who was happy to lie with me in his arms, happy only that I was happy. Although I never did, I always felt that I could cry with joy when I was with him.

Okay, so we had to be secretive about it. I understood secrets, they were part of my life. It was worth the risk, worth all the rainless Gladstone dirt I ever kicked, played on and fell over. It was worth the sky.

Luke... Luke Doherty enabled me to trust in others; gave me the possibility of hopefulness, of pleasantness and yearning in the flesh, gave me a kind of optimism with beams of sunshine that shone through my cloggy pores. With him, I could almost see it, that light...

Two whole months, that's how long it lasted. That's all. And yet it seemed... forever.

What I do remember almost as much from school at that time, was our middle-aged geography teacher, Mr Bloom. One day, trying to be comforting, trying to be nice to me, he placed an arm around my shoulders. It was in front of the whole class. Something in me froze and I peed myself.

Yes, at fifteen, when Mr Bloom, out of the kindness of his heart, put his arms around me, I peed myself. I caught such a fright at what he was doing, I went to ice and lost my bearings. For a moment I was not sure what he was on about, what he was going to do to me. My mind lurched, spun, tripped over, and I weed down my legs, seeing black clouds open like thunder in my head.

It became clear to me: it was different when Mr Doherty did the same. It sparked a whole set of other connections in my head. Signals unrelated to my past, unrelated to my going from one lap to another, unrelated to graphic pictures shown to me in lurid magazines.

147

When Mr Doherty touched me, the memories were warm like winter fire. I loved the intimacy. And even though it was wrong, all plain wrong, I never freaked out like I did when a simple, concerned man like Mr Bloom tried to sincerely comfort me. Then I became a mess: it told me I was still a dark and sodden clutter of disorder.

Enter Chris Pyke.

Because of the secret nature of our relationship – mine and Luke Doherty's – I still hung around with the boys and girls I met at school. And while Luke lived out his teacher life for the most part separately, I lived my maturing schoolgirl life with my school friends. The result was we both often did different things at the same time, met different people, hung in different crowds.

One of the people I met during this time was this other post-school bloke, Chris Pyke, another of the older lads who had the girls' tongues sweating.

In the blur of Mum's comings and goings from our home at Perenjora Dam, there was a night I recall that was one of those community barn dances. Dad was with us, and as usual with shotgun like precision he was watching over our every move. But at one point I went – or shall I say, was allowed to go – with a couple of girlfriends to the toilet. At the stairwell next to the toilet, was standing, or rather casually leaning, this longhaired, surfie looking, sought-after young guy. This was Chris Pyke.

I cannot tell a lie, seeing him leaning so confidently there, I could hear not just *my* heart beat but *all* the girls'. And then behind me, I heard a voice call out, 'Hey, spunk bubble.' I felt tingles going up my spine. All of us girls turned around, of course, each of us hoping. But my heart started to rush and then miss a whole stack of beats when I realised that voice was meant for me.

I waved and he nodded back in his smiley, charming way. Throat banging in my forehead, for the time being that was the end of that. But it was the spark that would lead to other things, other meetings. Dates.

I had actually first met Chris when I was about nine, when Dad, as always ready with a hand, helped the Pyke family out with a place to stay until they could rent a home of their own. I also went to primary school with his sister and brothers. Small world.

Totally unknowing of my relationship with my teacher, yet a friend of Luke Doherty at the time, after that barn dance Chris began to call me at home and ask me out. Obviously, I was never allowed to go but occasionally he turned up to see me, was allowed to visit, and we became friendly. My chest breathed with a flutter.

One night in Burrum Sound, Luke Doherty still secretly an intimate part of me, Chris Pyke called and asked if I wanted to go with him and a couple of friends to the drive-in. Knowing the answer from Mum, I almost felt like only pretending I had gone to ask her and then going back to the phone to tell him the only answer it could be. Only, on this occasion, I decided to take my chances, and Mum, *Mum*, I could not believe it, said yes. For some reason, this time it was OK.

I was beside myself. I was going out to the drive-in with Chris Pyke – after Mr Doherty, probably the most sought after fella in Burrum. I didn't give poor Mr Doherty a second thought.

Chris picked me up that Saturday night, and in the street, as though waiting in his car for me to come out, was Luke Doherty. Yes, Mr Doherty, my lover, my teacher, my bent guide, was parked there, car humming, just sitting there and waiting for me.

He called out, I could see, a little dismayed as he saw me and Chris leaving the house. He asked what was happening. Chris, a man with an apprenticeship and almost a trade already, called back firmly and matter-of-factly, 'Going to the drive-in, mate. Do you want to come?'

'Naaah, it's OK, mate,' Mr Doherty intoned. 'You young ones have fun.'

I tried to wave at Luke Doherty, to smile courteously, but he revved his car, turned the wheel boyishly, and was gone. It was the end of two of the most wonderful months in my life. How much could they have meant to my teacher, who I saw then as my life coach and priest, as well as my educator, I don't know.

I can only say I must have meant something to him, because we remained friendly while we still lived in the same area. I knew, at a gut level, Luke was who he was, even though he must have been aware that he was taking advantage of his position. Yet, at that earnest primal level, I craved the security of real love.

My beloved teacher and I stayed in contact after that, for many years. After all, he was also a mate of my new mate, Chris Pyke.

Now it was over to Chris Pyke, the man who would steal my heart, in a sense steal, because over the years, after the good times, I had to fight to get it back. To struggle and claw, and yes, even grow up some more.

31.

THEY ALWAYS SEEMED TO HAVE LONG WAVY HAIR, and Chris, when I met him, was no different. Only with that sixties middle parting, it made him look a bit like Jim Morrison from The Doors. But even more so than Jim Morrison, he had small penetrating hazel eyes that looked like they were undressing not just your clothes but your flesh. The brows that stood above the eyes were so strong and curved it was like they were "seeing" – like an owl. I guess those eyes were his temples – that hid within them his own hard upbringing.

Chris, too, had had it tough, witnessing at an early age the attempted hanging suicide of his father. He also, as I would discover, had his own bouts of depression, his own ongoing moods. Yes, those moods...

But in the beginning it was fun. It was exciting being with Chris. From the next door city of Gladstone, he was a guy of his times – with his open-neck shirt, tightly-hung surfie leather necklace, early seventies droop moustache, and tiny goatee beneath a kind and full bottom lip.

His lips. They were bowed and sorrowful and weighted with unknown bitterness, but they could be warm, and more important than anything, they were honest. At least in the beginning I thought they were.

It was good to be around Chris and his friends, and the best part was our relationship could be open. There were no secrets. Dad did not really say whether he approved or disapproved but by now he knew I was well out of his clutches and Mum was only too happy to have someone take me safely out of her sight of a weekend.

The trouble was I was still in Year Eleven. It was a big year, Year Eleven. Probably bigger than most kids would want to shoulder even when they were much older. But it was also filled, however wrongfully and darkly, with rounded corners of softness and radiance. And now with Chris, I saw this illumination burning ahead.

The important thing was I felt like I was beginning to have faith in my own ability, my own sense of decision-making, my own maturing outlook on life, and I was beginning to make plans. I had crossed a mountain, or felt like I had crossed a mountain, and in the road on the other side I finally saw straightness and direction.

I wanted to finish school. Not only that, I already knew I wanted to become a nurse or something closely related. Maybe a pre-school teacher? Remember Mum's Mum had a little girl, my Auntie Beatrice, and I tried to lift her out of the cot? I loved children. I absolutely adored them.

Whatever, even if it wasn't nursing or caring for the little ones, by finishing school I knew, as they all told me, especially Mr Dreamboat Doherty himself, a far bigger and better world would open to me.

Mum had other plans.

There was a young couple who ran a very wealthy Appaloosa stud farm in the area, at Rodds Bay, and Mum organised that I would go and stay over there in my school holidays and on the odd weekend -- to look after their infant son and do other domestic chores while they went about their business.

Nigel and Alysha Godbolt, the owners of the farm, may not realise it, not even to this day, but as it turned out, they had one of the most positive effects on my life out of anybody. Young and already wealthy as they were, rather than braggers and snobby there was something about them that was "together".

I loved being around them. Unlike my family, it was like they did not have to fight to breathe. There were no battles for the oxygen around them. They lived and inhaled easily and were phenomenally at home and loving within their own little family unit. To begin with, this included their two-year-old son, Jay, but later came a second boy, Eli.

Their stud farm ran, literally, for thousands upon thousands of acres, and just after Year Eleven, right at the very end of the Christmas school holidays, something happened that would tie me more closely to the Godbolts and their immense stud farm than I could have ever thought.

It was about the third last day of the holidays and I was due to go home and prepare to go back to school – happy I had only a year to go to finish my Senior. Then, of course, it would be onwards and outwards to who knows where? Nursing, yes, nursing or pre-school teaching were still definitely in my sights.

As I packed my bags and mentally prepared for my final onslaught at school, outside the house, through the Godbolts' large lounge windows, I saw this small sky-blue car. It was Mum's. She was at the house a day early.

'What's she doing here already? She's only meant to pick me up tomorrow,' I said to Alysha Godbolt.

'What do you mean?' Alysha's eyes flicked and she shook her short, mousey brunette hair. 'Mum's just dropped off your clothes.' I must have looked at her like a brainless white rat shaking with an experimentally injected head of big, bushy brown hair, because Alysha stared back at me like I was some kind of deformed rodent. 'Don't you know this is your new job? You're working for me now, silly.'

I felt my head go cold and shrink, or is that sink? Sink and shrink. My stomach, too. My gut drew inwards like it had been kicked in fury. It was all news to me. I couldn't comprehend. It was like someone talking behind my back in another language and I was only slowly beginning to figure the not so kind truth of what they were saying about me.

The sickly translation, it turned out, was Mum had made a life-changing decision for me. All on her own, without a scrap of consultation, she had decided my future. She had decided I was not going back to school – ever. I was now to be a full-time, live-in nanny to the Godbolts.

Staring across into the blameless, deer-like eyes that were

Alysha's, I could tell Mum had not told her the truth either – that I had absolutely not in any way been conferred with in this life decision. I was hearing it now, as I was living it, in the white, blinking horror of the moment. I felt like the tip of a sharp sword was piercing through my neck.

'You really didn't know...' Alysha's eyes looked like they were genuinely drinking in the revulsion of it.

'No.' I burst out crying. 'No.'

'Oh my goodness. Oh my goodness.' She was suddenly mumbling and holding me around the shoulders.

Little white rat with wild bushy hair, I looked at her thinking what's going to happen to me now, but understanding only too well. And it was like Alysha knew in that timid look of mine, I had caved, I had already given in to those greater elements that stepped everywhere into my life and stood between me and that massive force out there. Alysha, slim but muscular in a Roman boy way, walked away like her heart would crack if she had to make any decisions for me in that moment in time.

Like everything in my life so far, I took it on the jaw. I cried and protested in my head, but there was no way I was going back to Mum. Dad? That wasn't even a question. So I decided I had to do what I always did in life, I immediately set to making my new job with the Godbolts as good as it could be. In effect, once again, even if with buckling knees, I stood up and called on faith. This time it was in the future.

The positive part, and I have to admit this was an attraction better than school, I lived just outside the main house, in "my own rooms" – which in this case was a caravan, a small caravan that was warm and comfortable and to me, even if it did leak in the occasional rainstorm, had more than enough space. Room. I did not need much at that time in my life. A bed, a dressing table, that was about it.

On the down side, there was no electricity, but I could read to my heart's content by candlelight. Actually, it was amazing to me how I could live in a big house with my parents with acres and acres of empty property around us, and could feel like I was being suffocated. Whereas here, at the Godbolts, I was in a little caravan with a single room and burning candles all around me and it felt like I was living in acres of fresh air.

That was the thing, the air around the Godbolts was always positive. Always guiding. Even when firm, their breath was always pointed in a definite direction. I liked that. I liked the security of it.

Nigel Godbolt, the man of the house, the husband, may have been nerdy to the extreme, with his binocular-thick glasses that were so dense they were like coke bottles, but with his "goggles" sitting astride his enormous Roman nose, he cared. He and Alysha wanted to see me prosper. They wanted more for me than just earn my keep and stagnate. More for me than my own parents.

In fact it was them, Nigel and Alysha, who I would sit down with at the dinner table of a night and who would ask me as naturally as any real parent might, what I thought I wanted to do with the rest of my life. I don't ever remember Mum or Dad doing that. I can't even remember them asking what I thought my interests were or what excited or attracted me at any one time.

The Godbolts, on the other hand, would even offer suggestions, ideas that were plausible and possible. From day one, seeing my reaction to being summarily dumped there, it was like there was an implicit understanding that I was not going to be their nanny forever.

Unlike my parents who wanted to plant me in the dry Gladstone ground and were satisfied to leave me searching in the dirty soil down there, rooted only to some vague concept of family and whatever weird and whacky ideas occurred to them, the Godbolts wanted to see me grow. They wanted to see the sun flicker in me. They wanted me to make up my own mind.

The Godbolts only had one rule about "my rooms": Chris, my boyfriend, could visit whenever he wanted – which in its own way was like a big satisfying breath of fresh air – but he could not sleep over. Not under any circumstances.

I heartily agreed and welcomed the rule.

32.

CHRIS PYKE WAS MY KNIGHT IN SHINING ARMOUR. He was almost four years older than me and already out there working in the "real world", and I felt like he had come to rescue me. That he was such a knight and wore such shining armour would soon be tested.

One night at the Godbolts, we did what we shouldn't have. We broke the golden rule. We both fell asleep in the caravan, me tightly wound in Chris's wiry, sun-kissed arms, and we slept in.

That morning Nigel Godbolt came out to the caravan to see where I was. Nigel knocked on the door to see why I hadn't surfaced for breakfast, and when we didn't respond, it must have been evident even to him that Chris was in there with me.

Only my knight in shining armour didn't stay around to argue the point, or even to apologise. Instead, he dressed his lean surfer-boy frame into his clothes – quicker than Mick Jagger could shout Jumping Jack Flash – and as soon as Nigel moved off from the door he was out of there.

My knight had abandoned me. I should have seen the tarnish on the silver then, but I was young, willing love, and "forgiving" could have been my middle name.

In essence, I didn't mind being caught. I was, I suppose, a big girl now who had done things. And it was no secret Chris and I were sleeping together. What disappointed me, as I suppose it did the Godbolts, was that I had broken their rule. To that extent, I had let them down.

Nigel Godbolt, as I found out, did not take the episode lightly. A much older man than his muscularly-thin and taller, Italian looking wife – I would say about in his mid to late thirties while she was in her mid to late twenties – he could be quite stern.

He walked away from the caravan and from a distance called out to me as I poked my head out of a crack in the caravan door: 'Get up here. Get up here *now*... we need to speak to you in the kitchen.'

With Chris having done a runner, I was left alone in the caravan, slowly getting dressed, scared and crying, thinking how I had upset these people who were so good to me.

I walked into the kitchen like a little child, my mouth and throat so dry I thought I was not going to be able to breathe let alone speak. I was scared in a way that reminded me of when Mum or Dad called me before one of their hellish inquisitions. I stood there shivering, ready for a beating.

'Sorry,' I spluttered quickly, trying to ward off the damage. 'Really. We didn't mean to fall asleep. We weren't doing anything.'

'I don't need to know what you were doing,' Nigel's coke-bottle spectacles considered my chin. 'We gave you a rule and you've broken it. That's what disturbs us.'

Disturbs us, I remember it going through my head. *Disturbs us,* that's all? He was speaking so calmly, so politely in his firmness, it was obvious I wasn't going to get a belting after all. It was so different to Mum and Dad. I looked across at the Godbolts and saw two human beings facing something they themselves weren't quite sure how to deal with.

Nerdy and ridiculous – *a wuss,* Dad would have said – Nigel Godbolt continued to look at me with his binocular eyes, and in both of them what I saw was a sternness that did not come with that dark black line of anger that I was used to. There was something comforting in the way they considered me. It was almost reassuring.

'We feel responsible for you, you know?' Nigel Godbolt eventually pressed with a small tongue that looked like no more than a red smartie in his round face. 'We know you and Chris are close, and that's fine by us. We have never had a problem with that – but there's another side to it... you know. Are you being safe...?'

The tears were welling in my eyes, realising the Godbolts' concern, and I tamely nodded my head. Their language, their way of speaking, parents to a child, I had never experienced it in my life before.

By the end of it, Nigel Godbolt simply brought his massive nose fairly close up to my face, and with his thick glasses, said, 'As long as you're here we're responsible for you. You should know that. That's all. We're not here to judge or condemn. Just please obey the rules.'

I breathed out.

'And one more thing. Where's Chris now?'

I blinked up. This was it. The backslap, where the real trouble started. Chris would never be allowed back on the property.

I breathed in, not sure if I should say anything. Eventually I stammered truthfully: 'He's probably waiting in his car.'

'Well, tell him to come on in and have some breakfast with us. He's probably damned hungry by now.'

And that was that. I ran out to get Chris and we all ate breakfast together. Human beings. Or, was that exceptional human beings? For me, at the time, yes, definitely exceptional. At last I had found a good example of what real parenting could be.

In return, the Godbolts got a good nanny. At any rate, I like to think so. I loved their little boy, Jay, and their other boy, Eli when he arrived in the world.

Alysha Godbolt used to joke that it was because of me that Jay was walking at seven months old. They were proud of their boy – but they brought it down to me. And I was proud of that. There was not much I had achieved in life. But I had done that. I loved working there, and I like to imagine from the way they treated me their children have grown into two – there was a daughter later – so, three magnificent human beings.

At one point in my employment at the Godbolts, Alysha sat me down with grey apprehension in her eyes. Always so blue like solid marbles, her eyes looked concerned. She asked me what I wanted for my future. I shook my head, dull-faced. No one had ever asked me that question in my life.

A nurse by profession, Alysha only worked on the property now, but she had that caring of a woman dressed in all-white, and with the concern of a mother she made me sit down at the kitchen table and together we brainstormed all the possibilities.

Taking into account my education, or rather lack of it, finally we came down to a position that might be good for me: a nurse's aide. But she did not leave it there. Sitting with me, she helped me through the really arduous task of writing letters of application to numerous hospitals and nursing centres around the state. We even wrote a couple of letters to nursing centres in Sydney.

'I can't do that,' I pleaded to her. 'I can't leave here. It's so big, Sydney. What'll I do there? All by myself?'

'You'll do what you do here. Of course you can go there. You can go anywhere, Debbie. You're just as capable as anybody.' She looked at me with the certainty of a woman kneading dough. 'You've got everything a young girl needs. You are now showing more confidence and I know you have the ability. You'll get along. Wherever you end up.'

I smiled, nervous as hell, and went ahead with the applications anyway. In the end, though, with only a Year 11 to my name, I recall getting less than a handful of replies. All of them said the same: there were no positions available.

Was I despondent? Of course. But to me, what was really important was the time *she, they,* the Godbolts, took with me. It was like having parents, maybe even an older brother and sister for the first time.

In the end, without a future in the world, life went on as normal at the Godbolts. I carried on cleaning and helping in the kitchen and caring for their children.

What I didn't know was there was yet another – Mum-induced – incident to come.

33.

I was in the bathroom, keenly as normal wiping the grouting in the tiles, when the phone rang. I raced out to the kitchen to get it.

It was Mum. But strangely, with no hello, no anything.

All she said to me was: 'Get Alysha!' I just stood there, trying to think, only to hear her squawking voice shout again into my ear: 'For heaven's sake, Debbie, get Alysha! Now!'

I went to get Alysha, and put her on the phone. I stood there curious, hearing: 'No, Julie, no, she's fine.' A moment later she was putting her hand over the receiver, waving her short crop of hair, commanding me, 'Deb, just go to the bathroom. Go finish what you're doing there.'

I left the room.

But I did not go far. I stopped around the corner in the passageway and pricked my ears like radar.

They picked up: 'Well, Julie, I don't know. I really don't know what you're saying. She is a bit dreamy, I suppose. Or floaty, if you like. But it's always struck me it's because she misses Chris. You know, they're very close. Yes, it's like she wants to be with him all the time. Every time he leaves on a Sunday, it's like she's pining for him. I probably wasn't so different at her age, you know.' Then I heard Alysha as though stiffening her mouth into a large "O": 'No, Julie, no, I have never seen anything like that. Really. Never. Nothing at all. I honestly don't think so.'

I didn't usually bite my nails, but I was behind that wall biting them now, muttering to myself, 'What...? What the bloody hell?' I could tell from Alysha's voice, from her surprised replies, that she was defending me as best she could from an accusing, irate voice on the other end of the line. In some ways I was even glad Mum's voice was rattling through the phone into her ear rather than mine. I would already be crying, I know it, already falling in a heap.

Then the phone clunked down and I quickly ran back to the bathroom and my cleaning.

Alysha stepped into the doorway. With her firm, compact body and her – to me – noticeably firm breasts that to a young girl were "to die for", it was like those breasts were pointing right into me. She stood there for a few moments like that, in silence, the silence of an ancient Roman sculpture.

Compelled to speak, I felt my voice rasping, 'What was that about? What did Mum want?'

'We'll have to talk tonight, okay? Later…?' She tapped her face, it was drawn and flustered. 'I've got to get back to the horses now.' And then she turned like a solid concrete statue.

My heart was pumping like all the valves in there were suddenly leaking. I had not the faintest idea what the call could be about – short of a death or injury in the family. Or something else very sordid, something in our family that no one wanted me to know about. That the world would die of shame from. Inside my chest there was a feeling of anger – and guilt, and I could not help but think, multiple times: 'What's Mum got the shits in for me now?'

That night, not during dinner but afterwards, when everything was cleaned up and put away, on the promise that I could watch a commercial TV channel, I was called in to sit with the Godbolts in their living room.

Although often invited to do so, I seldom watched TV with them – mainly because they only watched shows that had little or absolutely no interest for me. All they wanted to watch was that boring ABC stuff, which was not on my playlist right then. If anything, I preferred to have my nose in a book.

As it turned out, and to my disappointment, they did not, or forgot to change channels to any of the commercial channels. So, instead of the ones I was expecting to watch, like *The Great Temptation* or *The Box* or *Blankety Blanks*, I had to stay tuned with them to the ABC. On the screen was some documentary that looked so boring I would have fallen asleep after five minutes had it not been for my racing heart.

I was still well aware they wanted to talk to me. And I knew it was about that call. My heart was crashing on stone and there was this lumpy clot in my throat. I stared forward at the TV set, and then suddenly, it seemed like hours after their show had started, almost out of the blue, Nigel Godbolt lifted his nose as though it were a heavy paperweight – which it almost was – and started telling Alysha and I in a slow and steady voice this story of driving to Brisbane once.

'I was driving along, a little bit tired,' he breathed very calmly, 'and after awhile I picked up this guy hitch-hiking on the side of the road. He had quite long hair, down to his shoulders, you know, a bit of a hippy...' He sucked in some air on that small red tongue of his and then breathed out as though allowing the air to run through his thick goggles. He went on, 'You've got to help people, you know. It doesn't matter who they are. Everyone can do with a hand.' He breathed in again, this time a bit roughly, prickly. 'Anyway, after a bit of chitchat in the car, this fellow starts talking to me about something else. In fact, to be frank, he was offering me this stuff... God's weed... '

Nigel was staring down at me, and I interrupted him, 'What? What's that? What's God's weed?'

'You don't know what God's weed is?'

My heart wasn't racing or pounding any longer, it was zooming. Whatever Nigel Godbolt was talking about sounded deeply contrived and suspicious. I began to think now, it was like he was trying to catch me out, test me, but I had never in my life heard of this "God's weed" stuff. I was shaking my head – and he was looking at me like I should have heard of it.

'You know, it's what some people use... you know, smoke... when they want to get high. You know, marijuana...?'

'Ooohhh,' I breathed. I had at least heard of that. Yes, of course I had. Without saying it then, I immediately thought of a couple of Chris's friends who I knew even smoked it.

'Well, have you ever had any?' Nigel finally asked flatly, glancing through his spectacles, the retinae of his eyes all of a sudden like wild suns staring through these tremendously thick magnifying glasses into me.

'God no, of course I haven't.' I shifted backwards in my chair.

I actually was quite affronted. Not only had I never smoked marijuana, I had no desire to, even though I had been around it when it was being smoked. Like Chris's brothers and his surfie friends. But not Chris, well, not anymore; he was dead-set against it and even warned me never to get into it. There was something going on. I knew it; it was beginning to feel like an interrogation. I should have known, I should have bloody known.

'So, you mean you've never even tried it?' Nigel's fiery eyes behind the huge magnifying glasses, pressed. 'You mean you've never even wanted to try a bit when others have smoked it? God's weed... marijuana?' He must have only seen in front of him a shaking head, because he persisted, 'So... Chris and his friends have never asked you to try it? I mean, they must smoke it themselves? They go surfing, don't they? It's quite popular these days.'

I was scared now. Chris may have run away the time we overslept in the caravan – my knight in grand armour – but I was no "dobber". Never. Not on anyone or to anyone. That was one thing Dad and Mum had brought us up never to do. Our secrets were always *our* secrets. Well, except for the small matter of that court case that brought no relief anyway. But I certainly wasn't going to dob on Chris or his friends. Chris, if anything, had always said to me, 'Don't ever touch it. It's evil that stuff. It's bad for you.'

'So, you've never smoked it?' Nigel went on, his thick glasses and little eyes gauging me like a detective.

I looked back at him, still shaking my head, and noticed something. He was actually not looking at me angrily or even accusingly; his look was rather more inquisitive.

I saw something then in Nigel Godbolt: he was a man who first got to the truth before jumping in and dishing out conclusions – or punishments. I respected that in him. Unlike Mum. Or Dad. I realised then what I was doing, in my fear I was reacting to them, Mum and Dad, not to the man who sat in front of me. Nigel Godbolt with his Asterix but honest nose.

I eventually exhaled, 'Chris has told me about marijuana, but he always says it's bad for you. You know. He's very anti it.'

'The reason I'm asking all this stuff,' Nigel spoke very slowly and evenly now, 'is because Mum thinks you're into drugs.' He must have seen the wild, stunned look in my eyes, my head shaking as though I was going to faint, because the next thing he said to me was: 'You know what? I don't think you are smoking drugs. I don't think so at all.'

Thick gushes of oxygen were whooping out of me. I felt dizzy, relieved, confounded, but more than anything behind all that schoolgirl gawping and quivering, I felt ashamed and angry. Ashamed that it was Mum, my mum who without even trying to communicate with me, thought I was off my tree, "floating on drugs". And angry as hell because she had gone straight to the Godbolts, and her suspicions had been channelled not into my ears but into Alysha's. Like I didn't exist.

It was true that I did "moon" and "float" about a bit, but as Alysha Godbolt had said: it was about missing Chris, about growing up, about being in love, about listening to the group Bread and crying to their sad, soft-rock love songs like "Hooked on You" and "If" while pining away for my beau...

But drugs... no. It didn't even occur to me. Ask me about sex... yes, sex, sex, sex, especially bad sex... and I would have to admit it, and say yes, of course yes! Why didn't Mum ask

164

about that? Ask about it in the way she was asking about marijuana – *God's weed* – instead of bringing me into her trust and then belting the Christ out of me when I told her the truth?

Nigel Godbolt, even-handed, even-tempered Nigel, launched into a lecture then... about drugs, about what they can do to you, how they play with your brain and mess with your thinking... but I could see that through it all he was just being a responsible adult, being a man responsible to someone's else's child. Being, in effect, a dad.

I should say this of the Godbolts: although they were not touchy-feely types, they were more than just ample mirrors to a future I was uncertain of. They were like well looked after windows, clean, straight up, clear and assured; they freely let the light shine in while I fought against the brown, wind-blotches outside. From their example, I learned maturity was about keeping the windows clean. About Windexing away the secrets.

Mum never spoke to me about that phone call... I only heard later, a fair bit later, that she had discussed "my problem" with my sister and even informed a policeman friend of hers... But what her attitude typified was this: a thoroughly broken relationship between a mother and daughter. A mother who did not trust her child, a mother who did not even attempt to communicate with her own daughter. Who got others to do her dirty work for her – like the Godbolts, the police, the courts.

It rang through my head that visit to the police station in Gladstone we did not even know was going to happen until the very last minute – because, essentially, she was a coward. Mum was terrified and weak. She did not know how to speak to or approach us or look us in the eye and have a decent conversation with us.

Definitely not me. And yet I cannot help in my way but feel sorry for her as she phones me every weekend in her old age now and pleads her love to me. I know she is merely trying to make up for the past, the hurts, the injuries, the insensitivities, the cowardice. I know that. But it is confusing. Still confusing as ever.

At sixteen, willing now to rebel, as if to prove her right, I did go ahead and try it: God's weed. With Chris's friends. But even I had higher expectations than it turned out. In the event, I coughed my eyes out like that first time I tried cigarettes – everyone laughed – and nothing happened.

The only high I got was from lack of oxygen and the deep whooping from the back of my nose and throat. The big high that they all used to get off on – and talk about incessantly – just didn't happen for me. I was spared that, at least that one injustice I was spared. The potential for addiction.

A few months later, with the help of the Godbolts, I did finally gain a more or less meaningful job – in a nursing home looking after old people. And... I moved back in with Mum. Yes, Mum. It was convenient. The location of my new work was nearby Mum in Burrum Sound and I could be close to Chris again, could see him every day.

Despite living with Mum again, and despite a surprising equilibrium we found in our relationship, what saved me was love. This new love of my life, Chris Pyke.

We were both young and enthusiastic and got away – out of the house – whenever we could. Mostly we went camping with his friends who spent whole weekends down at Agnes Waters on white empty beaches that appeared as infinitely long and assured as our love.

Chris's friends were always looking for a wave and a bit of fun, and yes, smoking God's weed. They also drank and snorted what have you.

We all used to sit around listening to music on an old battery-operated cassette player and would sing along by a fire. We also sat and lay in the hot sun, sat and lay much more than we should have by today's "slip-slop-slap" standards, and had sex, yes, lots of sex.

We were at that age when we were old enough to think we knew what we were doing. And that was half the fun... just believing in ourselves, having faith in ourselves out there in the hot-hot sun and swimming and surfing through large, unending waves. We were, in plain English, having a good time, enjoying ourselves, and for once in my life I actually felt like I was in control, like I had some power over my life.

I remember once, during a sudden wind on the beach, just as the sun was setting, one of the tents came down, and we all watched expecting someone to come running out of it shouting for help, yelling what the ef was going on. But instead of any bodies springing out of the tent, we watched as the now floppy nylon clung to a strange looking configuration of curves.

Set against the dying sun, the massive insect that seemed to reside inside the nylon, bobbed crazily up and down. We had no choice but to sit and watch with curious interest.

And then slowly we realised what was going on. And in the end all we could do was laugh and laugh and just laugh some more, realising it was not one insect in there but two – both of them intent on finishing what insects do. Replenishing the earth.

Those were some of the best memories of my life. So giddy, so absolutely liberating; I felt free and in charge of my own head.

Could it last? The moon hovered white and pasty above.

34.

WE BELIEVED IN ONE ANOTHER, CHRIS PYKE MY SHINY KNIGHT AND I. We were in love and we knew it because we could laugh and play and make love together at the same time. He was always there for me. Well, most of the time – if one remembers that little incident of the caravan.

And then one day, like all men, he asked that question: 'Why did you let your father touch you?' And I should have known. I should have known then. Rather than seeking understanding, he was... I don't know, not quite angry but annoyed and mystified. Like other men. Like the rest of them.

'I don't know. I don't know why,' I replied, needing to think. Asking myself: *Why?... Why now? Just like this, out of the blue?* I felt like I was being judged all over again. Not just judged but accused. Life, love, mateship, nothing but nothing would ever let it go. He was no different to Brad, my first male friend, just a fella, just another fella who always thought the girl was somehow weak or just plain deviant or wrong – maybe even the coaxer, the temptress.

Yes, the temptress and teaser, like men never did anything wrong, never broke things, were only ever led by all these serpentine Eves in their magnificent Gardens of Eden to do ill.

Dad was right, in his way right again – no one would ever understand. But what they wouldn't understand, just like him, is what *he* did, *he* did. It is a strange and immature thing, but it seems to me when some men grow up with an idea about women, about girls, the opposite sex, or get an idea about them put into their heads, it is like trying to cut through metal to change their thinking.

But in the end, Chris, like Brad, I guess out of expediency, perhaps out of love, I hope out of love, turned away from it, turned the other cheek. That is not to say that he forgave, or ever really understood, but that he stuck by me. Or was that *with* me? I don't know, I really don't, but he stayed the course, the long, long course, through thick and thin. Just plenty, plenty thick. Much more than I could have expected.

Who is to know these things? Who is to know what is below the shiny plating that men on white horses wear? You see the signs but you ignore them. You are a human being, needy, wishful of acceptance. But you find out in the end. It just takes time. So much time. It is slow. It can be gruelling. But I was used to gruel. I could stand it for long, long periods of time.

Chris joined the defence forces – the Royal Australian Air Force – in September 1979. He was sent to Edinburgh, South Australia, and I went to live in Brisbane with his relatives, so that I could feel closer to him while, for three months, he undertook his basic training.

At the end of that year he was posted to Melbourne, to do his radio technical training, later to be called avionics, at Laverton Base, and so I followed him there too. We lived together during that time, until July 1981 when Chris was posted to Newcastle, and of course I followed him there too.

It was obvious Chris and I were made for one another, and on January 2, 1982 we married in a chapel at Sandgate, near Brisbane. I was nineteen.

Exactly three days later, Chris was transferred again – this time to Malaysia. Talk about a honeymoon. Yes, exotic, it was exotic all right, in a different sort of way, because RAAF wives were at that time not allowed to work. Only have children.

One exciting thing about Malaysia was that my Grandad, Dad's father's grave was nearby, at the Kranji War Cemetery in Singapore. We went there for a visit once, and I found it. Not only did I find it, I unexpectedly found the whole experience very moving and kind of surreal.

Looking down at that white headstone with the ANZAC emblem on it I felt both dizzy and kind of elevated, knowing this man, my biological grandfather, died for something he believed in. He gave his soul to our way of life... the lucky country we live in today. And he did it despite Dad. With no thought to how he would turn out.

There it stood, that white headstone, and I saw it with my own two eyes – set against a yellow, buttery sun that looked like a bullet would never cross the air below. And yet so many died there. So many. It was something Dad would never do. See that heroic tomb. Never in his entire life would he see it except in that way he always saw things, by living and seeing inside me.

I am completely sure he must have seen it through my eyes as I lay my retinae on Grandad's well-scrubbed but gallant tomb and thought of Dad drunkenly bayoneting and karate-kicking all those Jap bastards who killed his dad and changed his life forever. I wished that day I'd had the chance to know this man. This man – an Aussie hero – who gave seed to my dad. Perhaps the war could have come earlier and I would have been spared?

Because I couldn't work in a paid job in Malaysia, I became a Red Cross volunteer and played sport. I loved the team interaction of playing in the netball and softball teams. I also won the ladies dart competition. Being involved in these things was good because I at least got to mix with other RAAF wives and other expats and saw a bit of the Malaysian world outside, a world which otherwise would have been denied me.

What wasn't so good about this time was that the year we arrived turned out to be the year Aunty Bev died. I received a letter from Mum telling me the news. For once she communicated to me. That day, that night, was a sheer nightmare.

I walked about sad and crying, mourning from deep inside my gut for the woman I loved so much and who suddenly drifted away because of Dad's misdeeds. And while this was going on, while Aunty Bev with her warm hands and cool eyes that never judged and only ever saw into the best parts of me, was fresh in her tomb, Chris, my shining RAAF husband was changing out of his Air Force blue, readying himself to go out with his pals on a boys' night out.

'What's your problem?' my knight shimmered, turning to me, his skin smoothly shaven, his moustache still drooping but now immaculately clipped.

Yeah, what was my problem? How long could a person mourn? An hour? Two hours? When I tried to tell him, he just fobbed me off. I was here and she was thousands of miles away. Plus I hadn't seen Aunty Bev in years. That was true. That was the absolute truth. Other things were true too.

What, for example, did he know about those hands? Those hands which had warmed my skin, which had rushed like warm water through my brain in a world darkening with stones on all sides around me? What did he know about that smile? Those eyes, those grandmotherly eyes that looked not into my eyes but always into my heart? Those eyes that saw only the good in there? That breathed oxygen into a human soul?

Chris looked down at me with what I can only describe as an invisible upper lip that sat as cruel as a common pirate below that little moustache of his. His mouth gazed with a hidden tongue so bitter it sunk into my chest with the sting of a caning.

In front of his morose, puzzled face I felt I could not mourn. In front of him, Aunty Bev did not exist. He had better things to do. The boys – as boys do – were waiting. They would not wait for long. They would go on without him. I stared after him, seeing the back of his paisley shirt going through the front door. My knight, my knight in wild shining armour was at my side but was no longer at my side.

There was worse to come. I did not know it would happen so soon that my knight's horse would fall over.

That night when he got home, I knew, I could smell it through his alcohol breath, I could see it on his still festering lips, the quickly dehydrating colour of his mouth, that he had been with another woman. I could just see it; nay, I could feel it. A woman knows these things even though men cannot figure out how. I didn't scream or shout. Just looked him in the eye, questioning, silently.

As I lay beside him, that full and white Malaysian moonlight shining through our windows onto our faces, I asked why. *Why?* He said he didn't do anything, but I knew he was lying. So I fell asleep with tears trickling silently down my face, wondering why. I was a good wife; I loved him with all my heart. I was so hurt and knew I loved him still. Obviously, it crossed my mind, I wasn't giving him everything he needed. I suffered in silence and couldn't bear to tell anyone what he had done; I had failed him, not lived up to expectations.

The very next day, close friends of ours, the Robertsons came to pick me and Chris up, to take us into George Town, Penang, to set up bank accounts. Jan Robertson, especially, could see that I was very upset, but I just did not feel I could share my agony or grief. I did not want to share it, not so much for my own protection or because of shame but because I did not want the Robertsons to look at Chris differently. I think I was defending him. I must have been.

Over the coming months, I tried to find out more from Chris, I just needed him to be honest with me, not that I ever considered leaving him, not a hope in hell, I loved him too much for that. But like a true man, like a true military man, he kept his silence. His indelible code of giving out only his name, rank and number.

But I found out, eventually I found out – three years later, after three whole years, when we got back to Australia he finally admitted it. After three years!

The trouble was, by then, I knew it wasn't the first time – I also knew it wouldn't be the last time. It was a normal RAAF night out with the boys, part of the runway, so to speak – playing up on your wife. Or did they think of it rather as simply "playing without your wife"? She would understand. Yes, yes, of course, what reasonable wife wouldn't?

I wasn't one of those "reasonable" wives. I didn't like it, it hurt like hell. It turned out, it hurt like crazy. But I never spoke of it to other RAAF wives. I never spoke of it to them even though they all talked about the "poor wives" whose husbands used to go, regularly, to Hat Yai, a town in southern Thailand, close to the Malaysian border… to enjoy their time off.

These wives who were sympathetic towards others, to so many other moral causes, said it was normal, but I did not like it, no, no, I did not like it. I could not understand, could never quite make the leap in my head, why the men needed to be with other women.

Betrayal was a word that kept jumping into my head. Betrayal, even in my marriage, seemed to be my friend. Only it seemed so soon, so soon after we had pledged our vows to be with one another and no other.

I suppose, in retrospect now, what affected me most on that night was Chris had not allowed me to mourn. Chris Pyke, my husband, my lover, my friend, my knight in shining armour, had not been at my side to serve me like the true soldier he was meant to be. Didn't even care – was only interested in serving himself and his military buddies. Was only interested in getting it off with some unknown exotic dancer or whatever else offered itself to his hungry lap. Yes, a night out with the boys from the base was so much more important than an angel. Than the death of Aunty Bev, the only woman in the entire world who had touched his lover's soul.

There was another thing that upset me about my husband's betrayal – something else that really, really got to me. It was not that he had put his proud soldierly male penis like a machine gun into another women, it was that his tongue, his male tongue that had touched mine, was kissing this exotic other. Some young so and so he had only just met. *Kissing* her.

The lips... the mouth, so sacred to me. Just ask Mr Grove, who I offered my tongue to for nothing. For a birthday greeting. Just ask Dad, who used my lips like a common girlfriend, my lips that had saved my sister from the evil in her path.

He knew – Chris should have known what it meant to me. The honesty that resided in there. In the mouth. On the edges of the tongue. The knight's shiny armour hadn't just become tarnished; it was beginning, so soon, piece by piece, to fall off.

In the end, and despite everything, it was not all bad in Malaysia. In fact, there were still some good times, even fulfilling moments of deep love between Chris and me, well, as deep as they could get knowing what I knew now. One of those times, one of those moments, was in Phuket, Thailand. While on holiday there, I fell pregnant.

It may be a normal part of the sway – and nature – of life. Especially for married couples. But for me becoming pregnant was like a silver-lined dream. It was the gold I had dreamed of since I was four years old and tried to lift teeny little Aunty Beatrice – Mum's Mum's baby girl – from the cot and nearly got beaten for it.

It was a dream ever since Dad and his mates held and caressed me and showed me what a cute little girl I could be. I wanted my own. I wanted my own family. My own tribe. I wanted something normal and non-creepy in my life. Something I could cherish and grow... if only I could... and this, this was it.

Through children, through my own child, I could achieve that. Maybe. No, yes, not maybe, I could. I had more confidence in that act of becoming pregnant than I had in anything in my entire life.

As though a confirmation of my vision, it was at this time that I won the Ladies Dart competition. The vision ahead was as clear to me as that bull on the dartboard.

35.

MY DREAM. JUST LIKE IN THOSE ROMANTIC BOOKS I READ ALL THE TIME, THIS WAS IT – my dream coming true to be a mother.

With pregnancy it all came racing before me, that need to live and love and cradle. To hold in my arms my own. To show I was better, to show I was better than my own mother, to show I could be the best mother on the planet. Only I *really, really* wanted to be that. The best mother on earth.

I know, I know, who doesn't say that? But it was a passion with me, like a job one loves, a musical instrument one holds and caresses out of sheer devotion. I really and truly wanted to show I could be a parent and a mother – something more than a mere biblical stick figure causing chaos because the Lord hath handed us down His seed and said go forth and multiply.

I wanted to multiply, I did, but I wanted it to be with love and show it could be real. I wanted children I could love, children who, maybe, with a bit of luck, would one day love me back.

Sarah eventually came – four weeks after my twenty-first birthday. My mother and my sister Marge came to visit around this time, my sister arrived with her toddler son, Samuel, and already pregnant with her second child.

Though younger than me, I did not deny her. Did not want to take any attention away from her. I just wanted my own. It didn't matter what I looked like. I was so big, so round, so fat – like Mum at her worst. Like Mum in her plastic astronaut weight-loss suit. I had put on 20.5 kilograms.

Even the doctors were concerned. Ironically – *Dad, if you're listening* – they put me on a salt-*free* diet. Maybe it was to annul all the bad genes? To annul all that could have passed through my over-salted blood into my own? I don't know for sure. But I believe it was because of the fluid I was retaining, giving me such a bloated look. I honestly didn't care what I looked like, only that I was carrying my own child at last.

It didn't matter to me one iota either whether I was having a boy or girl, I just wanted a baby. I really didn't know all that much about birth or pregnancy, but I read a lot of books and followed the months of my little one's arrival. I believed in myself, in my impending motherhood, and all I wanted was to physically see this child who resided so heavily in me. Who had resided in me since I was four.

In the end, Sarah delayed not for days but weeks her presence in the world. Her reluctance to pop out came much at the frustration and chagrin of Mum who was only in Malaysia for a five-week holiday and thought I would come on early, if anything.

So frustrated did Mum become that she and my knight Chris put me on this exercise bike and made me pedal and pedal and pedal, in the hopes of bringing on labour.

But it wasn't happening – nothing was happening. The only thing that happened instead was my sister being rushed into hospital – the "hostie", as the RAAF hospital was called – in what appeared to be a possible miscarriage.

The day after this drama was taking place, Chris, Mum and I, along with my little nephew, Samuel, went out for dinner. I'm not sure why, maybe a pre-celebration thing, or sheer frustration, but we "chowed" ourselves fatter than fat on chilli crabs, which was one of my favourite local dishes.

The date was April 11 and earlier that day I had had my doctor's check-up. He said if no labour came on soon, I was to go into hospital the day after the next to have myself induced.

The next morning, the morning after our night of feasting on chilli crabs, I awoke feeling deeply bloated and uncomfortable, and went to the toilet. I went in the hopes of having a bowel motion to settle things.

Wiping myself, I saw a thin smear of blood, and not sure what was happening, I panicked but laughed, telling Mum, who after all had had four of us: 'Hey Mum, I think I'm peeing chilli crabs?'

It certainly was possible, the amount we had eaten, and it certainly was the right colour. She laughed too. And then I explained the bloated feeling and the pain of it – and, I suppose, after four children she was on the money when she made the statement that somehow never sounds like a cliché, 'I think you're going into labour.'

Marge, who had just returned from care at the hostie, foetus still safely tucked in her belly, but totally incapacitated, agreed, 'Yeah, Debbie, I think this is it.' She pressed a square smile.

I bit my nails and held my tummy tight. It felt bad but not urgent. I was in no way afraid, so felt no need to go rushing to the hospital. It was like I had waited so long for this, and if it was finally starting to happen it was better to be cautiously patient than over-optimistically anxious.

I chose to wait at home for a while. It was eight in the morning, there was time. There always seemed to be time in the mornings – the whole day ahead, when you didn't really have to go anywhere.

At eleven am, the pains were coming on about ten to fifteen minutes apart, like real labour, like I was told to expect, and finally I phoned the hospital. They said I should come in – immediately. This was it. It was going to happen. I was going to – *Please God. Pleeeease…* – see my first.

They offered me an ambulance, but I refused knowing Mum and Marge would not be allowed to travel with me. It was good to have family, any family. I wanted them to be with me. This was *my* moment.

So, the only way was by car. Marge, because of that near miscarriage, was out of action, and well, to be frank, could one really trust Mum? So, guess who was going to be the driver?

We all climbed into the car, my sister, immovable as she was, her son too young to know the difference, Mum, overweight and almost immovable as well, and me, massive tummy and all, behind the wheel, making myself as comfortable as I could.

Everybody finally at ease in their seats, I turned the key. It wouldn't start. A bead of sweat fell on my forehead; I tried again. Same thing. And then I tried again and again with the same result. In the end, we had to crank it. Yes, you heard right. We had to crank it.

The car was a really old Morris Minor, and Mum, with no choice as the only "fit" one amongst us, in all her overflowing plumpness, had to get out of the car and crank it. Only, huffing and sweating, much as she tried, she couldn't get the motor to turn.

So, with Marge sitting frowning and disabled in the backseat, and Samuel too young to do anything, there I found myself again, out on the street this time, looking like a Dr Who TARDIS with this massively obese parcel stuck in the middle of it, taking deep breaths and puffing with contractions as I cranked the car, ready to give birth to Mary Magdalene.

Mum's final revenge? Dad's final intrusion? Who knows? In all seriousness, it was a reiteration for me that we all have to live with what we have. That is to say, as I learnt in those anxious moments of cranking the old Morris, we have to start from where we start. There is no other choice. And then, if necessary, we just have to get out of the car and goddamn crank the engine for ourselves if we need to.

There's no use sitting there and bagging or blaming God or anyone else for it. It's just the way it is. If you want to know how really bad it can get – go and read a romance novel!

And so there I was, not quite feeling blessed or happy at that precise moment, fat as a TARDIS, madly cranking this old jalopy like I should have had my togs or gym gear on and been working out on the treadmill.

Holding my back at times, crying silently with the oncoming bursts of Mary Magdalene inside me, while I shifted and rotated the twisted steel shaft with the enthusiasm of a weightlifter, it was like the car didn't want a bar of it. No matter what I did, nothing worked. The car was uncrankable.

There was no other choice – we had to go to Plan B. Luckily Chris and I lived on the flat bit of what after a few metres became a downward sloping road, and so the cranking became the only other thing it could be – pushing. Only with Marge the way she was, and me having to drive, Mum was the only one with the strength to push the old hunk of metal so that we could get it ready for its descent.

She tried, I'll give it to her, Mum tried. But it was no use. So, bloated like that TARDIS and puffing even heavier now with contractions, I had to help Mum. I did this by pushing from the side of the car. Passers-by probably thought it was one hell of an advert for the circus coming to town, but there we were, fat as a barrel mother and puffing, TARDIS-sized daughter pushing this old heap to the crest of the hill.

Somehow we managed it. We inched the car to the beginning of the downward slope and got the car off to a good start. Barely hanging onto the door now, half way down the hill I just managed to jump into the old scrapheap, and not to overpraise my incredible driving skills, I was able to clutch start the battered thing and hold it there like some badly rusted old show-ride.

I revved and revved and revved until Mum, sweating like a KO'd boxer, caught up with the car and managed to jump in, squeezing her barrel-flesh into the front passenger seat.

I guess she was used to a few clutch-starts in her life, Mum. Just nobody wanted it to be right then. That was the other thing about the car, the brakes weren't working. The brakes were as good as not there. So the whole way down the hill – and all the way to the hostie – I had to keep the car revving with clutch and accelerator, and using the handbrake.

If there was one thing that worked well on the car, thank God, it was the handbrake. And well, there was also my immense driving talents – thanks to Dad. Finally, finally... a lesson from Dad had borne fruit.

There was still a ferry-ride to come, which was part of the journey from Penang Island to the hospital at Butterworth on the mainland, and I was by now in a great deal of pain.

But we got there, too, finally we got to the ferry. But even on the ferry I had to keep the car revving lest we had to push again.

So there I sat on the Penang ferry, surrounded by my invalid sister and near invalid mother, still wildly revving a now dead-still car, my contractions increasing to about five minutes apart. It was hard to think Mary Magdalene would ever be born safe – or sane.

36.

IT WAS ABOUT TWO IN THE AFTERNOON WHEN WE FINALLY – AND
GOD KNOWS HOW – SAFELY REACHED THE RAAF BASE HOSPITAL AT
BUTTERWORTH. I had done it with my foot on the pedal all the
way. I felt a bit like Mum that day she was racing into the
drive to beat Dad into the house before he could catch her,
but I had made it to the hospital and could now flee the car
just before everything ended in a heap.

At precisely 10.28 that night, with Chris my renewed
knight in reinstated armour at my side, and having had
exactly what I did not want in my push for a natural birth, an
epidural because of the extreme pain, Sarah came spinning
out into the world. I say spinning, because, well, they had
to spin and drag her out with forceps in the end – and
everything in my head and upper body felt like they were
swimming and rotating with her.

But I have to say, the negatives aside, it was amazing. The
most astounding episode in my life. Well, let me put that
into perspective. She was bloody and purple and I was a
little shocked and afraid when I saw that tiny squashed face.
At the same time, separating her crimped and bedazzled
expression from all that muck and gunk that comes with
childbirth, and which I had somehow forgotten about, and
she looked beautiful. Absolutely the most beautiful thing I
had ever seen.

Mire and bile, sludge and gall aside, I know how they
say you love your child in that moment of first sight as she
comes pouring out of the womb, well it's true. I felt it like
a wave. Like love was oxygen speeding from my eyes into
her heartbeat. And vice versa: I could feel her miniscule
heartbeat on my tongue. We were both tapping absolutely
in tune.

I wanted to cry I was so overcome. That little pattering heartbeat of hers, that little purple body struggling for breath, writhing and hanging in the air waiting to be laid on my stomach, her lips somehow already groping for Mama's breasts.

They took her away from me after a short while, to clean her up, and despite the presence of Chris and Marge and Mum, I sat up and then fell back over because of the epidural. I had no control over my body. Life was showing me its ways again. Like at home. One minute everyone laughing and singing and having a grand old time, and the next everyone falling over, Dad kicking me and everyone else in the backside, including all the Japs in the world for what they did to his dad.

The sanctity of life. The privilege to bring new life into the world. It is sacred. It is still sacrosanct to me. It would be the same for each one of my children to follow – Ruth two years later and Dean five and a half after that.

But at that time, in those first few days, weeks, months, although I did not know much about child-rearing, it came to me as the most perfectly natural thing – despite the occasional pains of breastfeeding and a baby crying with heat rash because of the unrelenting Malaysian humidity.

In the end, after the first few harrowing days following Sarah's harsh birth, she was such a delight, she even started sleeping through at a mere 10 days old... giving me some peace, my little sparkle of light. In fact I used to call her "Sparkle" – because of her striking, luminous blue eyes. Motherhood for me was exactly as I expected it, the most extraordinary thing in the world; I felt privileged in an absolutely human way to finally do something right.

I often wondered if it was ever like that to Mum. How fatherhood felt to Dad. It is hard to imagine. Sometimes, even through the tears, I look back at them, and see them, Mum and Dad, in the same way I saw Chris and myself in those first anxious, astonishing moments of giving birth. I see them smiling, relieved, happy in a way they never expected to be.

And then I see Dad inspecting my body like an amateur doctor, like a grubby woodchopper, to make sure I was a girl. That the sawdust was his. That he had his human flesh to sever. And I see Mum, the smile fading, finally disappearing completely, becoming a weight on the world. In front of her, bin-load after bin-load of grey washing hanging on a thin line, the sun beating down on her back until the soil is hard like rock.

I also knew in my heart I would never trust Chris with our newborn child, or with our children to come. He was a man. He had shown what kind of man. The fear was too great. I knew he could never, would never do what my father had done, but I guess that was how deep it went, my experience, the fear, the absolute fear… of the so-called love between a father and a child.

After having Sarah, she came everywhere with me; there was no way I was letting my cherished daughter out of my sight. During my sporting days in Malaysia, our maid or *amah*, whose name was Penata, would be in tow, to take care of her while I was on the field or on the court playing. But always Sarah was there, somewhere near enough for me to see.

With Sarah safely in my arms, I felt I had something no one could ever take away from me. Except perhaps the hand of that great, inexplicable force that meanders through the universe. I understood that. I also understood its kindness.

37.

BY THE TIME OUR SECOND DAUGHTER, RUTH, CAME ALONG – MAY '85 – Chris was stationed at Australia's well-known Amberley Air Force Base and we were living in Leichhardt, Ipswich. We even soon moved and bought our own home in Bellbird Park, a fresh, newly developing suburb with lots of space and open areas

Initially, we were so excited to be back in Australia, our marriage once again purring along like an old tabby cat, sort of all furry and cosy... well, it seemed that way to me at any rate. Chris was his fun-loving self and it all seemed so positive.

Ruth's birth soon after also reminded me and made me believe in that miracle of life again. Well, in her case, for a short while. She started out with colic, but that seemed to quickly settle until she actually slept right through the night. Then at about six weeks her colic developed into reflux and projectile vomiting and maybe I should have seen it then, as Chris and I nearly climbed the walls with frustration, there was more to come.

But we somehow lived through that phase, and for most of the rest of that year our new baby was a very contented girl, often sleeping right through and enjoying her food and playing with her big sister, Sarah.

Then came her first birthday. And our little Ruth became a difficult child. There was no other way to put it: suddenly there was screaming and tantrums and fits of obstinacy that were almost too difficult to bear.

In retrospect, I think the reason for her trying ways was quite simply the fact that I'd started looking after other people's children. Doing it too soon – when Ruth was only six months old. She must have sensed there was just not enough time to spend with her like I was able to do with Sarah at the same age. She demanded attention.

I know, blaming myself again. Well, once again it was my fault, my responsibility, wasn't it? In this case, I have no doubt. I had a child, I had wanted another child desperately, and there I was taking on the childcare of other people's children.

On the other hand, there was also a mortgage hanging over our heads, electricity, food, clothing and other bills, and very little money. The reality was Chris was at base most of the day and sometimes even at night he was out working in a second job as an electrician, at Rosewood, near Ipswich. The result: I was doing it almost all on my own. I don't want to make excuses, so I have to confess: I felt responsible. *And terrible.*

The problems with Ruth continued, it seemed forever. From age one to three, which included the mythological "terrible twos", which I can say very confidently now are no myth at all, it went on and on. It wasn't until her third birthday that she returned, almost like a miracle, to her happy, joyful little self.

From that time, almost as though the sun had come out of the sky for the first time in the history of planet Earth, things eased out. Ruth became a pleasure again, my lovable, adorable child. I'm not sure how exactly it happened, but it happened. I am sure there is some psychological/scientific/sociological/paediatric explanation, but for me at the time I was just rain-away happy it happened.

For Chris, however, it seemed too late. For him, a screaming, crying, obnoxious child combined with the constant nagging to somehow squeeze out extra money, made life too difficult. And even when Ruth returned to normal, it would remain that way for him.

More and more, he was becoming bleak. And doing his own thing. More and more, I was beginning to know, on a deeper level, what I already knew – Chris was a depressive.

With our new baby-rearing burdens combined with his moods, Malaysia was beginning to seem like paradise.

The elation, the softly whispered words, the laughter were slithering away from us, and in their place a cold and difficult to comprehend vacuum was beginning to suck out all the energy between us.

Chris could sink so low at times that he would hardly talk to anyone for days. I know I should have felt sorry for him – and I did – only he would never even want to open his mouth and tell me what was going on inside. Not even a clue. I had to surmise it. Had to conjure it out of the chilled air from the stories I had heard along the way about his own harsh upbringing. About his dad literally hanging from the bowing rafters. About his older brother Phillip who, in the nick of time, cut their dad down from the ceiling.

But in the day-to-day reality, without being willing to open up about anything, Chris became more and more difficult to live with. I think I could safely say, in his moods, he was more difficult to live with than my child Ruth in her most horrible moments of reflux and tantrum throwing.

Like a child, he demanded things, demanded attention, had sex without saying anything, without whispering a word, merely staring at me with an almost uncaring resentment at how difficult and hollow life had become.

By the time Ruth was about eighteen months old it became too much to bear. We were going to split up. I am not sure what held us together, other than the fact that the RAAFies, the guys and girls at the base, might say something, might think badly of us, might point fingers and say that Chris had failed, couldn't even keep his marriage together.

Chris could not stand the thought of that, of others pointing fingers at him as though he had messed up. From my perspective, feeling the emotions of what he was feeling as well as having to consider my own needs, I couldn't bear the thought of taking the girls from him; I felt I didn't have a right to do that... to rip our family apart.

I also, at all costs, it played on my mind like a plague, like a dark, rotted cheese, did not want our girls growing up in a dysfunctional family like mine or Chris's was. He did not want that either.

So we held it together – like glue without the sticky substance. Like cheap ineffectual adhesive that has already gone dry and no longer bonds. It was around this time Chris' brother, Aidan, moved in and lived with us, so our house wasn't just for us anymore. Aidan's girlfriend also stayed over most of the week. Then about a year later, my brother Sam and his partner Annie and their baby girl moved in as well. I could hardly imagine it myself – I was just like Dad. Like "have-a-chat, come and stay at our place" Dan Gallagher.

I cannot say I didn't enjoy it. I obviously enjoyed the company, especially at dinnertime when we all sat around the table chatting and sharing the day's events. But in the end, I can only say it made me think it must have been much easier for Dad inviting the world to stay over than it could ever have been for Mum.

As the so-called "stay-at-home" mum, I had to do everyone's washing, all the cooking, all the cleaning, most of the looking after the kids, as well as looking after other people's kids.

The only thing I did not do – at my firm insistence – was Annie's baby's nappies. Annie also kept to herself, while privacy, time to myself, time even to be with my own husband, what was that? All I saw on my brow was fog and sweat and people, big and small, spinning around my eyes.

Yes, Mum, I understand that part a little more now; it couldn't have been easy. Actually, I was desperately tired most of the time. I needed something else. I needed more than to just wake, work, and breathe.

Enter Josh Kelly.

38.

YES, ENTER JOSH KELLY, AND I HAVE A CONFESSION TO MAKE. I HAD
AN AFFAIR. I did exactly what I said Chris had ever harmed
our relationship by doing. Don't ask me where I found
the time, but somehow I did. Everything was splintering
and fracturing around me, and in the cracks, in the little
peepholes of light between, spilled Josh Kelly.

A little like Chris in the early days, he was another saviour.
Someone I could talk and chat to and that I felt understood
by. He was unruffled and even tempered and seemed to take
the time to listen to the day-to-day stuff. That was important
to me, especially since the fact was Chris was no longer there
for me.

We, Chris and I, that is, never even fought – because we
did not want the kids hearing us yelling at one another. We
were literally scared out of our boots to have the kids see
us like our own parents, caterwauling and yowling at one
another like jungle animals fighting over dead prey. We did
not want that. That much we knew about each other. That
we did not want to set that kind of example. But even on
quiet terms, in good moments, we hardly spoke anymore.

The reality was we didn't argue or raise our voices when
we needed to because there was simply no communication.
We were unhappy, unhappy with each other, so, so unhappy,
and it was there – loudly and clearly – for all to see. Only for
us it existed silently within our heads, within our bones, in
the anxiety of our body language. In all these ways we were
fighting with one another – like robots violently bumping
and pushing against one another all day long, we were a
long, silent noise.

Exacerbated by Chris's depression, his moods, by the
comings and goings of visitors, by working out how we were

going to pay for things, and maybe worst of all, by Chris continuing with his boys' nights out, there was nothing left between us.

Feeling exonerated by circumstance, I did what I shouldn't have done.

I had known Josh Kelly since I was sixteen and his family were like family to me. His father was in the same timber-cutting business as my father. In fact, his older brother and his wife were to become one of Chris's and my closest and best friends, and are Dean, my son's godparents. Chris and I are godparents to one of their three children.

And so all I know is that at that time, when I was going through all this turmoil and trying to break through to Chris, Josh was kind to me. He was sincere and considerate. At any rate, he was definitely more understanding than any man I had met until then. Well, except perhaps for Mr Dreamboat Doherty, my schoolteacher. But at that time Josh Kelly was the tree-stump, the maturity, the emotional fixture I needed.

He also had a beautiful voice and would sing directly to me when we would go to watch him perform at local venues or even at parties that we held at our house. One song in particular he would sing to me was Chris de Burgh's "Lady in Red". Not only that but at these public events he would let my daughter Sarah sit up on his knee and he would sing Billy Ocean's "Suddenly" with her.

He was so good with both my girls and they loved him in return. Maybe, maybe, I like to think so, he is the reason Sarah has a great love of music today.

Josh Kelly represented the absolute opposite of my marriage, the absolute opposite of everything in my relationship with my once knight in shining armour, and yes, yes, we went that extra distance together. It was love, I am sure; I am sure it was love.

But I had caused it to happen, I was a woman, I had the maturity, the presence of mind. Even worse than with Dad, I was a mother and a fully responsible human being now. I could make or deny these decisions. And in this case I had chosen to go ahead. To go all the way. To enjoy and lap up the moment.

To that extent, in the final analysis, I suppose I was as bad as my husband, maybe even worse, because Josh, unlike Chris's girls, was no "floozy". He wasn't just the result of a girls' night out, a bit of alcohol-driven fun; he meant something to me. Not only that, he was a friend of both Chris and I and regularly stayed in our home. I guess that's how we found the time, he stayed in our home. Another visitor!

If I can be kind to myself for just one second, here's the heart of the matter: Josh was single at the time and if Chris, my husband was not around, I could have married him. I could have easily sworn my vows to Josh Kelly, a man who stepped back into my life like a responsive anchor to hold me calm and still at just the right time.

On the other hand, that I could have sworn vows to him was easy to say, even to think in retrospect, because at that time it really, really was at gravel end between Chris and me. Even having sex with Chris, my once lover and friend, had become a duty. It was an echo with no voice, I just had to lie back and literally think of my flower garden. I could do it no other way.

As a point of fact, as a young teenage girl I would love to sit and look at the water lilies growing in the dams on our property at Anondale... I always had a sense of peace looking at them. And through my life I often think of those beautiful singular white flowers with their bright yellow centres and the glossy green leaves and remind myself of the "exotic quietness" they gave me during those stressful times. When Chris and I were making love, it was those floating lilies I thought of.

People can judge me now, as they did then, throw the Ten Commandments at me, but what happened between Josh and me was an affair that I could feel burning through the stomach and peeling in the chest. I am at least sure of that.

The intensity of it. It happened only once, that is the truth, and it happened when our hearts leaked over and were unable to say no any longer. It did not happen again, though the feelings, I have to be completely honest, remained.

Josh even, at one stage, said he would help set me up in a place of my own and be there for me, but still I didn't have the heart to take the girls away from Chris. So I made the decision to stay married to Chris, but went as far as to tell Josh that he was one of my biggest sacrifices in life. It may have been a bigger sacrifice than I could have imagined.

Like the tide beneath a wave, Josh and I continued to feel that ripping pull for one another for years to come but we never repeated our unfaithful act. Eventually, Josh fell in love with Clare, a girl who was a barmaid at the Acacia Ridge Hotel, at the other end of town, where he sang more often now.

I was truly happy for him. I remember thinking, even though I was married, how I had to let him go and just suck it up. I believed he deserved to make a new life with someone that was free, that was available to him. Someone who was not such an entangled mess.

And as these things happen, we all became great friends, Chris, myself, Josh and his new wife, Clare. Occasionally, I would even look after Justin, Clare's little boy from a previous marriage. He was the same age as Ruth and they got on like a dream.

Josh and Clare even asked Chris and me to be part of their "wedding party", but there are some things in life I have to decline. I just could not stand up beside them on that sacred platform; it was still too raw and painful for me, seeing him marry someone else.

Chris and I did, however, go to the wedding. It was a fine and bright ceremony, but I cried so much that day. So much. I explained it away by saying that weddings always did that to me.

Tears dripping through his own musical green eyes, Josh even told me at the end of that day, his new wife only metres away, that he would always love me. I guess it was love. I guess it was. Despite my infidelity, despite my self-flagellation, at least I can carry that around in my shameful bush of locks.

But it had all become too much for me... Chris, visitors, lovers, boys' nights out, everything had become like the weight on bare flesh of a rough and itchy blanket in the summer.

I had to get away, even if only for a short while. Even I knew that. So, I took the children and went for a two-week break from everyone and everything. I went up to my sister Marge's place in Burrum Sound.

Only even that short break would turn into something darker than I could have ever imagined.

39.

IT WAS ONLY MY SECOND NIGHT AT MY SISTER'S AND CHRIS WHO WAS GOING TO CALL EACH NIGHT TO SAY GOODNIGHT TO THE GIRLS, CALLED WITH AN ULTIMATUM: if I did not come back home immediately he would hang himself. Yes, hang himself. Do exactly what his father had attempted to do.

'I have a rope around my neck,' he said with the desperation of a long-suffering prisoner of war, 'and if you don't come home I'm going to kill myself.'

I saw in front of me the image of his hanging dad that had implanted itself in his every brain cell, and I knew well he suffered from depression. But it was the noose he was holding around my neck that right at that moment I resented. He was using it to squeeze us together. Only the more he squeezed, the further I wanted to drift from him.

To my mind, it had already come to a head. The storm clouds had already let their guts out. What he was doing only confirmed every riling feeling in my veins I had against him. But at the same time, I felt guilt, overwhelming guilt, like it was because of me that he was doing what he was doing, like I had let him down.

I was trapped; it pricked through every pore in my flesh and I could not shake it off. It only made me feel more resentful. Holding the phone, I put my foot down and refused to go.

The reality is, in my head, in my heart, I think well and truly in my soul, I had already parted from him. This threat had made sure of that. Only, on the other side of the line, his trembling voice was desperate and real; it was getting louder and more insistent. Still I refused. His voice lowered and he begged, even cried and howled, but I remained firm. I was not moving an inch.

In the end, he jumped in his own car and came to fetch me.

But rather than seeing in his heroic trek, love, passion and devotion, I detested him for it. The fact that I knew he needed help didn't help me – or us – at all. And now he was at my sister's doorstep, hundreds of kilometres from Bellbird Park, ready to whisk me away – or commit suicide. He was, in plain English, holding a knife to my heart. Not only that, he insisted that my sister look after the girls, that they remain behind, and I saw in his mood, in his determination, that he just wanted me to himself.

I had never left the girls by themselves anywhere before, other than when Marge stayed with Chris to look after Sarah while I was in hospital having Ruth, and he knew that. He could see in my balking eyes that I hated and despised him for his demand, but he just stood there, waiting for me like an expectant child, like he didn't care.

His need – I could see it in those curving "temple" eyes of his – was greater than my not wanting to be parted from my girls. It was that stark.

Maybe I should have shouted and screamed and thrown a fit. But I wasn't like that. When I looked at him, I saw every sinew in his muscles pressing me to obey or else. Like a chattel, I sometimes think of it like that, I agreed. I left my girls behind with my sister and went with him back to Bellbird Park.

I would never get over it, though. It may not have been quite obvious then but in my system there was something I needed to flush out, and everything but my mouth was saying it was him.

I remember when we finally got back home, Chris was trying really hard to reconnect with me but I just wanted to be left alone. I was missing my girls and deeply abhorred him for taking me away from them. I was so sad, so in a way lost, but in the end, as in all things, our life together continued and within a few weeks the girls were back with us...

It is a funny thing, even in a horrid, empty relationship, especially once we have children, have a mortgage hanging over our heads, time somehow passes, the grass grows and needs mowing, and life moves on.

I thought about the horror and emptiness of it every day. And I was reminded of it every morning and night as I saw that spousal face next to me. The nights were always the longest and the worst. But ultimately I had to get up every morning, get off my emotionally roller-coasting butt, and get on with it. I had to get the kids to school and preschool, help out at the school, do the washing, the washing up, make arrangements, go to my job, make sure I did more than my bit to supplement our never quite sufficient income. And so it passed. Time passes.

And no matter all my wondering how people can live in black holes, Chris, my old rusted knight and I, lived on.

To supplement our income, I continued with my day-care work, looking after other people's children in my own home while they in turn went about their business. The truth be told, I wasn't prepared to leave my children with anyone else while I went out to work, so working from home seemed the only solution to bringing in the much needed extra dollars.

For some of us anyway, the more our partners fall by the wayside, the more we put ourselves into our children, and this is what happened to me. I did not see anything wrong with it. Nothing. It is a mother's calling. I was already devoted to our two girls, loved them like the day they were born, but without that partnership, without Chris really there, it was like everything became even more about the kids.

Through the hot, wretchedly humid days at our home in Bellbird Park, a kind of little miracle happened. There was this one little girl in my care whose name was Rebecca, and I don't know what it was but with each day I saw her the more my heart wanted to encircle and embrace her.

Maybe it was that with her awkward little running body and bushy head of dark brown hair, she reminded me a little of that tiny girl from my past; that skimpy girl, free and loving and full of heart that I could have been? I don't know. But I literally fell in love with her.

It actually pained to hand Rebecca back to her mother of an afternoon. Yes, I said pained. With Sarah by now in Year One and Ruth at preschool, I cherished this little bundle that did not even belong to me.

I don't know if it was purely hormonal, or if perhaps like a miracle it was a "word" from the great mysterious forces in the universe, but the almost daily sight of this little girl, despite the black emptiness between Chris and I, was changing the way I saw things. I began to view Chris in a more positive light and soon I realised what I wanted, what I really wanted.

It took a while for it to dawn on me, but when it did, I felt immediately it was right: what I wanted was to have another child. Through that little girl Rebecca, almost desperately I was becoming maternal, clucky, chirpy, whatever you want to call it, but the obsession grew, and grew; I had to give birth to another one of my own.

Chris, who was not even so sure about having any more children after Sarah, and had only reluctantly agreed to becoming pregnant with Ruth (ironically his favourite now, I guess now that all the temper tantrums were over), was very sceptical again about this new urge in me.

But somehow, I think it was that paradoxical twist, that remembering how he did not under any circumstances want to have another baby after Sarah – because he did not believe he could love another child as much as he loved her – and then seeing the flowering of Ruth into his favourite, that made him eventually relent.

Perhaps it could happen again? Perhaps, better still, we would have a son? What soldier, what knight in shining armour, no matter how rusted and worn, does not want his own male progeny? His own little knight?

Chris agreed – and the strange thing was that through this little girl, Rebecca, this little girl who was my past and possibly my future – Chris and I stepped out of the shadows and began to love again. For a while it was like the dark brooding shadow over our house that burnt a strip of emptiness down the middle of our queen-size bed, was moving off and would never come back.

It returned to me the faith that even in the darkest of times the dawn can eventually make its way to your address. I pinned it down to that little girl. The great big force out there had sent her like a Moses-child to us, to rekindle, to re-spark, to give us another chance.

I fell back in love with Chris all over again. Here again was the man of my dreams, the one I "moonily", "floatingly" thought of and missed so badly every day when I was working as a nanny for the Godbolts at Rodds Bay.

Life was starting again.

40.

WHEN I WENT TO THE DOCTOR TO TEST FOR PREGNANCY AND THE RESULT CAME BACK POSITIVE, I stood in the man's office and cried. Just stood there and cried.

'Is this what you want?' he asked with a face offering a backstreet abortion, and between sobs I squealed back for everyone in the waiting room to hear: 'Yes. Oh yes. This is exactly what I want.'

I was so happy that even as I was leaving the doctor's rooms I continued to cry in front of everyone waiting there.

So seriously was the universe speaking to us, that Chris, my soldier, my knight, when he heard about my pregnancy, even opted out of the Air Force. I loved him for it. My heart raced and touched him because of it. He was my hero again.

Only... only... unbelievably, he wanted to go back to Gladstone. To Gladstone! I couldn't understand it. The idiot, the fool, the wombat, what was he thinking? Taking me back to that messy, ramshackle, dirty, drought-drenched place of my worst nightmares, the last place on earth I wanted to go.

'Are you sure this is what you want?'

'Yes,' he said. 'Yes.'

I don't know, I don't know. I guess I was pregnant, thinking differently, had this new chance at life and love, and relented. As bad as the thought of going back to Gladstone was, there was still something there; I had to admit it, there was still something in that hard soil, in the chaos of scrap metal and poisoned timber that positioned me there.

Another harsh truth: Dad was still there, running his sawmill – Dan Gallagher Enterprises – on that exact spot, Perenjora Dam Road, Anondale. In fact, during our time at Ipswich and Bellbird Park we would even go and visit from time to time.

Talk about life going on. Talk about sweeping dirt under carpets. Not just dirt but mounds of fetid, rotten, over ripe, smashed up, fermented slices of old pumpkin and watermelon under the carpet.

That's the way it was with Dad, with my entire family. We'd go and visit – I'd keep a very, very careful eye on the kids – but nobody said anything. What had happened should not be repeated – not to anybody. Not even among ourselves.

Was the past really the past?

You would think so. Mum was there too, in the same region, living in Gladstone in a house with her new partner, Ray. And knowing it was impossible for me to sleep under the same roof with Dad again – something "intuited" rather than openly stated by anyone – we actually started out our existence in Gladstone living with Mum.

It was also a money thing. We were waiting for the sale of our house in Bellbird Park to eventuate and at the same time saving money to build a new house, our own brand new castle in Gladstone. We even had the plans drawn. And then they were redrawn.

That was the funny thing, each time we had plans drawn up, Chris would sit with them for a while and there would always be something he objected to and we would start all over again. He kept finding things he did not like about the plans, kept delaying signing off on anything.

Talk about a woman's prerogative, I sure gave him his man's prerogative, kept on giving and giving, until what? – we moved back out to Anondale. Yes, I had completely given in by then, willing to move back to Dad!

Well, it was not quite under the same roof, because it was all part of a new deal: Chris and I would buy the house and two acres of the property off Dad, and Dad – that thick wooden casing who once held the entire structure of the house together – would be relegated to the old shed, the original structure that was our abode on the property when

Mum and Dad initially dragged us all to go and live there.

Talk about circles. Talk about living in a small, round world. Talk about going round in rings. Now I was taking my own daughters to live in that house where I grew up – or was it to that house where I was "ground down"?

My son Dean would be born there... The entire sin of humanity, Original Sin itself, the entire planet seemed to revolve around Gladstone and Perenjora Dam, around Anondale. A world without stars. A world without sky. A world of darkness and sins, of big black crows and beasts. And there I was going back forever. Going deep back in there...

The reality was Dan Gallagher Enterprises was struggling and Chris saw an opportunity to buy the house and property at a good price and help Dad out in the process. We even loaned Dad a further fifteen thousand dollars, which was written up by solicitors as a proper loan at a fixed interest, to be paid back in a reasonable amount of time. But this too would become a bone of contention between Dad, Chris and I.

Dad had said he would be able to pay us back within three months, but as it turned out I finally agreed to a lesser part of what should have been the final amount – sixteen years later.

I suppose, from a purely pragmatic point of view, buying the house at the time made sense. My knight in shimmering armour – now more like my knight in scalded, sinful rags – was taking me back to my roots.

In the event, from the day we moved in, I refused to have Dad's and Mum's bedroom as our bedroom. Even though it was the only room in the house warm with carpets that still looked good – that's where we stored our boxes.

I could not help but see Mum and Dad there, king and queen under that royal white veil. Could not help but see Dad laying me down on that bed, my legs wide open, my jaws echoing with theories of royal families and long lost tribes that loved and cavorted in their incestuously small, simple circles. Could not help but see Mum standing there, peering over Dad's shoulder ready with a slap of denial to my face.

No, no, no, I could not bear to step into that room. Me, "the dirty little girl who had done such secretive things".

I hated that house, hated it. And the first thing I did was paint the walls. Actually, Chris and I were the first to ever paint the house. Until we painted it, it had always been bare fibro and unpainted timber.

We painted the insides a whitish blue and the kitchen a fiery red and white so that it stood out like a British flag to the dam, to the highway, to the rail line, to ourselves, and so even the thick wooden beam near the kitchen that was so much like Dad in its solidity, looked different. Looked rustic, yet modern – nothing like Dan Gallagher.

We determined to make everything we could look new and like our own.

And in the background the trains chugged by and the cars whooshed forwards and backwards as in the days of my black past.

41.

WERE WE REALLY ABLE TO CHANGE THAT HOUSE? Or maybe more poignantly, how did I get along with Dad? Well, the answer to that question is I got along with Dad fine. Just fine. As long as he was never too close to my girls.

Dad, in a fatherly way, would try to hug me – and my bottom would stick out three miles. Also, on no account would I ever leave him alone with my children. Babysit? I wouldn't even let the idea pass my forehead.

In actual fact I never allowed my father to stay in any of our homes, not even when my sister would try to convince me to have him sleep over. I just couldn't bear the thought of him sleeping that close to my daughters.

Which makes me think of an incident while we were at the property – the strange but telling incident of the mung beans and the feeding of the sheep.

One day, while I was still heavily pregnant with Dean, without knowing anything at all about feeding sheep, Sarah and Ruth got it into their little heads that they knew all about it. In fact, they decided that Dad's flock of about 15 sheep looked so desperately hungry that they opened up a big 20kg sack of mung beans for the purpose.

From the top of it, they started whooshing out the beans like they were building a mountain of food on the ground for the poor, starving animals.

The sheep were, so to speak, happy as Larry with their huge mid-morning hors d'oeuvre, but even I knew that less than a twentieth of what the girls had given them was more than enough to feed the entire flock for a week. In point of fact, it took a mere litre bottle of the beans to feed all of them of a morning. And here were the girls dolloping out an after-breakfast treat so huge it could kill them.

In feed terms, the beans were as filling as concrete; just a small amount would swell in the sheep's belly and digest slowly through the day. And that would be more than enough to see them through a twenty-four hour cycle.

In the distance, the dust – earth and sawdust – gathering around him, I saw Dad's tall, gangly body like an agitated emu bouncing toward us from his shed. And God, oh God, knowing Dad, knowing that brutal temper, I was so afraid I started shouting at the girls, yelling words I didn't usually use with them, telling them they were 'idiots' and 'stupid' and should have known better and asked before they acted.

Dad arrived.

'Jesus bloody Christ, what the fucking hell is going on here?' Just as expected, he began roaring, seeing the sheep bleating and merrily eating at the mound of food around them. And then more urgently, his voice blew like a hurricane: 'Pick up the bloody beans, for God's fucking sake! Get the fucking, goddamned sheep out of here!'

Chris, my knight, who it has to be said very seldom touched the girls as a means of punishment, totally freaked out. Next to him stood Sarah, our eldest, and he let out a yell and then gave her such a hard smack across her backside that it sent her flying to that dirty, awful, dry soil.

Trembling together after that, Sarah and Ruth stared up at Dad, and everyone expected the sky to explode. In truth, we were all heaving, waiting for the inevitable: Dad to beat and kick the hell out of our kids, out of each and every one of us perhaps – just like he kicked the crap out of all those Jap soldiers, like he made Jacko Johns dance that night with his shotgun, like he nearly strangled Mum to death, like he nearly squeezed and shook the air out of me until there was none left.

Only something else happened. Suddenly the earth seemed to stop and calm, the sheep moved off, and the mung beans lay silent.

Dad shook his head at Chris: 'What the ef d'you think you're doing, mate? Just bugger off and leave the girls alone. For goodness sake, can't you see they're just kids? They don't know what they're doing!' He pressed his teeth in that "mulling" bird way with his tongue.

Dad, Lord Protector, was on night watch again. Batman, our hero, the protector of darkness, of everyone, especially children. In a similar situation he would have beaten the living daylights out of us kids, but here he was displaying his full, bright, spinning wheel of human colours. Displaying his glorious chummy heart that was a shield to everyone but his own. The face we show the outside world, the worms that reside within.

I think the incident shook Chris more than it did me. But being me, and in the circumstance, I determined to persist and make the best of things. To scrape away the past. To sweep it as far from my mind as possible. Chris and I now even set about cleaning up the yard, that filthy rusting mess of overgrown weeds and useless, wiry trees.

In the end, the problem was Chris, once again it was Chris. His moods came back, slowly but surely they came back. And they were dark, at times so dark it was difficult even for me to see.

I'm not sure if it was in one of those moods, it must have been, but at a certain point Chris, who had been working as an electrician at the Nebo Smelter nearby, decided he was much better off re-joining the Air Force.

So, guess what? The week I was due to have my much-desired, wished and prayed for third baby, Chris was travelling back down to Brisbane to get himself reinstated into the RAAF.

As it turned out, he may have missed the birth of his son, but he was so happy to be back in the Air Force, so glad he hadn't lost his sergeant ranking and that there was now a great possibility of being posted back to Amberley, that despite everything, despite it all, I had to be happy for him.

The highlight at this time, beyond anything, was the birth of Dean. It was quick but painful. I had to be cut twice – and without painkillers – to let out Dean's broad shoulders.

But almost greater than my delight at giving birth was seeing the emotional high that heaved through Chris's body when he knew he had a son. His own little knight.

I was so happy for him, so happy that I'd finally given him the son he desperately wanted. Happier for him than I was for myself, if that was possible. I just felt blessed to have my new baby, boy or girl. Almost more amazing to me was that I had one of the Grove girls as a ward sister. Talk about small world. Talk about full circles. I still tasted the shame of that kiss on my tongue. That birthday kiss planted in her father's mouth.

But in the end, even Chris's high with his little knight didn't really matter – because his moods came back, continued to roll from his eyes, continued to gather like constantly darkening clouds.

The reality, the sad reality because it came despite the upsurge in our relationship with the initial pregnancy of Dean, was that the moods were always there now, forming and then clearing, but never quite clearing altogether.

With the constancy of those clouds, with their changing shades from grey to black to a kind of blotchy purple-green, our relationship was just a huge and damaging hailstorm waiting to happen. It hovered above us, always there, shaping and reshaping.

Luck was on my side. When Dean was four days old, we found out we were going to Melbourne. It was nowhere near Ipswich, like we had hoped, but at least we were going.

I guess I should have been over the moon we were leaving Anondale. Leaving Dad. Leaving that sordid, unenchanted world of memories. That House of Horrors. But next to me I had Chris. Chris and that purple-black cloud that was his head.

It sometimes briefly passes my mind that maybe Chris was in some way punishing me – by taking me back to Gladstone, to the mess that was my past. Perhaps he even wanted to see how I stood up to it, to Dad? To see if I was still so meek, so available? But in the end he saw he could not stand up to it either.

Knowing we were about to depart was like a triumph, like I had won something special. Like I had, in a way, beaten Dad – and Chris – at the same time. It brought back a memory. I was fifteen and at the time together with my first real boyfriend, Brad. Well, one day at about the time I was beginning to see Brad, Dad accused a school friend of mine of being a slut. Of smoking cigarettes and being a bad influence on me.

The girl was not there, nowhere near our house at the time, but I was so mad at Dad, madder at him than I would have been if he had said those things of me. Instinctively, I don't know what got into me, I slapped him. Slapped him so hard it split open his lip.

I stared at him, my big Dad with his hard crow eyes and steel jowl, waiting for the retribution, waiting for him to knock my block from the one side of the room to the other. To strangle me. But in the end, breathing out and snorting like he was still capable of anything, he brought his big fist to my jaw – but just touched it, merely scraped the pores of my skin with it, and then humphed a second breath of sliding air and walked away.

As he turned, in an almost proud way, he looked back at me and said: 'You have a bit of Gallagher in you after all.'

I was astounded, in the act of facing up to the beast I had vanquished it. At any rate gained some respect from it.

Man is a strange animal. If I had stood there trembling I am dead sure he would have truly knocked my block off, but seeing me stand there staring at him with some defiance, he did nothing. Just walked away. Praised me. I see it as a sign of an inherent cowardice: when there is weakness, Man, men, show no mercy.

Like the time I fought back and injured that girl, Dad had now stepped aside. If I had lost, if I had stood there shaking, I would have been seen as weak and almost certainly been trampled on.

I remember feeling after this incident a little bubble inflate in me. It blew out all shiny like the whole world could see it expanding in me. I was actually proud as hell.

Now, once again, Chris, in what was quickly becoming his very dishevelled armour, seeing that I could, if I wanted to, live near Dad, was whisking me away. My knight was becoming a real soldier again.

We spent that Christmas, me, Chris, the girls and our new baby Dean, after those intense few months in Gladstone and that badly bent and twisted Anondale house, in an upmarket, self-contained luxury apartment in inner Melbourne.

We were celebrating the Christmas of 1990, getting ready to set up our brand new lives reattached to the RAAF. At the same time, the rest of the world was beating its feet and making jungle sounds, planning the First Gulf War. Fear, the thought of wars looming, didn't even cross our minds.

It was a good Christmas. Both the girls raced around the apartment, swam constantly in the luxury pool, and had lots of fun with their dad. Even baby Dean behaved and seemed to enjoy it as best a newborn can.

Soon after that Christmas we were placed in our new RAAF house in Clayton South. The date was January 2, 1991, the same day we were married, nine years earlier. It was a stinking hot day of forty-two degrees, so much for Melbourne's cold weather. It would change our lives forever.

42.

BAR THAT ONE UPSURGE IN HAPPINESS, DECIDING DEAN'S CONCEPTION AND BECOMING PREGNANT AGAIN, which lasted a matter of months, it seemed Chris and I never really reconnected. We would have bursts of happiness and then the gloomy darkness would set in again; it was like a long drawn out boat ride on seas that refused to stop swelling and dropping. The sharing, which was there at times, would inevitably find its way behind a black rising wave and then sink down into a hollow and an energy-sapping vacuum would re-enter.

Little Rebecca's "miracle", was, I saw now, no more than about the birth of Dean, perhaps a moment of light for Chris and I, for the two of us together. But no more than that. A moment.

To me, it was becoming more and more apparent the longer we stayed in Melbourne, the less I felt for Chris. I wanted to disentangle. I was a stronger woman now, an idiot, yes, but no longer a fool at anyone's beck and call. I had made up my mind, I was not going to let any man bribe me with suicide again.

The good thing is that by the time Chris and I got to Melbourne our girls were both at school age and I did what I think every parent – not just abuse victims – should do. I threw myself into their schooling. Whether it be husband or wife, I believe strongly – based on my own experience – at least one parent should always be "right in there", at least in the first few years of a child's life.

Despite my lack of education, despite my lack of experience, despite my lack of skills, I helped in the children's classes, I helped in the tuckshop, I became an active member of the "mothers' club", I put both hands up to be on the school council, and when it came to it, without thinking I had any abilities whatsoever, I even put my hand up to be the note-taking secretary at school council meetings.

Yup, I know, know it only too well, that especially in the position as secretary at school meetings, I could have failed. I could so easily have made a complete and utter fool of myself. But at the time I thought what the hell, who cares, the worst that can happen is they can criticise me, call me stupid, a failure (so, what's new?) and beg around for someone else to take my place.

But I discovered something at these meetings and other related school meetings: I had this uncanny knack at quick and accurate note taking. It is something I would never have discovered had I not put my hand up. Something I would never have known about if I had just kept my neck in my shoulders and called myself a victim, an uneducated dysfunctional, and stayed silent, doing nothing. I could easily have let others, the school system, do the work of bringing up my children for me.

This was not what I wanted. Life, my children's lives and safety had become too precious for me, and in the event, having stuck my neck out, I actually discovered my experience also counted for something.

People were actually listening to me. Even relying on me. One day it would also start me on a course of further educating myself, but right then I was happy just to be directly involved in my children's education and their growing up.

Not only my actions in being a part of the school community, but my note-taking became such a legend and so appreciated, that the principal would one day write in reference of me, lines to the effect: *Deborah Pyke has been an important and active member of our school community. She is a concise and word-perfect note-taker, a great contributor to her and other people's children's education. I have always maintained she needed a bed at the school – because she never left it. We do not know how we will ever fill all her voluntary positions.*

That was probably the first open praise – in writing, in black and white – I had ever had in my life. I was already thirty, and I felt a lump in my throat when I read it.

When I think about it, it could have only come from what I always said, which may sound a little trite now, but at the risk of overstating, it is this: Read and learn about others, take note of their bruises and failings and their tragedies, and remember through it all there are always people much worse off than you.

Above all, don't ever feel sorry for yourself. Rather go and read a romance story. It is true, trite or not, we have to get off our butts and do something. The idea of magic wands and knights in shining armour coming to rescue us, as I was slowly but absolutely discovering, has a much better place in movie theatres than it does in our lives.

Talking of which, my marriage was in pieces, almost a formal vacuum now – and yet, to be totally honest, neither Chris nor I wanted to face it. So, no progress there. Not only that, with all his moods and depression and expectations of me, I found out he had another woman on the side.

Back to square one.

I remember him saying that they were only "good friends". But as we were all going to a RAAF function at the Comedy Club one night, he thought he should warn me to be aware of the talk as everyone in his section thought he was having an affair with her.

Once again my heart was in my throat – I knew intuitively what "good friends" really meant to him. I could see what he meant by "everybody talking"; I could see the lie quivering on his lips. Yes, his mouth was telling me, he, Chris Pyke, my knight, my mate, my lover, my husband, however hollow those terms may have become, had a real, live, girlfriend staying not that far away from us.

She would even give him a lift to and from work. He grew really annoyed one afternoon when Sarah and Ruth ran out the front of the house to greet him as he was being dropped home by her. They were jumping up and down and were running around, laughing and giggling.

They were shouting out to me: 'Hey Mum, Daddy's girlfriend has brought him home.'

As he came inside he became so cranky with the girls for "talking such rot" that he actually swore at them and told them, loud and roughly, to get to their rooms for being "so silly". What he really meant was for demeaning him and showing him up. He who I had come back for. He who I had stayed with in order to rescue. It was me who was "so silly".

Like that first instance of disloyalty, of denying me my day of mourning for Aunty Bev in Malaysia, I had a choice now: I could either curl up and accept it and go on living emptily, using the excuse of the children and the sanctity of marriage as the reason for my choice, or I could get up and do something to change it.

Unfortunately, it seemed, we had both lapsed into that great Australian, perhaps all-Anglo-Saxon cure: ignore it and it'll eventually go away.

I know now that is a very dangerous thing. Taking it on the chin and saying nothing. Avoiding conflict because our children – or our neighbours – may hear us or think less of us if they do. I am not talking here about calling each other idiots and useless pieces of shit; I am talking about really having it out and raising voices when you need to, because there is reason to. Because it is better than holding it in until the heart and the liver and the spleen blow up like children's inflatables and burst.

It's something I know now and something I *should have* learnt from the Godbolts – if you talk and argue with thought, with mutual respect, it is possible to love and admonish at the same time.

I knew one thing: from the lessons I had learnt, from the lessons life kept dishing out to me, it was time to find a way through. I was a woman now, one who had learnt from ample experience and I had to do something.

In the end, I chose not a fiery path as I easily could have, but what I thought was a sensible way ahead. Nevertheless, it took courage. To be firm rather than fiery. I had to face up to Chris and let him know I was unhappy, that our marriage was not working, that we either had to do something about it or things might happen that would grow beyond both our control.

Eventually I convinced my knight – even he by now could see through that not so shimmery armour – that our marriage was in breakdown, that we had to at the least go and seek counselling.

It was probably the best thing I ever did in my life. In *our* lives.

43.

EVEN AS WE SAT THERE BEFORE THE MARRIAGE COUNSELLOR – EMPTY IN OUR MARRIAGE AND YET SOMEHOW OLD AND ANCIENT FRIENDS, HOLDING HANDS – the counsellor sat on the other side of the room, not looking at appearances, not looking at our tightly-sweating, clasping hands, but reading instead into the tone of our words, the slant of our bodies, the blinking of our eyes.

And what she heard, once I was able to finally open up – from the bottom of my gut – was how Chris had tried to manipulate me, was continually befooling me, saying that he could not exist or carry on without me. She also eventually saw how I had allowed myself to be deceived, had allowed myself to be lied to.

Finally, it also came out: how Chris had threatened to kill himself if I left him.

He sat there shaking his head in the negative, defiant.

'Is that true?' she asked.

'Yes, yes.'

Only it was me replying.

Chris said nothing.

I looked across at him.

He looked down. His eyes dark and upset.

'He's done it before. You have to believe me.' I was sounding desperate. 'You have to believe me. He does this to me all the time with his self-harming and "can't-live-without-you" threats.'

That was among our first counselling sessions. But so it went, on and on. At home, we lived like ghosts around one another, but finally, finally, seeing us still holding hands, there was only one conclusion that could be reached: *This marriage is over.*

For my part, without actually saying it, the counsellor had in effect given me the power to say to Chris, my husband of almost thirteen years, father of my three children, my once friend and saviour from Mum and Dad, 'I neither want nor need you anymore. Our marriage is done.'

For Chris, in his corner, ultimately there was only one piece of advice, and in the end it had to come from the counsellor herself, 'You have to let this woman go.'

'Okay, Deb,' he finally acknowledged, 'if this is what you really want. I won't harm myself. I won't even threaten it. I promise. I'll let you go. I just don't want to tell people at the base yet.'

I understood what he meant. I nodded. Accepting his fear of social failure.

Thinking back on it, strangely, or maybe not so strangely, I had at first resented the counsellor for what she brought out in Chris and me – the ultimate realisation that we were really hanging onto nothing.

And then, suddenly, at that particular session, knowing it was over, knowing I would soon be free of him, there was this sheer relief like my mind had suddenly opened up and oxygenated like a massive flying air balloon. I had finally managed to internalise it, that this *really* was what I wanted.

But the beating pulse, the light-headedness, the sense, or rather the true meaning of that relief in all its more subtle and terrible permutations, would only come in the moments after the session.

Chris and I had quietly exited the counsellor's rooms and were going down in the lift. He was standing opposite me, chest throbbing like a frog in that small, confined space. There were tears rolling down his eyes. And the more I looked at him, the more I saw he was not saying goodbye, or even *au revoir*, or even it was good knowing you; he was standing there reneging on everything he had agreed to in front of the counsellor. He was denying everything he had confessed to.

He stood there, legs crossed at the ankles, leaning against

the wall for support, telling me that I still meant everything to him, that I was still bound and tied in every way to his life. He needed me. Could not live without me. I was his world.

To me, at that moment, rather than like a man, my friend, my soldier, my once shiny knight, he looked like a little boy, like a little schoolboy whose parents had never allowed him to grow up, a boy in a playground who needed others weaker than him to lean on, who needed others to exert control over by making sure – no matter how darkly and emptily – they will remain weak, and in effect always be there for you. He looked not just sad and tragic, but perfectly selfish.

I gazed at him, into those intense hazel eyes whose curving arches, like temples, had once stared into my flesh, and saw only eyes now that were red with self-concern, like a little boy's.

'What! What's wrong with you now!' I said it without feeling. And when he did not respond, I told him with firm assuredness to stop the crying, to stop the mewling, and reinforced with my harsh breath that this was it, this was the end of our marriage, whether he could accept it or not. I also told him it was time he grew up. I told him that, irrespective, we were both now going to have to do that – but separately and apart.

He sobbed on, 'You're not going to leave me. You're not!'

I stared, feeling my eyes pinching into his chest, feeling every fibre in my body rejecting him, telling him that I didn't care how much he self-harmed, how much he threatened and manipulated, I was separating from him.

That was one of the valuable things I had learnt through the counselling. I was not responsible for anything he wanted to do to himself. Even to this day it holds no weight with me if you threaten to self-harm. I can't abide by anyone trying to hold on to someone by doing that – it is not a way to prove love. Only deceit.

Finally, finally, half looking into my eyes, still whimpering, he nodded as though he had heard. The weight and strength pouring off my shoulders in those moments was enormous. I didn't have to think twice about it, it was just there, I think now, had actually always been there, but being the snail and pacifist avoider of conflict that I was, I had to wait for a marriage counsellor on a defence force base to allow me to express it: this inner strength, this independence of thought; to allow it to finally exhale from me.

I was not responsible for any other adult person, and standing in that lift I told him so. With my words, my unsympathetic words, I let him know it. The bubble of pride that I felt when I slapped Dad as a fifteen year-old and he walked away, was back, even bigger and shinier in my breasts than before. I was glowing. I didn't even know why.

And yet there was another thing that was to come up through counselling, counselling this time that I went to alone, that I went to towards the end of the marriage counselling – mainly because my school, that is the school my children went to, saw that there was something wrong with me. Saw how it leaked on my face and caught in my thick, shameful forest of hair.

44.

ACTUALLY, IT WAS SARAH'S TEACHER WHO NOTICED SOMETHING WAS AMISS WITH ME. Mainly, she noticed it because she found out I wouldn't let my girls play at any of their friends' houses; I only ever allowed their friends to come to our place. The teacher, Theresa Rose, was the first person ever to tell me, face to face, that it was a normal and healthy part of growing up for children to go to their friends' places. I was surprised. Of course, I know I shouldn't have been.

Not only that, with a sense of urgency, it was she who put the school counsellor on to me rather than the other way round. And while I could have taken it as a threat, I saw, reading the honesty in her mouth, reading the pressing body language of that teacher, that there were only the best of intentions there. I *knew* what it was, I knew I needed it. Perhaps for my children too.

In the end, I buckled and accepted the help.

Again, like the marriage counselling, this proved the best thing I ever did in my life. Admit to an outside source with the professional background what I had kept secret and hidden in the darkest corners of my soul.

Once again it was not long before I was given "the permission" to breathe. To exhale my real power, to breathe it through my larynx and chest and gut and right up into Mum's snorting nostrils and Dad's hard bird nose. Yes, tell them to their faces the truth. Tell them the way I saw that thing in me that distinctly reeked of reality's shame.

First came Mum's turn.

Chris and I and the three kids were up in Brisbane, visiting my sister Marge. Mum and her new husband were there too. I don't know how it happened, but as it does so often in families, only perhaps that little bit easier in my malfunctioning one, an argument developed, and like a typical Queensland storm it grew from grey to black to purple and then a ghostly dark green before anyone could do anything about it. Soon it was hailing big emotional rocks, with Mum doing her usual, packing her bags. My sister Marge was standing behind me, encouraging me to stop her.

So, eventually I trudged heavily into Mum's bedroom, and said, 'Mum, what are you doing? Why do you have to do this? Maybe we need to talk? Why do you have to go?'

Only if it sounded like a plea, it wasn't. It was merely questions from stiff, cut lips. I was not being sympathetic, I was only doing what anyone would do. What my sister was urging me to do.

And Mum, sobbing, turned around but like I was begging, like I was that little girl asking forgiveness, and she yelled at me, at my sister, at everyone: 'What have I done? All I've ever done is stuck up for you kids. All I've ever done is help you!'

It hit me like I had seen kangaroos punch, brutally, with cruel beating might, and it connected right in the nose like one of those mighty kangaroo fists had got through my guard. My eyes went foggy, my lips drooped, only I was not going down to the dirt. Oh no, no, no longer. Counselling had given me that much;

I looked into her eyes and hit back: 'Oh my God, no you didn't!' And then glaring I repeated it. 'Oh no, you did not!'

'What do you mean?' Her eyes heaved. 'I always tried to protect you. I always stood up for you kids.'

My cheeks, I could feel were red and bursting. 'Oh no, you did not. You did not *protect* me. Did not *ever* protect me!' I was so angry, so tired of the lies, so tired of the self-deceptions, I could feel the bones in my chest bursting out into her lips. 'You *never ever* protected me.'

And still she persisted: 'I did. I always protected you.'

'No, you did not. Oh no, you did not. You were not there when I needed you. You never were. You never protected me from Dad!'

That seemed to startle her, actually bring her to a halt, quieten her. Her nose was sniffing, she was rubbing at it with a fist, in that way she always did under duress. I could feel the hairs on my head digging into my skull just as hers must have been stabbing into her head. I saw myself standing before her: a little girl, unprotected, set among miswired adults, groping through a darkness that they explained away as normal light of day.

Horrified, unable to talk, she stormed off, crying: 'How can you say that? How can you say that?'

But I knew she understood. I knew she did. If anything, it was like she was crying those words to herself. Only she couldn't make it sound that way. She did not like to be defeated.

I did not chase after her. I did not feel sorry for her. I felt I had had my day. And really, taking the whole history of my life that went before, it was just a small moment, a small if powerful blow back to the human being who had constantly punished and neglected me. At last I had done it, had my moment with her. That balloon in my chest bubbled again, just a little, just for a small moment I felt it swell.

Until my sister Marge came running up to me: 'You're nothing but a bitch! How can you be such a bitch to Mum!'

I was stunned. Gob-smacked frozen. Absolutely stopped in my tracks.

Marge was fully aware of my counselling sessions, knew very well about *our* childhood, *my* childhood, even if she didn't know how I had put my lips and tongue out to Dad one day in order to save her. She had even agreed to my face, at some stages, that life had been difficult for us growing up. But as they say, life, families, even bad, rotten families...

All I could think was at least I had given a punch back, at least I had stood up and rattled a nose – so that Mum did not go through the rest of her life without knowing what I thought. *Felt.* What dwelt like an unkillable worm inside me. Hitting back made me feel that little bit more empowered.

And I was proud of that. My sister had her own life, there was nothing I could do about that.

And then it was Dad's turn next.

It may seem a bizarre thing, but through all my relationship problems with Chris in Melbourne, through all my groaning and tears of despair about our continuing financial problems, aside from one or two significant others like my sister and Chris's older sister Rosita, who I confided in, it would be Dad, yes, Dad with an attentive ear who would phone me of his own accord on a regular basis and listen to my woes.

It reminded me of when I was younger, even at the height of my abuse, if there was anyone I could somehow talk to, it was not Mum, it was him. He was always there for me. And like then, perhaps even more so now, he sat patiently at the end of the phone and listened to what I was going through. Sometimes he would even offer rather wise fatherly advice.

But this is what I mean... that man, the beast who had tortured me... who treated me worse than a car rag... had infiltrated my skin, had drilled through the hard bone in my ribcage, had seeped into my very brain cells... and become a part of me. In the end, I believe, he really cared.

Only with counselling – through counselling – I now had this power, and not even a thick-skinned idiot and fool like me was going to let Dad get away with it.

One night during one of these calls he was telling me about his own problems, one that was particularly bothering him, how he had sub-leased the mill – *Dan Gallagher Enterprises* – to my older brother Jim. Only Jim had not made the lease payments in months and it was doing Dad in financially. He was at wit's end, not sure how to get the money out of Jim, money that he needed to live on, and he was angry.

'I've always done the right thing by you kids. I've never ever hurt or harmed any of you,' he groaned.

Dad groaned *that*.

Now a veteran of counselling, I felt my chest thunder and then roll, but with the utmost control into the phone, I said,

'Oh yes, you did. You hurt me. You sure as bloody hell did.'

'What the hell are you talking about?' his voice blustered back, a badly bent trumpet totally off-key.

'You hurt me, Dad, and you know it. You hurt me like no child should ever have to be hurt.'

As though seeing him on the other end of the line looking down that long distance of lean, muscly, awkward body of his, I heard a pause, a thick silence, and somehow I kept expecting to hear the line shake, the phone to grab hold of my neck and strangle me to death.

But in the end I could barely pick up this small voice that cried: 'Oh my God. Oh my God. I didn't mean to, Deb. Really. I didn't mean to. I know what you're talking about. I know I have hurt you very badly. But... I only ever meant to love you. That's all. I'm sorry, Debbie. Really, I'm sorry.' His voice was breaking up, struggling. 'You have allowed me to stay in your life, Deb. I can see. I know what's going on. I know what I've done. And I don't know why you have forgiven me. I don't know why, but you have. I am eternally grateful for that.'

Dad, my dad, my – *You don't ever mess with Dan Gallagher* – giant dad, sounded so shocked and staggered, he almost sounded defeated. Almost.

But it was too late, all these words, it was too late. Just as it was too late with Mum, so with him, but in my soul, in the circling pulse that was driving through my chest, I knew I had survived, I had come through. And I think it was because of that, inside myself, I could forgive him. He knew, in his bones, in the bones that linked us, he knew, even in his own badly processed head, I had somehow forgiven him.

The truth is, though, as I have found, a heart forgives, in fact can forgive as much as it likes, and yet still it carries the pain. At best we manage to put distance between ourselves and that thing that is hurting us, even sometimes put up actual walls and geographic miles between us and that haunting thing – something I achieved by living apart from him, in Malaysia, in Newcastle, in Melbourne, in Brisbane, in Ipswich – but still the pain does not simply depart. Just as it does not, like magic, depart with that single most charitable of Christian utterances: *I forgive you*. No, no, no, it does not.

Dad thanked me on the phone for forgiving him. But it was clear I didn't want him anywhere near me, not when I was by myself and definitely I did not want him anywhere near my children. He seemed to accept that – accepted it, I suppose, as part of his "hard-earned" punishment.

Knowing him, though, right until the very end he probably believed that because he did not intend to hurt or harm or in any other way abuse, but only to love, that somehow he wasn't altogether crazy or wrong and should not really even have to apologise or be forgiven.

I am sure he believed, right to the end, there was still something perfectly reasonable and harmless in his actions. If only others could understand. Would "get it". I could... and I could not.

At least I had had my day with him, albeit in separate rooms on the other end of a telephone line. But I had done it. Stood up to him. Not only to him but to *him* and *her*. *Them*. To both Mum and Dad. And although I am an idiot for letting Dad – and Mum – back into my life, maybe even a complete moron for doing so, I cannot be an altogether out and out wombat... because, before anything, I have realised I am a human being and therefore not perfect.

And that's the way I believe we should all be given the chance to live... not just as human beings but as *imperfect* human beings. Idiots, morons, wombats or not, it is true none of us should have to endure abuse by gender, race or sex, yes especially *sex*, but more than that, we should never have to endure neglect. Not on account of anyone's beliefs – or imperfections.

But there is more – and there is a twist. Because on the verge of packing up and leaving Chris, what did I do, I went to see a clairvoyant...

45.

I DON'T KNOW WHAT IT WAS THAT DROVE ME THERE. But something told me I had to seek "other" help, some other form of guidance, some alternative which looked into the stars and the heavens and aligned me with that greater, ever more knowing force that could see even deeper into my soul – and, hopefully, the future. I still seemed to need something, something spiritual to fill the gaps, the gashes and the wounds.

As a result, just before I was going to split from Chris and take the children with me, I was led by someone whose children I was day-caring, to a spiritual counsellor – a clairvoyant.

I was a little nervous at first, sceptical, but something had driven me there, was driving me in that direction, and I would not be satisfied until I had entered that "temple".

The actual, physical place – the clairvoyant's room – was dark and warm, and the woman before me sat tall, her back long and erect like the very earth rotated upon it. She looked at me – or was that into me? – with deep brown eyes that were confident, mesmerisingly aloof, and yet somehow down to earth.

She looked so assured in her seat, it was difficult not to trust that bearing; it made me feel comfortable, at home, and at the same time like I was at the cusp of another realm. Gazing into those infusing eyes, things happened at that visit, things I absolutely believed in. They were the things that had my heart pounding, my shoulders shuddering, and my eyes sobbing with gratitude.

After only a fairly short process of getting me to breathe deeply, to empty and bare my mind, I felt my entire body beginning to fill with a teary and sad warmth, and then slowly, almost chillingly at first, I was enwrapped by hands, by tepid flesh, flesh so smooth that it startled me at first. After a while I became used to that touch, and as I did so it seemed to invite me into it. It dwelled on me that I knew that touch. I had felt it before. As it warmed, it came to me; it could only be one person. Aunty Bev. Yes, I had been put directly in touch with my Aunty Bev.

All my life after Aunty Bev's death, I felt a need to touch her, to somehow feel her close to me, to communicate with her one more time. And maybe therefore I was "open game". But, whatever, sitting in that clairvoyant temple, I was lifted into a space where I was literally bathed in a sense of Aunty Bev being around me.

She touched me and I touched her warm hands and arms in turn. Tears welled and dripped from my eyes. Everything around me was an ancient fog clearing into a brilliant crystal realm. At last I was able to be with Aunty Bev again, to thank her for being a part of my life, for being a part of my sordid world; at last I was able to say goodbye to her.

More than that, I was able to thank Aunty Bev for being! The very idea of it, the idea that I was there with her, even as she lay dead in the ground, had my shoulders and heart quaking with relief and joy.

Those butter-smooth arms around me, it was like her hands, one last time, without judgement, without criticism, were peering – as they had in life – into my heart and soul.

I had desperately needed to say goodbye to her – desperately – and finally I was. It gave me a sense of the closure I had always hankered after. Hankered after since Chris turned his back on me and even before that, as she left my side as Dad was brought into that cold and distilled courtroom.

Believing in this experience, in this feeling of absolute reality in another realm, gave me the faith to listen to the clairvoyant when she said there was someone in my life who needed me. Someone who needed me urgently, who I needed to be with right now, whose life I could literally save.

And in this way, listening to those words, I was convinced not only about my closure with Aunty Bev, but of this thing also – not to leave Chris, my husband.

Coming out of that clairvoyant's dark temple, I knew staying with Chris was the right thing to do. I had to at least give it a go. My knight was burning, his flesh was singing and flaking, and now I had to rescue that melting armour.

When we experience something so powerful in our lives as touching and farewelling the dead, someone who meant the world to us, it is amazing what else we will listen to. Life and relationships are so complex, yet, with a little prodding, we often do with the ease of ants what we would normally, rationally, shirk and run from.

So there, obeying the voice of the world beyond, I was back with Chris, giving it another go.

Maybe, as the clairvoyant had indicated, it is true, this period was for him, just for him? Maybe I was actually saving him? I don't know. I really don't.

The truth is, I tried, I really tried to love Chris again, and in fact we did in many ways reconnect.

Together, for a while, newly returned to each other, we saw some essence and energy in one another again. Even had moments of plain downright fun, just like in the old days. The beginning days. The days when we camped on beaches and rolled in the waves.

Only when you build with bricks that are second-hand, that have already been well and truly used, it doesn't last long. The house eventually falls over. Yes, old bricks. They say a leopard never changes it spots, but there is more chance of that happening than resurrecting old bricks. They just eventually crumble and become sand.

And still I waited. Trying to build with old bricks.

Chris was posted back to Ipswich in this period but with him came his moods, his depression, his expectations of his loyal wife, and they were to be the most uncomfortable and longest months of my life. Eighteen months that would seem like a double lifetime. A tenfold lifetime.

Daily, I thought of when the time would be right to finally crawl from his bed and separate from him.

It is easy to say go back to someone. The reality, in the soft pulp of the human flesh, is that even if it is as a favour, as a rescue mission, it becomes difficult to disentangle from again. I just knew I had to. Somehow I had to. Only now it was like I needed some new reason to pin it on. Some new cause to give effect to what I essentially knew to be true so long ago in that rational counsellor's rooms.

Finally, the chance came – when Chris, in a foul, depressed mood, after a night out when he thought I was being too friendly to certain others, ran out into passing traffic. He was trying to hurt himself, obviously trying to say something to me, trying to hurt me, a cry for help?

But the worst part was that he was doing it in front of our three children – doing it in front of our precious human flesh and blood who were sitting in our car watching from the roadside. Who were sitting there, eyes wide and fearful, trying to understand. Three pairs of little child eyes pondering their father's death wish.

For me, having had that taste of empowerment, having had that swill of my own free will, this was the final straw. I was not going to put up with his controlling jealously, his selfish acts, his pure egocentric actions, not one inch further.

I put my foot down, very hard this time, and as soon as he sobered up brought him around to the inevitable. Exactly two days later, on June 16, 1996, Chris moved onto the base for a couple of days and then moved in with friends. That day in June was to be the final time we actually lived together as husband and wife.

It would have been obvious even for a mouse living in a dark hole in the wall to see it was over between us, there was no breath there, no oxygen, but it still took, I have to be totally honest here, a massive inner courage, a massive dose of strength and guts to face him – to make *him* face *it*.

The only thing I knew was that I was not stepping back this time, my counselling had got that much through to me; and finally, after nineteen years of being together, fifteen of those years married, we divorced on September 15, 1997. The final cut – the sawing of our once cherished but now tarnished love – had been made.

How did I hang on for so long? Hanging on to the word of a clairvoyant? All I can say is, aren't we all suckers sometime? Don't we all make mistakes? I like to think that maybe, just maybe in its own little way, black as it was, this period did help my once knight in shining armour.

46.

I WAS SINGLE AGAIN. I SHOULD HAVE BEEN HAPPY AS A PRINCESS, no, happier of course, except I had three children and life ahead of me looked like nothing but a steep hill.

Once again I had to tell myself to get up off the pavement and surge ahead into that black tar road, doing the best I could. The worst thing I could do was sit on the sidewalk feeling sorry for myself. I knew, and seeing the children around me kept reminding me, I had to throw myself into their lives – their education, their safety, their maturing. I had to make sure my life was worthwhile.

And that's exactly what I did. As before, I became involved in their schooling, their growing up and socialising, making sure they had both firm borders as well as plenty of room to breathe, and, more than anything, unconditional support.

I have to admit, even though I craved the roundness of a relationship, a man around the house to help out, I felt happier now. I felt in control. I felt like my own set of emotions and healing and growth were more than enough to look after for now.

It was important to me then that I had escaped the dark gloomy cloud that was like some kind of menacing landlord looking over my shoulder all the time. No longer was I responsible or had to make excuses to the children for that ever shape-changing presence. The presence that was my once lover and knight, a man constantly falling off his horse, needing me yet betraying me, loving me yet denying me, and who I had to keep lifting back like a drunk into the saddle.

The one thing I also did – immediately after the divorce – was sign over to Chris my share of the Anondale property at Perenjora Dam. In return, Chris relinquished his claim on the loan Dad owed us both. I was now absolutely free of the house where I had grown up, if you could call it free. If you could call it a place where I "grew up".

I was only too happy to be rid of that house that had raged and reigned like a hurricane in my head forever. That house that I still see as a black spot that cars and trains ride over and the people passing by peek, rightfully but unhelpfully, through their windows to get a better look at. That place with all the rusted metal, utes and old engines piled up like a massive graveyard of ghosts in the back paddock.

That grave did not belong to me any longer. No, not in any way.

What I knew was I adored my children. I loved them. Even before they could walk, I was proud of them. That did not mean I did not impose firmness and restrictions. Ultimately, I believe, as much as we long for freedom and open space, what really we hanker after are borders and boundaries. But within reason. Borders and boundaries that give effectiveness and responsibility to our freedom. Make us see freedom is not just something wild and matter-of-fact. That we have to serve it.

What we don't want – a la Mum and Dad – is borders and boundaries so up-close that we can't breathe or that allows others next to us, literally, to live inside our flesh. More than anything, even within boundaries, we want safety with oxygen. These are the things we should not just want but should demand.

I made mistakes. I made big mistakes too.

The first mistake came while I was still together with Chris – before our third child was born. It came in the midst of those empty years before the moment of that too quick-lasting resurrection of our love when we decided to have our third and last child, Dean. This is no excuse, no excuse whatsoever, but I did what every decent parent would never do, or at any rate would be educated never to do.

I found Sarah, my then four-year-old, playing with this expensive lipstick someone had given to me as a gift – and that I had warned her never to touch. The lipstick was blue but when you smoothed it on your lips it came out red. It was semi-permanent lipstick that took twenty-four hours before it even began to fade. It was almost impossible to wash off.

I walked into her room on this particular afternoon – when she was meant to be having her afternoon nap – and found her standing there, a smile bigger than a clown, the lipstick smeared like oil paint all over her mouth and nose and cheeks and chin. Her face looked so "done-up", it was obvious she also had some blush and rouge on it.

Caught in a better moment, she would have looked... like a clown. And perhaps that's the point when I should have stood back, looked at the incident objectively, and laughed. I should have. Instead, I looked at her bed and saw it too had thick lipstick all over the pristine white sheets. The bedspread was painted red.

I snapped. I fully and completely snapped.

I turned around and slapped her and then because it did not seem to mean enough, I slapped her again and again across the face and head until she could no longer cry, could hardly breathe, she was shrieking so loud.

Thank heavens at some point a neighbour called out, 'Deb, is everything all right over there?' Else I don't know that I would have stopped.

The truth was nothing was all right "over there". I was shaken, shivering and trembling, and when I "came to" I saw faint specks of blood on the side of my daughter's face. I felt so ashamed I wanted to run from the house forever.

'What have I done? What have I done?' I cried to myself. I never thought I could be that person. That monster.

There was – and never can be – any excuse for my behaviour. But now I can see how parents can beat up their children – it happens when their esteem is low, when they feel their lives are out of control, when they are barely holding down jobs, and are in relationships they cannot get out of. When they feel, as I did then, like shit... like an absolute swamp.

That beating made me realise I was trapped in a bog with slippery edges, and I could not climb my way out. I looked inside myself and saw both Mum and Dad; they were coming out in me, Dad with his switchy-stick and Mum with her fists pounding into my back. I was a beast, a brutal ogre, I was my parents.

Yet somehow, in those moments, more than anyone it was Mum I saw standing in front of me, slapping me through my face like I was some kind of dirty washing on the line. If there was one person I did not want to be like – it was her. And my beautiful child was on the receiving end of this moment of being her, of standing up to my madness. Of being beaten for everything I hated and resented – and feared – in my life.

I felt so bad about what happened that I immediately called Lifeline. To tell them what had happened, to ask them if they thought I was on the brink. A strange thing happened, that does not, I don't think, usually happen with Lifeline. I was asked what had made me call, and when I told them I was told there was no one available I could talk to for the next three weeks.

Three weeks!

I was in despair. But in the end it made me realise something: I had to deal with this episode – with my life – myself. Maybe that was the lesson. If you can't get help, don't simply lie back and think of the world caving in around you. Get up out of the gravel and do something yourself.

And so I made up to Sarah for it. I made up for it – not, as would be so easy to do, by offering her lollies and material things, but by saying sorry to her – sorry without begging. Without expectation. And promising never to do it again. That was the only guarantee I could give her. I would not do it again. No matter what she did.

I also told all the people I could trust about it. I felt so embarrassed and ashamed, I felt I could not keep it a secret; I didn't want secrets in my life any more. Secrets that soiled our property and our upbringing on Perenjora Dam Road.

If I did something wrong – and I had – I wanted others to know about it. I did not feel I should hide it from those I could trust.

I realise now I wanted feedback, I wanted reassurance, I wanted people to know I maybe needed help.

I saw also I would rather be a serial confessor than keep things hidden like black holes in my chest. Ever since I witnessed that little girl, Grace, getting beaten by her mum for eating the Devon sausage I had so hungrily munched into as an eight year old, I wanted to confess, to tell people the truth, to let them know what I had done when I had done anything wrong. I swore to keep confessing, but never to snap again.

And yet... and yet... I did it again. Only it happened much later, when Chris and I were living in Melbourne, and not with Sarah this time but with my now little two year-old. With my cute, adorable son, Dean that I had promised a safe and loving environment to, an environment filled with reasonable discipline and masses of open space and oxygen.

Again, I don't know if it is an excuse, and I don't want to use it as one, but I was lying half asleep on the couch in our lounge room, one pretend eye on the kids, the other in dreamland, when Dean walked up to me and blew a trumpet in my ear. The little devil. I don't know if he realised what that does to a giant sleeping eardrum? To any eardrum? To the daughter of beasts?

I sprung up and walloped him hard all over his nappy covered bottom... Mum, Mum, Mum, Dad, Dad, Dad, coming out all over in me again, until something, probably the yelping tears and the sound of a child, my own child Sarah pleading, begging me to stop, brought me to a halt.

I looked at both of them, Sarah and Dean, and felt guilty. Guilty before her as well as before my little boy that I had damaged. Back to my senses, once again I had to apologise – and once again I did it without material or sweet-tasting things. Once again, I did it without begging. Or expectation.

And once more I gave that guarantee: I would never do it again.

This time I kept my word. This isn't to say they didn't continue to get the odd hiding. But not like that. Nowhere ever near like that. And they only got it when I had judged, after the best judgement I could make in the time allowed, that it was necessary.

That firm discipline – combined with the effort and time I put into their school and schooling – seemed to bring off a pretty well rounded upbringing.

In the end, my eldest daughter, Sarah, aced her classes most of the time – was at any rate totally an "A-plus" student, worked obsessively, and eventually graduated from The University of Queensland with physiotherapy – honours. It seemed the harder the birth the saner or at least the cleverer they came out.

My second daughter, Ruth, although also a diligent student fell into some difficulties in her Senior year – her grades went right down in the last half of the year – but she immediately got a job and came back to her education soon after her days of trauma. She is happily married now and firmly Christian and religious. Even today it saddens her that I haven't taken the Lord as my Saviour.

She believes, as a result, I won't go to Heaven. But I believe I will be fine. Belief in myself is what I have learnt. That is what I need, and with that belief the Universe will take care of me.

My daughter works as an administrator for the government – ironically, in their child safety section – keeping meticulous notes and files on the many aspects of child abuse cases. Talk about coming full circle.

Another full circle: Dean, my son, a mostly "A" student, followed his dad into the Air Force. He studied exactly the same course as Chris had done all those years ago, becoming an avionics technician. He loves it. His moods are softer than his dad's.

But also, not only encouraging them but encouraged by my three children in turn, especially my eldest, Sarah, giving me the confidence to push myself, I began to study, to further my own education. I started with short certificate courses and then slowly built my studies and training up. I finally qualified as a skilled and efficient (or so I like to think) teacher aide, a job that has kept me going to this day, even though my children are no longer at school.

To get to where they were, however, my children still had to live their lives, much of it with me as a single mum. And seeing my relationship with my parents, with my own family, they intuited there was more to my own growing up and becoming their mother than, to put it mildly and blandly, met even a child's egocentric eye.

Particularly Sarah, maybe being the oldest, started being curious fairly early – asking questions. Only they were not the questions that a parent looks up in a dictionary or encyclopaedia, they were the questions I did not ever want to answer. Questions that brought back all the pain, the dirt, the anguish, the unknowing shame.

I had kept it all secret, so, so secret, I did not ever want my children or anyone else to know who did not already know. No one was talking about it any longer, I was happy with that, my secrets were my own.

How could it all suddenly – like a rogue storm cloud – spring into the air above us again?

47.

YOU MAKE THE BEST OF THINGS. YOU TRY TO SORT OUT THE WORST. I have done my best to scrape away the past, to bury it in the ground at my feet, but eventually, in some way, at some time, it comes back and grabs you like spikes at the ankles.

I made a point of teaching each one of my children three things: 1.) Your body is your body and no one else has a right to touch it without your consent.

2.) Always stand up for yourself. It doesn't matter how big they are: Stand up to em. As I had learnt, it frightens them away. Even the big ones.

And finally, 3.) I taught them, if there is ever anything bothering you, tell me, and tried to make them feel safe and comfortable enough to do so.

But knowing children, in case they didn't feel comfortable telling me, I taught them this: If you can't come to me, that's fine, but make sure you go and speak to someone – an adult person. Someone you think you can trust. And keep talking until you have been heard. If you are not satisfied with the response, choose another adult person until you feel you have been understood.

I made sure my bedroom door was always open to them.

With this background, Sarah, nine, came home from school camp one day and told me that one of the kids in her class was very upset.

'Something very terrible is happening to her, Mum. Something to do with her stepfather.'

I stared down at her, every fibre in my being knowing, already wriggling. 'Yes...'

'Everyone knows, Mum... but nobody will say anything.'

Oh my God, I thought. Oh my God, here we go.

'He's probably hurting her in some way, Sarah, and she just doesn't know how to deal with it.' I tried to talk in a way sufficiently responsive but uncommitted enough for the subject to be dismissed and forgotten about.

She stared back at me. 'How would you know that, Mum?' Just like that – a child's adult-eye to a mother's dishonest eye. 'How would you know that, Mum?'

'I just know, sweetheart. I know.'

'Well, you tell me how you know, Mum. I want to know how you know.'

She wasn't letting me off the hook. Not in any way. It was obvious to me she knew more than she was letting on, in fact knew, at the least, a lot more than I thought she knew about that awful word "hurting".

But I did not want to continue that conversation, not at that time. Not with Sarah so young and innocent. I still felt too ashamed. Was too afraid that my own dark ghosts, my own lies and deceptions and hurts would come bumbling from my lips and I would not be able to control what I said.

I was having counselling at the time, but there was one thing I still did not want, even though the counsellor gave me "the permission and the power" to confess it, was for my children to know.

I could stand up to my father, the culprit, the beast, "the murderer", but the wounds were still too raw to tell my children. Still too close to the veins to wipe away the veneer of innocence and joy when they greeted their tall as a house, loving and jokey Grandad – their "Grandy", as they affectionately called him.

The grandfather they looked up to with the awe of puppies.

I tried, strategically, feigning disinterest, to leave it more or less at that, explaining to Sarah a little further what I thought she already knew, that that girl's stepfather was hurting his stepdaughter by touching her without having the permission I always warned about. But exactly how he was touching her was not for me to say.

She gazed at me sceptically, and I felt my heart diving. I had to tell her something more. It was also important, I could see it in her bloating face, that I *did* something. Did something rather than just listen and feel sorry and turn my cheek.

She was eyeing me with those blue, doe-like eyes of hers, and they were insistent, not letting go. Eventually I told her, yes, I would do something and resolved at that moment that I would. I would phone the police – *the police* – because, I had to be honest with her, her school friend was obviously feeling so much pain she felt compelled to tell her mates about it.

My decision, my decisiveness, made Sarah happy. Her eyes finally let go of mine, seeing I was doing something about it, actually willing to stand in the road for someone else.

That same day, I called the local police station, albeit anonymously, and was put through to the Protective Behaviour Unit. I told them what I had heard from my daughter, and, in the end, in the weeks ahead, that family was successfully investigated. That is to say, The Devil, the Dark Perpetrator within had been brought into the daylight, and there was some justice done. The stepfather was brought to heel, made to confess, and desist. One hopes forever.

But Sarah never let up. This idea of "hurting" and "being hurt" by being "touched" was growing in her mind. I think too, even at her young age, she was seeing in my own bulging lips that they were thick with shame, guilt, there was something wrong, something I was hiding.

Sarah was intuitive for her age – there was just nothing I could do about it. And over the next days, weeks, months, she kept at me, kept at me as badly as any obsessive child over a toy they desperately wanted. She kept asking about "hurting" and "touching", and how I knew so much about it.

One day, it must have been as long as a year later, Sarah, ten then, Ruth, eight, I decided I had had enough of the questions. It was time to speak. I knew the truth, at least some of it, a small quantity of it, had to come out. Dean, my son, was still far too young, so I sat my two daughters down on a kitchen bench and told them as simply as I could, my story.

'When I was a little girl,' I told them, seeing them peering up at me from their miniature two-seater wooden bench, 'I was touched by someone... in the wrong way. You know, in that way I said to be careful of. In my private parts. Like that girl at your school.'

'By who?' Sarah's response, in her typical child-adult way was like an exclamation mark I couldn't get around.

I shook my head. 'That, I am afraid, I can't tell you.'

It hit me like a massive rock, just how hard it was to tell anyone, to tell my children something that might crush them, that would definitely change their world, which would destroy the mystery and joy in it. How could a simple truth be so difficult – that the person responsible was the lovable, affable, always ready with a joke creature whose head reached so high into the air at times it looked like it actually touched the sun.

'Tell us, Mum. You have to!' It was Sarah, coaxing.

I could see the concern, something motherly in her, something protective and at the same time sharp and already mature and judgemental abiding in her. Next to her, I saw Ruth, eight, her long flowing hair like a doll's, her still feline greenish-blue eyes interested but not as interested, her eyes merely following her older sister but not caring in the same way.

All I knew at that time was that I did not want to reveal the truth to them – I did not want to devastate, did not want to shatter that "Father Christmas/Tooth Fairy" illusion for either of them. I did not want them to see their grandad – their loving "Grandy" – for what he was, a monster. Not yet. Not yet.

'The only thing I can say,' I eventually struggled, 'is that you are safe... safe from the person. I can assure you... you will always be safe from that person.'

It is so difficult this thing – to shatter illusions. To shatter a child's illusions about people they cherish and love. It is even more difficult when the person is a relative, is a part of their skin and blood. A part of the same seed.

As with all the exotic lies we tell in order to keep our children happy, I wanted my children to be protected from the real world, from the real beasts in their family tree for as long as possible. I looked especially at my tough little interrogator, Sarah.

'Sweetheart,' I said, 'all you need to know is that I'm not hurt anymore. I'm fine now. So, there's nothing to worry about. Everything is okay.'

She and her younger sister trundled off then, into the garden to play, perhaps even, by the looks of their body language, to ask questions between themselves. And in fact that is probably just what happened – because it was obvious Sarah was not satisfied with my explanations or my reasoning. In the weeks and months that followed, she still never let up, still kept asking, 'Who did this thing to you, Mum?'

She would ask at bath-times or bedtimes or in those quiet moments when I thought I was safe. 'Why did they do it to you, Mum?'

Shaking my head, I would shush her quiet, but eventually in her grown up-child way she would continue by saying, 'My mum and dad would have protected me.' And then she would give a wry smile. Even at her age, a wryness on the lips.

Yes, that hurt. Really, really hurt. *Her mum and dad would have protected her.* They would have, and they did. But what about mine? It could have been so easy to fall into self-sorrow then. Into that feeling of woe is me. It could have been so easy to show her my sobbing face and say, yes, yes, it is true, it is absolutely true, and have her feel sorry for me.

But I did not want that. If the day came that I eventually told her, told all my children, I wanted them to understand, I wanted them to be able to reason, I also wanted them to know I was a person in my own right now, that I was no longer that shy, hurt, guilty little girl they had to feel sorry for. I wanted them to know I could stand up on my own two feet – no matter what happened in the past.

That time of telling, that time of shattering illusions, would come. Yes, it would, I could see it in those moments. It is impossible to turn off the interrogative tap of an enquiring child. Especially one like Sarah.

What I did not want is the story of my growing up, of their family tree, so dark and black, to burgeon and explode on them through other means, other people – and then I would have lost control of my own story.

The only thing in my favour was that, as things stood, no one else in the family wanted to admit the past. No one. I could wait to release it.

48.

I KNOW I SHOULD HAVE LOATHED THE SOUND OF TRAINS OR MAYBE EVEN TRAINS THEMSELVES, but a whole couple of years later, I remember it distinctly, there we were sitting on a train going somewhere, and bored with looking out of the window into other people's yards like others used to do to us, Sarah, a twelve-year-old now, started asking her questions again, trying to figure out her game of Family Cluedo, and she said to me more maturely than ever before: 'Why didn't they protect you, Mum? Why didn't Grandy and Nana protect you from that awful man?'

My lips must have been quivering, the hooting sound of shunting trains rushing back to my head as I lay there with my legs sprawled open and my head back on a mattress, restless, because all I could do was look down at her, and then it was like she saw the light – or was it the darkness? And she said, 'I know why, Mum. I know. Because it was them. Wasn't it? It was Grandy and Nana who hurt you.'

I did not know whether to shake or nod or turn my head in shame. I wanted to cry. She knew, Sarah knew, she had worked it out in her own little head, and now she had effectively spilled the beans to my other two children who were listening to every word.

And still I could not say that word "yes". Much less breathe the full statement of truth, 'Yes, it was Grandy. Your grandfather. My father!'

It hurt, it hurt too much. I know I probably should not at that time have done this, but I left it in the air, the timing not yet comfortable for me, still managing to leave it dangling in that world of the illusory. Of rattling trains. Of passing cars. I neither confirmed nor denied, knowing inside me that my children were already seeing their grandparents in a different light. Would never feel as comfortable with them again. Were confused about the people they loved. The train rode on, my lips still quiet and fracturing.

Amazingly, it was not until Sarah was nearly fifteen – yes, nearly fifteen, that's how long I managed to hold off – that I found I had to make a full and truthful confession. Sarah was just too insistent, she never let up, not over all those years; there was always, at some time, the questioning, the judgement, the knowing in her eyes. And all I wanted to do was keep up the façade and maintain that terrible secret which I thought made me such a dirty person. It was not even so much that I wanted to protect their love for their Grandy. It was that feeling of dirt written over my body.

And then finally it came out one day, bumbled like Snow White dressed in black and covered in blood from my lips. First to her and then to the others, telling them the truth, the absolute and God honest truth, well, as far as I could tell it without damaging my children as well.

In any event, no matter how I said it, no matter what I said, it tarnished them all. Grandad was no longer Grandad anymore. Grandy was over. Which was just what I knew would happen. But Sarah, Sarah the eldest and the most inquisitive, took it the hardest.

While the other two, in their way, were more forgiving at the time, more willing to let the darkness of the past reside in the past, Sarah immediately began to hate him, to hate her Grandy for what he did, and not only him but her Nana for doing nothing to protect me.

She hated them both from then on – and with a passion that never receded until the day her Grandy was buried. She hated them in a way that perhaps I should have hated them? But especially him, Grandad, her Grandy, she did not want to be anywhere near him again. The sun had faded from his tall, mythical head, and his strong, music-loving hands were no longer a joy to hold. They were cut and scarred with sin. He had blood – and flesh, *my* flesh – on his hands.

To this day, despite my counselling, despite what I felt was an ever-growing inner strength in me, I do not know why I hid the truth from my children for so long. Or maybe I do, the honest truth is I do know: it was because in some way I wanted us to be a normal family, a family perhaps with warts, a few warts and pimples here and there, but not with the massive corns and carbuncles and stab wounds that were the reality.

I wanted to keep up the damned Father Christmas and Tooth Fairy tales and hide my children from their real world. I suppose, in a sick, bizarre way, I still felt that irretrievable link – like a chain – to my abuser. To my children's Grandy. It is the deceptive nature of that terrible venom. At the same time as we should be running away, it ties us. That – that is the true abuse. It is not something the next – safe – generation can ever begin to comprehend.

I recently heard in a court series on the ABC, the proposition that "a fear of abuse leads to a learned helplessness". Maybe. I would say, in my humble opinion, not even a "learned helplessness", but a kind of acceptance, a tolerance. A way of being. And in the end, as in my case, that fear, that so-called fear was not even fear at all, it was a deep sense of obligation to keep up appearances – the appearance of the "happy family", the "normal family".

But I am happy that, in the end, no matter how late, the truth of my family, of my family relations and history, at least came to my children through *my* lips. Even if they could not forgive, especially as in the case of Sarah, I am sure because of my telling her, and the way in which I told her, she did not have to feel sorry for me in a way that I was incurable, an invalid.

I could show her how eventually I fought back and stood up. That woe definitely was not me. And nor should it ever be on her or my other children.

The amazing thing, especially to her, is that, even on my father's deathbed, each day I went to him, those afternoons I drove from Ipswich to the hospital in Brisbane where he was being treated for his cancer, I fed and comforted him...

49.

WHEN I WAS TOLD BY THE DOCTORS THAT MY FATHER HAD TERMINAL BRAIN CANCER, I CRIED. The tears just rolled. I could not hold them back. Although, in retrospect, when I think about it now, that he had brain cancer was maybe some divine justice, some poetically fair end to the brain that had diseased all those around him.

By the time he was flown back to Anondale, he was so weak, this once big strapping man, this wood of my life, this tough, hand-hardened man who as a boy ran the Olympic torch through Gladstone; now he had absolutely no control over his body.

Dad's one regret was that he never got to see his father's grave. Never got to see the tomb of the father who he grew up without, the father who served his country and died a hero but left everyone's life inextricably changed behind him. The least I could do, on his deathbed, was to forgive him. It was an opportunity I would never be able to visit again.

Pressing all his strength to his cracked lips, his tongue flicking not against the gap between his front teeth in that old, menacing bird way, but flicking nervously right through almost invisible lips, he said to me one day, 'I know, Deb, I know. I hurt you. I did some terrible things. I am sorry.'

It was like the court in his head had finally ruled against him. And he had accepted the judgement. I felt immense pity for him. Pity that in his life he had got it so wrong. Pity that he had turned other people's lives upside down and did not even acknowledge his logic may have been arse about face.

I think in the end though, to be perfectly honest with myself, I felt pity for him because in his now dull, cancer-riddled eyes, much as I should have hated those eyes, much as I should have passionately resented the sick, white tongue that struggled to breathe to me now, I saw despite everything, despite the ever searing harm he had done, he only ever meant to love me. In his head that remained true.

Of course it upsets me, upsets me still, this strange love. But in my heart I know he loved me. He did! It was conditional. It was a sick love. I wanted to believe it, though. I wanted to. What little girl who grew up believing in the man that was the central wood-structure of her entire life, whose height was capable of reaching the sun, would not want to believe that?

He was no danger to anyone on earth now. The damage had been done. A pragmatist, forever the practical minded soul, I knew there was nothing I could do about it. It was a time for forgiveness and healing.

I know many may see this kind of pity, this softness of approach, as a weakness. But I do not. I see it as a strength. For all my lack of schooling, all my torrid, mixed-up experiences of growing up, that is my biggest lesson in life: Dad could die with his darkness and lies; but I had to let go. I had to continue to grow. What I demanded was honesty, and I think in the end, he at least gave something towards that.

When I think about it, rushing quickly over my life to those times, I see two hardworking people, my parents, Mum and Dad, so busy trying to eke out a living and a bit of enjoyment from life that they spent no time on the three things they needed to do most in life: educate, love and bring up a family properly.

Probably not unlike many other parents, everything was in effect experimental with them because they did not know what they were doing. And in a sense that is all I can say in their favour. They had a deep lack of knowledge, a lack of everyday familial know-how, and it did not make it easy for us.

I shiver when I think about it: Dad's crazy, screwed up way of seeing things, the stubborn, heavy-handed axis he rotated on, so far removed from the modern universe that he was closer to Neanderthal man. Mum, washed out, bloated and overworked with chores, a woman who saw but did not want to see.

This is my siren-call, my human scream, because I know the truth. And the worst part of it is that to outsiders we looked – at least most of the time – like one big happy family, grandfathers, grandmothers, daughters, sons, sons-in-law, happy, happy grandchildren. But it was a façade. What a bloody façade.

I know from the inside now, we human beings put up that veneer, and as in the case of my family, when we should be wearing the truth on our foreheads like banners for all the world to see, we keep it hidden. Hidden like birds hide their hatchlings in a nest.

But the truth is this: if I had the choice all over, for all Dad's so-called love and good intentions, I would never want to live through it again. Sometimes I am still not sure how I survived.

I sit in my Flinders View lounge room in Ipswich and take out a picture of their wedding day, of Mum and Dad's great day of coming together as one, and look over it for the signs of love, for the signs of my beginnings...

On my father, standing there like a solid upright tree in his immaculate dark suit, I see a rebellious, James Dean smile. I see a man a little reticent yet confidently looking out of the photo.

He is tall, obviously young, dashing, standing straighter, with more bravado than a "switchy-stick". Mum, beside him, is smiling more widely than he is, is in fact showing white straight teeth and a round, gushing face. She has a petite little body that is clothed in fairy tale white veils and virginal white dress.

I see the future for a moment: while I am left to fend for myself in the company of rum-sodden, music-thumping adults, she will blow up ten times her size and run around in a full-body plastic astronaut suit trying to lose weight.

I suppose it is not surprising, barely reaching up to Dad's unbending shoulders, that she carries an uncertainty in her rosy cheeks and even in her well-known "c'mon lips" and beguiling brown eyes. I see the uncertainty especially in the bloated smile. It is like her lips and teeth are trapped; it is a smile she may never wear again.

In her daring eyes she wants to be optimistic, desperately wants life to work out. Wants to ride away, as in a fairy tale carriage, from the fights and drunkenness and broken pieces of her own upbringing.

In that moment of the photo is a belief that her parents' ill fortune will not visit upon her or her children. They both look like that. Mum and Dad. Untouchable. Ready to love and reach out to the world.

What is really sick about the photo is that Dad has white gloves. Perhaps almost like a sign, one white glove is on and one is off. The one white-gloved hand is holding the other empty glove. A real gentleman. This, no country bumpkin. This, a man of honour. The camera cannot see the warnings, the duplicity, the hands behind the gloves.

Next to his naked, barely visible hand, I see Mum's whiter than white dress and already it somehow looks soaked in the sanguine clots of the future. One day his hands will hold her like that dress. Strangling. One day he will hold us like that, the hands naked, the gloves given back to the hire shop or buried in the paddock. I see children in the linen of Mum's dress, full of hope yet struggling to breathe. Mum wears us on that expansive tight dress and yet she has not even had children yet.

But it is those gloves, those white-white gloves of Dad, which really get to me. The perfect, perfect henchman to his lady. I see those gloves around my neck, pulling my spine down into all that is old and second-hand and dilapidated in our back paddock.

Old fashioned and dated now, the white gloves carry the promise of integrity, of valour, of decency, and yet they will strip me of mine. Already, just hanging at his sides, without lifting a finger, I can see – *feel* – the damage those hands will do. Yes, the gloves will come off as soon as the ceremony is over, and the giant hands that they hide will saw not only wood but children.

It is hard to believe a marriage that looks like this can really be made in a witch's stew. It is Father Christmas, the Tooth Fairy illusion we all want to abide by. It is the innocence we wear on our rouged cheeks, the ceremony put on for the gifts.

Studying that picture, I see a kind of hopefulness sitting in Dad's high-cut cheekbones, that they too have no idea what lies ahead. Behind this gentleman and his lady, behind Mum and Dad there are massively long-hanging curtains. They hang as in a grand theatre, partly open, as though eager yet unable to reveal what's inside.

And now, back in the hospital... in the world of darkness, I see myself crying, hearing a voice full of cancer, eyes like Old Jack Frost, confessing, 'I did some terrible things... I know. I know. I wish I could have done things better...'

There is no retort I can give to this, other than to brush my hand over his cold forehead and tell him to rest, that it is a time to be calm. The solid wood that stood at the centre of our universe – at the centre of my life – has been felled.

I forgive him with my eyes.

50.

RATHER THAN TWELVE MONTHS, DAN GALLAGHER DIED EXACTLY SEVEN MONTHS AFTER HIS DIAGNOSIS, at the eleventh hour on the eleventh day of the eleventh month – Remembrance Day – sorry he never saw his dad's foreign grave and wishing he could have his life all over again.

My family could not believe the tears that flowed from my eyes. They saw it and did not want to see it, knowing my story, knowing their own story, but finally they came to terms with my unfathomable grief.

My own children – who did not have a dime of respect for their grandfather at the time of his death – all came to his funeral to be by my side. They wanted to show that great human dressing: *our family concord*. But more than anything they did it to support me, to support me from the bloated watercourses wending down my eyes.

I think, seeing the monster's body safely housed in that polished casket, there was a kind of forgiveness in them too.

Behind my own tears, I saw a practical woman. I saw a life – mine – that was yet beginning. Even as my father lay on his deathbed, struggling against his cancer, I had told him, 'You know, Dad, you are going to die. You are not going to beat it.' That was the least I could give him, honesty.

Today, I look at my children and see them as adults before me. Dean: tall, manly, easy-going and ambitious in his RAAF way, a young person following in the footprints of his father but with his own escapades to look forward to. Never ashamed to tell the world of his love for his family. Ruth: very attractive in an almost exotic way, with easily tanned skin and long, dark glossy hair, a person deeply loyal to those she cares about, also intensely religious, pious and honest with a good dash of stubbornness. And then there is

Sarah: small, tight-boned and beautiful to look at, classically fair in that English maiden sort of way, witty and clever, and, yes, yes, perhaps a bit like me, a woman with attitude.

I also see in her, besides her compassion and empathy, a little of the judgemental and self-opinionated, but always there is reason. In her own words – she is a perfectionist. As she justly said to me on that day she was let out into the world to be a physiotherapist, 'You know, Mum, I'm the first on both sides of the family – to go to university and graduate.'

And she had done it with A's – and honours.

People often say to me what a wonderful job I have done with my children. And maybe I did impact, but what I always reply is that they took the steps themselves, weighed up the odds and made their own choices.

At best, perhaps I gave them the confidence to make those choices, gave them the safety, the openness and discipline of a home that allowed them what my parents never allowed me: to grow up according to the best of my abilities. There was something waiting to burst in them, my children, as there is in all of us, and I think in my small way I was able to help release it.

For me, the safety and openness of reasoning with adults that my children had from birth did not come until I was about thirty. That was when I first went to counselling. Until then I believed that everything that happened to me was my fault.

If anything, I deserved whatever demented actions and punishments were dished out to me. Just as I had pulled Dad into me on that bed as he read to me from his dirty books, I was guilty. Guilty, guilty, guilty.

In many ways, thank heavens for my marriage breakdown, because without it the chances are very small that I would have been led to this one positive thing: further professional counselling. Everybody tense, miserable, maybe even suicidal, I would still have been married to a man I no longer loved; would still have been burying my secrets, deceiving my children, and blaming myself for everything.

It is my message, my one big message to the world: Seek help if you need it. If it is true and proper it will give you the tools, will unleash the strength and acumen in you, and by God, I think there is in all of us that have been felled by "the hand that saws" a need for insight – and valour.

It is something we should be given in school – before reading and writing and history and geography and even arithmetic – the lessons to prevent the damage committed by our own blood. The knowledge to combat the seemingly wonderful families and adults around us.

I was a warrior now. I had a "counsellor's shield" as my guide; I was no longer anybody's exotic instrument or any kind of plaything. I had received warmth and light when I needed it: through Aunty Bev, through her beautiful warm hands and eyes that did not judge; through that school principal who allowed me to lie my banging, mixed-up head down in her office and keep my secrets to myself; and through the Godbolts who showed me more than anyone what it was to be a normal, loving family.

The smell of candles in their caravan, that thickening beeswax with its creamy, smoky flavour still brings a shiver of warmth to me – both for the Godbolts and for the early days with my knight in shining armour.

Why do we open up the door and let them in? I should mistrust men, but I do not. I take them at face value. I look at their lips and try to read their mouths. Maybe it's a fault, a weakness in my character? But somehow when I see – or feel – honesty in the mouth, I still do not mistrust. I give benefit of the doubt. Except when it comes to my own children. Then, don't even come near me. Stay away. Most men don't know how to play with small girls anyway. They are too rough or overcompensate by being too soft. At any rate, and in any event, they can be awkward with female children. It makes me feel protective.

I suppose before I put it all on Dad and men, there was Mum too. She did nothing – absolutely nothing – except in the most absurd ways – to protect me. In terms of Mum, it was useless.

In a twist, recently when I visited her at my sister's place I became emotional due to a conversation I had with her where she asked me if I'd forgotten – or forgiven – Dad and her brother (yes, Mum even knew about that) – for the terrible things they had done to me. I faltered and held in my reply. I didn't really want to talk to her about it.

My sister, after realising what had happened, later sent a text message to me saying she was sorry Mum had upset me. My sister told my mother that she should not bring up that stuff anymore as Dad was dead now and couldn't hurt anyone again.

She also told Mum the reason I get upset with her now is because I don't understand why she didn't protect me all those years ago. Mum's reply, quite simply, was that Dad had threatened to kill us. She felt she had no other choice at the time but to let things be.

What I learnt from Mum was that, in the end, I had to grow up in myself. That was the only place it could ever be resolved. Even if I came out losing it was always good to know that.

Another thing that's good to know is the excruciating pain and exquisite joy of giving birth. There is only one thing more wonderful and more magical than giving birth, it is watching your own child giving birth to her child.

I have experienced that too now, only just two years ago, and there is nothing more sweet, more delicate, more spicily miraculous, especially as that ripping, shooting, bloating pain does not belong to you – only the marvel of it. I could not believe it, I absolutely could not believe the sacred communication driving like a wave between mother and daughter and newborn soul, and all I can say, because I have seen it for myself now, is yes it is true, us women are truly amazing.

People already say of my relationship with my granddaughter, Sophia, 'You're going to spoil her. You're giving too much of yourself to her.' The reality is I always wanted to be a mother, now I want to be a grandmother. And I want to spoil my grandchild and all my other grandchildren when they come along too. I want to spoil them with affection, with love, with complete and soft pillow-like joy, with space and oxygen and safety.

Like that little girl, Sophia, already growing up, walking unsteadily, flapping her arms like ducks' wings with excitement whenever she sees me, I see myself sitting on the back steps of our house in Anondale, just near the passing cars dashing by on the highway, a small child unconsciously seeing the future, a small child with hope, and I feel the sun shining on the golden honey as it drizzles from my bread in lines of expectation from my warm little fingers onto my arms.

And in the end I am glad Dad didn't choke me that night on the way home from Grandma's, just so that... just so that, without malice, without venom, I can tell you my story. So that instead of saying woe is me, instead of simply being a victim, I can warn others.

And there is another reason. So that I can tell you of this: that behind the darkness, after the shadows of it, there are warm little places, tiny little holes where the light shines through. It is true, we are women, we are survivors.

I found that engagement ring, hadn't I? We can do it. I know we can.

Postscript from a Daughter

MUM'S STORY REALLY IS QUITE AMAZING. Well, the fact that she has become a caring, intuitive, empathetic and warm person and a fantastic mother is the amazing bit. How she managed to turn into the wonderful person I know and love blows my mind. I think some people have amazing resilience to horrible situations and Mum is a great example of this.

Mum always told us that all she ever wanted to be was a mother. She taught us to keep our eyes open, to listen, to question, to love and to be safe. I am so proud of who Mum has become. I remember bits of the "old" mum: the person who would try to hide her face if you spoke to her directly and compare that to now: a woman who is quietly confident and has learned to understand what happened to her was not her fault.

I'm not sure if Mum ever made a specific decision to tell us about her past. But somewhere inside of me I've known her story since I was a child. I was the one who figured out who the perpetrator was because Mum didn't want to tell me who it was (understandably).

I still remember it taking me ages to solve it... I kept saying to Mum over and over: 'But who could have done this to you without your parents knowing? Grandy and Nana would have protected you!' I guess that just goes to show my innocence and naivety at the time. I still remember the day I figured it out and I was so shocked it was difficult to breathe... I still feel bad that as an eight or nine year-old, I asked Mum why she didn't stop him.

When it came to Mum's past, she would only ever answer my questions in the way I asked them. She never volunteered information. Nevertheless, that's the main reason I knew more than my sister and brother: I simply asked more questions. For some stupid reason I thought sexual abuse was just touching (Mum had always told us that nobody is allowed to touch our private parts). I was nearly sick to my stomach the day I made the mistake of asking – in general

254

conversation – when Mum had lost her virginity.

I actually didn't think her father had had SEX with her. This was now really bad. Then I thought he'd only done it once! I almost couldn't bear the thought. I still can't. It's almost like my definition of hell kept changing with every new question and answer session. Looking back, I think Mum wasn't sure how much to tell me – for my own sake but also her own.

She was coming to terms with her childhood while at the same time trying to be honest with me. Looking back, there probably were times I was too young to know what I knew. Funny, writing this now, I still haven't made up my mind whether I want to read Mum's book cover to cover – except that I probably know most of it anyway.

I think, looking back it was hard to learn the details of what happened to Mum. I continually pushed to know more, it was as if by hearing the gruesome details I could somehow share some of her pain and hold her hand through it.

I remember getting to a point where I felt physically ill, and ANGRY. So ANGRY this had happened to her. I got to a stage where I refused to see my grandfather and I think I secretly told myself if he ever died, I'd be glad.

When Grandy did die of a brain tumour, Mum told me she wanted to go to the funeral and although I didn't intend to go, I told her I would go but only to support her. On the day of the funeral, a strange feeling came over me: I no longer felt angry anymore…. And I still don't know why. Everyone including Mum wore black/grey to the funeral (as you do), but I still remember Mum wearing a fuchsia pink hat on the day. I think it was Mum's way of saying – I'm not a victim, I'm free.

Sarah Gallagher
February 2013

Further Resources

- ACT for Kids – www.actforkids.com.au/– Provides therapy and support for children who have been abused or neglected. Telephone: (07) 3357 9444.
- Adults Surviving Child Abuse – www.asca.org.au – Self-help resources and Professional Support Line: 1300 657 380.
- Australian Childhood Foundation – www.childhood.org.au/home/ – Aims to strengthen community responsibility for promoting the well-being and protection of children throughout Australia.
- Bravehearts – www.bravehearts.org.au/– To educate, empower and protect Australian kids from sexual assault.
- Brisbane Rape and Incest Survivors Support Centre – www.brissc.org.au/– Services for women survivors of sexual violence and their supporters. Telephone: (07) 3391 0004.
- Bursting the Bubble – www.burstingthebubble.com/ For teenagers who are living with family violence.
- Child Abuse Prevention Helpline 1800 991 099 – www.childwise.net/Help-Advice/child-wise-national-child-abuse-prevention-helpline.html.
- Children and Youth Health – www.cyh.sa.gov.au/ – A South Australian government resource with practical health information for parents, carers and young people.
- CREATE Foundation – www.create.org.au/ – Non-government organisation connecting and empowering children and young people in care.
- DVconnect – www.dvconnect.org/– Provides free 24/7 help for women, men, children and pets affected by domestic and family violence across Queensland. DVconnect womensline: 1800 811 811. DVconnect mensline: 1800 600 636.
- Hands On Scotland – www.handsonscotland.co.uk/ – A Scottish government sponsored online resource for anyone working with children and young people.
- Healthy Start – www.healthystart.net.au/ – An Australia-wide strategy to support parents with learning difficulties and promote a healthy start to life for their young children.
- Kids Help Line – www.kidshelp.com.au/ – Confidential and anonymous, twenty-four hour telephone and online counselling service specifically for young people aged 5-18.

- Lifeline – www.uccommunity.org.au/– Provides twenty-four hour telephone counselling and services to assist people in Queensland communities. Telephone: 13 11 14.
- National Association for Child Abuse and Neglect (NAPCAN) – www.napcan.org.au/ – National organisation focused on promotion and primary prevention of child abuse and neglect.
- National Child Protection Clearinghouse – www.aifs.gov.au/cfca/ – Australian Institute of Family Studies advisory and research unit focused on the prevention of child abuse and neglect and associated family violence.
- Parentline – www.parentline.com.au/ – Confidential telephone counselling service providing professional counselling and support for parents and all who have the care of children. Telephone: 1300 301 300.
- Protect All Children Today Inc. – www.pact.org.au/– Services for children and young people aged 3-17 who are victims or witnesses within the criminal justice system. Telephone: 1800 090 111.
- Queensland Child Safety – www.communities.qld.gov.au/childsafety/protecting-children/reporting-child-abuse– Reporting child abuse in Queensland.
- Raising Children Network – raisingchildren.net.au/ – Joint Victorian government/community organisation website providing information to help parents with the day-to-day decisions of raising children, and looking after their own needs.
- Relationships Australia – www.raq.org.au/services/counselling/victims-counselling-and-support-service.
- Women's Infolink – www.communities.qld.gov.au/women/about-us/womens-infolink – Provides a state-wide free and confidential information and referral service about community services and government agencies supporting women. Telephone: 1800 177 577.

Other Prose @ IP

Frenchmans Cap: Story of a Mountain, by Simon Kleinig
ISBN 9781922120052, AU$33

The Terrorist, by Barry Levy
ISBN 9781922120076, AU$33

Blood, by Peter Kay
ISBN 9781922120038, AU$30

The Girl with the Cardboard Port, by Judith L. McNeil
ISBN 9781922120090, AU$33

No One's Child, by Judith L. McNeil
ISBN 9781922120151, AU$33

Write My Face, by Kathy Sutcliffe
ISBN 9781922120014, AU$33

Art from Adversity: A Life with Bipolar, by Anne Naylor
ISBN 9781921869846, AU$33

When Romeo Kissed Mercutio, by Kathy Sutcliffe
ISBN 9781922120281 AU$30

My Planets: a fictive memoir, by David P Reiter
ISBN 9781921869556, AU$30

Memories of Shinichi Suzuki, by Lois Shepheard
ISBN 9781922120137, AU$30

Past Perfect, by Karen Zelas
ISBN 9781922120311, AU$33

For the latest from IP, please visit us online at
http://ipoz.biz/Store/Store.htm
or contact us by phone/fax on 61 7 3324 9319
or sales@ipoz.biz